Legislative Voting and Accountability

Legislatures are the core representative institutions in modern democracies. Citizens want legislatures to be decisive, and they want accountability, but they are frequently disillusioned with the representation legislators deliver. Political parties can provide decisiveness in legislatures, and they may provide collective accountability, but citizens and political reformers frequently demand another type of accountability from legislators – at the individual level. Can legislatures provide collective and individual accountability? This book considers what both kinds of accountability require and offers the most extensive cross-national analysis of legislative voting undertaken to date. It illustrates the balance between individualistic and collective representation in democracies and how party unity in legislative voting shapes that balance. In addition to quantitative analysis of voting patterns, the book draws on field and archival research to provide an extensive assessment of legislative transparency throughout the Americas.

John M. Carey is the John Wentworth Professor in the Social Sciences at Dartmouth College. He has taught at the Universidad Católica de Chile, the University of Rochester, Washington University in St. Louis, Harvard University, and at the Fundación Juan March in Madrid, Spain. Carey's most recent books are *Term Limits in the State Legislatures* (2000, with Richard Niemi and Lynda Powell), *Executive Decree Authority* (1998, with Matthew Shugart), and *Term Limits and Legislative Representation* (1996). He has also published articles in numerous scholarly journals as well as chapters in more than a dozen edited volumes.

Cambridge Studies in Comparative Politics

General Editor

Margaret Levi *University of Washington, Seattle*

Assistant General Editor

Stephen Hanson *University of Washington, Seattle*

Associate Editors

Robert H. Bates *Harvard University*
Torben Iversen *Harvard University*
Stathis Kalyvas *Yale University*
Peter Lange *Duke University*
Helen Milner *Princeton University*
Frances Rosenbluth *Yale University*
Susan Stokes *Yale University*
Sidney Tarrow *Cornell University*
Kathleen Thelen *Northwestern University*
Erik Wibbels *Duke University*

Other Books in the Series

David Austen-Smith, Jeffry A. Frieden, Miriam A. Golden, Karl Ove Moene, and Adam Przeworski, eds., *Selected Works of Michael Wallerstein: The Political Economy of Inequality, Unions, and Social Democracy*
Lisa Baldez, *Why Women Protest: Women's Movements in Chile*
Stefano Bartolini, *The Political Mobilization of the European Left, 1860–1980: The Class Cleavage*
Robert Bates, *When Things Fall Apart: State Failure in Late-Century Africa*
Mark Beissinger, *Nationalist Mobilization and the Collapse of the Soviet State*
Nancy Bermeo, ed., *Unemployment in the New Europe*
Carles Boix, *Democracy and Redistribution*
Carles Boix, *Political Parties, Growth, and Equality: Conservative and Social Democratic Economic Strategies in the World Economy*
Catherine Boone, *Merchant Capital and the Roots of State Power in Senegal, 1930–1985*

Continued after the Index

Legislative Voting and Accountability

JOHN M. CAREY

Dartmouth College

CAMBRIDGE
UNIVERSITY PRESS

CAMBRIDGE UNIVERSITY PRESS
Cambridge, New York, Melbourne, Madrid, Cape Town, Singapore, São Paulo, Delhi

Cambridge University Press
32 Avenue of the Americas, New York, NY 10013-2473, USA

www.cambridge.org
Information on this title: www.cambridge.org/9780521711913

First published 2009

Printed in the United States of America

A catalog record for this publication is available from the British Library.

Library of Congress Cataloging in Publication Data

Carey, John M.
Legislative voting and accountability / John M. Carey.
p. cm.
Includes bibliographical references and index.
ISBN 978-0-521-88493-8 hardback
ISBN 978-0-521-71191-3 (pbk.)
1. Legislative bodies – Voting. 2. Representative government and representation.
I. Title.

JF511.C37 2009
328.3′75-dc22   2008019287

ISBN 978-0-521-88493-8 hardback
ISBN 978-0-521-71191-3 paperback

Contents

Preface   *page* ix

1 TO WHOM ARE LEGISLATORS
       ACCOUNTABLE?   1
       1.1. Introduction   1
       1.2. Decisiveness Problems   4
       1.3. Collective versus Individual Accountability   7
       1.4. Legislators, Principals, and the Structure of
              Accountability   14
       1.5. Plan of the Book   20

2 COLLECTIVE ACCOUNTABILITY AND
       ITS DISCONTENTS   23
       2.1. The Strong-Party Ideal   23
       2.2. Legislative Parties and Discipline in Latin America   25
       2.3. Trouble in Paradise: Partisan Representation
              Falling Short   29
       2.4. The View from the Chamber   36
       2.5. The Shift toward Individual Accountability   40

3 THE SUPPLY OF VISIBLE VOTES   43
       3.1. Visible Votes and Accountability   43
       3.2. Who Can Monitor Votes?   49
       3.3. The U.S. Experience   51
       3.4. The Supply of Recorded Votes in Latin America   55
       3.5. Conclusion   65
       Chapter 3 Appendix   66

4	DEMAND FOR VISIBLE VOTES	68
	4.1. Is Transparency Desirable?	68
	4.2. Incentives to Monitor and Publicize Votes	70
	4.3. How the Political Actors See Things	74
	4.4. Effects of Recorded Voting	83
	4.5. The Trend toward Visible Votes and Its Limits	90
5	COUNTING VOTES	92
	5.1. Party Voting Unity and Collective Accountability	92
	5.2. Measures of Voting Unity and Success	94
	5.3. The Silence of Nonvotes	96
	5.4. Data on Recorded Votes	102
	5.5. Describing Voting Unity	107
	Chapter 5 Appendixes 1–6	112
6	EXPLAINING VOTING UNITY	125
	6.1. Legislative Parties and Institutional Context	125
	6.2. Competing Principals and Existing Accounts of Party Unity	126
	6.3. Cohesiveness and Discipline: Weighted and Unweighted Indices	128
	6.4. Hypotheses: Legislative Parties and Competing Principals	132
	6.5. Picturing Party Unity across Systems	141
	6.6. Models	146
	6.7. Results	150
	6.8. Extending the Analysis	159
	6.9. Conclusion: Competing Principals Disrupt Voting Unity	162
7	THE INDIVIDUAL-COLLECTIVE BALANCE	165
	7.1. Transparency, Party Unity, Votes, and Accountability	165
	7.2. Reviewing the Major Points	166
	7.3. The Optimal Mix?	169
Appendix: Interview Subjects by Country		177
References		181
Index		195

Preface

Shortly after the 2006 election, in which the Democrats recaptured control of the U.S. Congress, the spoof newspaper *The Onion* ran a story in which Nancy Pelosi, the new Speaker of the House, reprimanded her partisan colleagues for supporting her legislative agenda without necessarily meaning it. Referring to a fictitious bill, *The Onion* had Pelosi admonishing Democrats not to "just pass it because *I* want it, but because *you* want it, too," and went on to describe Pelosi's "concern that her relationship to the House was based completely on voting" (*The Onion*, 42 [49], December 4, 2006).

Legislative decisions are about votes, and voting behavior is organized by parties. If we want to understand legislatures and the representation they provide, it makes sense to look at partisan voting. To *The Onion*, the joke was that Pelosi might care about anything beyond that bottom line.

It never got big laughs, but I had a similar idea in mind around a decade ago, when I started the project that became this book. At the time, the study of voting in the U.S. Congress was a bustling cottage industry, but there was almost no information about legislative voting outside the United States. The reason, it seemed to me, had to be the lack of available data on votes. So, to begin, I set out to collect data on votes in a number of legislatures, mostly in Latin America where I had some experience, but also in other assemblies where I could establish research connections. My first surprise was that, in most countries, it was exceedingly unusual to record how each legislator voted on a given proposal. What *The Onion* took to be the bedrock of legislative representation could not be taken for granted in many democracies.

As I explored the issue across more and more assemblies, it became clear that a prior question – before *how* legislators vote – is whether assemblies make it possible to *know* how legislators vote. So the research agenda evolved and expanded, and I spent as much time talking with politicians, journalists, and activists about whether they favored voting transparency, and why, as I did collecting and analyzing voting data.

As it turns out, I spent a lot of time on each, which accounts for the ten years that passed between starting the project and publishing this book. Those years have seen progress in the study of legislative voting beyond the halls of the U.S. Congress. This book takes a step toward mapping, and explaining, the world of partisan voting in legislatures. Data availability remains an obstacle in most assemblies. Many still record few or no votes, and those that do record often do not make vote records easy for outsiders like scholars, or citizens, to examine. The problem is more than academic. Lack of voting transparency is also an obstacle to accountability.

There is much more on this topic in the book itself. Here, I want to recognize and thank the organizations and the people who made my research possible. The book offers the broadest cross-national analysis of recorded voting to date, and all the data collected for the project are available online for other researchers to use. Doing field research in ten countries, and collecting the data from fifteen others, required resources, expertise, and effort beyond what I could muster on my own. Early financial support was provided by National Science Foundation Grant SES-9986219 and also by the Weidenbaum Center on the Economy, Government, and Public Policy at Washington University in St. Louis.

I received outstanding research assistance at Washington University from Christopher Kam, Connor Raso, Meg Rincker, John Bunyan, Sarit Smila, Alba Ponce de León, Erica Townsend Bell, Gina Reinhardt Yannitell, Adam Bookman, Rachel Kaul, Cheryl Boudreau, Juan Gabriel Gómez Abellardo, Amy Nunn, and (now Senator) Jeff Smith. Jeff Staton's contributions are better described as collaboration than as research assistance, and I continue to learn from Jeff. Rebecca Cantú provided solid assistance during my brief visit at Harvard. At Dartmouth, assistance from Anne Bellows, Justin Brownstone, Xavier Engle, and Seth Goldberg helped bring the project across the finish line.

In the course of conducting field research and in collecting data from assemblies far and wide, I drew on the expertise, and often on the hospitality, of dozens of generous souls. Eduardo Alemán, Mark Jones, Valeria Palanza, Roberto Sabá, and Mariano Tommasi shared data and provided insights into Argentine politics. In Bolivia, thanks go to Diego Ayó, Carlos Cordero, William Culver, René Mayorga, José Rivera Eterovic, and Eduardo Rodriguez. On Brazil, I am grateful to Barry Ames, Octavio Amorim Neto, Scott

Desposato, Argelina Figuereido, Wendy Hunter, Eduardo Leoni, Fernando Limongi, Scott Mainwaring, Carlos Pereira, Timothy Power, David Samuels, and Kurt Weyland. On Canada, New Zealand, and Australia, Christopher Kam was, and is, the man. On Colombia, thanks to Luis Fajardo, Ana Julia Ramos, and Elisabeth Ungar. In Costa Rica, Jorge Vargas Cullel and Aixa Ansorena, Rafael Villegas Antillón, and Leo Nuñez Arias competed for the title of most gracious hosts, and most insightful political experts. In the Czech Republic, thanks to Elena Mielcova and to Daniel Munich for sharing data. Felipe Cisneros and Andrés Mejía helped lead me through Ecuador's dense political thicket. In El Salvador, David Holiday was another dual provider of safe haven and deep political knowledge. Eric Voeten graciously shared voting data on France. On Guatemala, Harry Brown Araúz, Javier Fortín, and Reginald Todd all offered key insights. On Israel, the politics of which is pretty much self-explanatory to begin with, Itai Sened and Doron Navot offered yet further clarity. Thanks to William Heller for insights on the Italian parliament. In Mexico, Jeffrey Weldon, Joy Langston, Cecilia Martínez-Gallardo, and Alejandro Poiré all walked me through the politics of a democratizing legislature. In Nicaragua, Guillermo García showed me the ins and outs of the Assembly and provided critical contacts. In Peru, Cynthia Sanborn made me feel at home and also led me through the shifting post-Fujimori political landscape. I was happy to receive further help on Peru from Catherine Conaghan, Gregory Schmidt, and Rick Walter. Steven Braeger, Sheila Espine-Villaluz, and Carl Landé all shed light on the Philippines. In Poland, Wieslaw Dobrowolski and Jacek Mercik shared data, and Meg Rincker provided on-the-ground knowledge. On the Russian Duma, thanks to Moshe Haspel and Thomas Remington. Thanks also to Manuel Alcántara in Salamanca, Spain, for making data available from his Proyecto Élites Latinoamericanas. In Venezuela, Ricardo Combellas explained the politics of Hugo Chavez's (first) constitutional overhaul, while Brian Crisp, José Molina, Steve Ellner, Janet Kelly, Michael Coppedge, Miriam Kornblith, Berta Peña, and Juan Carlos Rey delivered all-around expert observations.

Drafts of various papers that eventually formed parts of the book benefited from critical feedback from participants in seminars at the Universidad de los Andes in Bogotá, the University of Chicago, Cornell, Duke, Florida International University, the Fundación Juan March in Madrid, George Washington University, Harvard, the Instituto Tecnológico Autónomo de México, Notre Dame, Ohio State, Oxford, the Universidad del Pacífico in Lima, Princeton, and the University of Vermont.

1

To Whom Are Legislators Accountable?

1.1. Introduction

1.1.1. Overview

Legislatures are, formally, the principal policymaking institutions in modern democracies. The most fundamental policy decisions – budgets; treaties and trade agreements; economic, environmental, and social regulation; elaboration of individual and collective rights – all must be approved by legislatures. What forces drive legislators' decisions? What different political actors place demands on legislators, and how do legislators' actions reflect these demands?

These are questions about what sort of representation citizens can expect from those they send off to deliberate and make policy decisions on their behalf. Citizens want legislatures to be decisive – that is, to resolve the issues before them without chronic deadlock. They also want accountability, which entails responsiveness on the part of legislators to citizens' demands. In modern democratic legislatures, the principal vehicles for delivering decisiveness are strong political parties. Decisiveness through party discipline, however, presents a dilemma in terms of what kind of accountability is possible.

This book distinguishes between collective accountability and accountability that operates at the level of individual legislators, which often make different demands on legislators. In modern democratic legislatures, collective accountability operates primarily through parties and requires legislators bearing a common party label to act in concert. Individual accountability implies a more direct link between a legislator and citizens and may require the legislator to act independently of party demands. Individual accountability also requires that information about each

1

legislator's actions be available to those outside the legislature and capable of being monitored. Because the informational conditions for individual accountability often are not met, maximum legislative individualism does not necessarily produce individual accountability.

Scholarship on legislative accountability tends to regard collective accountability favorably and legislative individualism with skepticism. Yet surveys from legislators and citizens and the substance of political reforms themselves in recent years all suggest that demand for individual accountability is strong, and technological advances have reduced the logistical obstacles to making available the information necessary for individual accountability. It is worth asking, then, whether individual accountability is feasible and whether it can coexist with collective accountability, in what measure, and under what conditions. One goal of this book is to examine whether the vote records that legislatures produce are a critical ingredient for individual accountability. A second goal is to use vote records to measure party unity, a key ingredient of collective accountability, and to explain why some parties are more unified and others less so.

To be clear, transparency in the actions of individual legislators is a necessary condition for individual accountability, and some measure of party unity is necessary for collective accountability, but neither condition guarantees perfect accountability. Legislators whose every action is known may still ignore their constituents' demands, and unified parties may pursue policies citizens abhor. This book merely suggests that individual accountability suffers when individual legislators' actions are unknown to constituents and that the failure of copartisans to act in concert undermines collective accountability. Beyond these sorts of lapses, however, the tension between individual-level and collective accountability is not fully reconcilable. Even full transparency offers access only to an accountability frontier where an increase in individual accountability requires trading off some measure of collective accountability, and vice versa. I reconsider this trade-off in the concluding chapter, but the empirical substance of most of the book examines whether the conditions exist to allow legislative representation to approach that frontier.

The book moves beyond previous research in the theoretical connection it establishes between individual and collective accountability and in its empirical scope. It illuminates the connection between legislative transparency and accountability by examining why voting is transparent in some legislatures but not others. It offers a simple and general account of the various political actors institutionally empowered to place demands on legislators and how their relative influence affects legislative party unity. This account, dubbed the competing principals model, generates hypotheses tested against voting data from legislatures in nineteen countries. By documenting what information is available about legislative votes and providing new tools to process the information, the book outlines the mix of collective and individual accountability that legislators deliver across an array of countries, as well as the potential for political reforms to alter that mix.

The rest of this chapter establishes vocabulary and concepts on which the book depends. After defining some key terms used throughout the book, I describe the unique role of political parties in organizing legislative processes and as intermediaries of accountability between citizens and their representatives. Then I contrast the ideals of collective and individual accountability and discuss how electoral rules shape the balance between collective and individual representation. Finally, I present the competing principals model of demands on legislators and outline the plan of the chapters that follow.

1.1.2. Definitions

1.1.2.1. Accountability. The expectation of accountability implies a relationship between a legislator and some other actor or actors (principals). Accountability means that legislators are responsive to the preferences and demands of their principal(s), that information about legislators' actions is available to the principal(s), and that principals can punish legislators for lack of responsiveness.

Accountability depends on professional ambition among legislators. Professional ambition may be a purely venal desire for personal advancement, or a purely altruistic desire to serve others by promoting policies that advance some conception of the public interest, or some combination of these. Whatever the motivation, ambition implies the desire to cultivate electoral resources – renomination, or else nomination or appointment to an even better office, campaign financing, and good favor among voters. It also implies that legislators value access to resources within the legislature itself, such as leadership positions, assignments to key committees, access to support staff, big offices, perks, and such. Ambitious legislators curry favor with political actors who can provide these key resources. The ability to withdraw favor, and so deny the resources that fuel professional advancement, is the enforcement mechanism behind accountability. Overall, accountability should maximize legislative effort and responsiveness to the principals' preferences and minimize corruption and other abuses of power at the principals' expense.

1.1.2.2. Principals. Principals are political actors who command some measure of loyalty from legislators, and whose interests a legislator might represent and pursue in an official capacity. Given that most legislators in democracies are popularly elected, we might think of voters as the ultimate, universal principals to whom legislators are accountable. Under some conditions, this is the case. Yet, as I argue in this book, political parties, and specifically their leadership within legislative assemblies, are in many cases the main principals that command legislator loyalty. In many institutional settings, the level of accountability of legislators to voters pales in comparison to their accountability to party leaders.

Beyond party leaders and voters, many political systems are populated by other actors who, by virtue of their institutional positions, their organizational capacity, or other resources, can command the loyalty of legislators. These include presidents, who are elected independently of the legislature but are often endowed with resources and powers legislators value or fear; governors in some federal systems, who may wield substantial resources, including control over subnational political party machines; interest groups, which direct electoral resources (funding, activist volunteers, mobilized voters); moneyed campaign contributors; and even those in a position to bribe or extort politicians.

1.1.2.3. Decisiveness. Legislative decisiveness refers to the capacity of legislatures to reach decisions on policy and to make those decisions stick. Criticisms of legislatures frequently focus on failures along these lines (American Political Science Association 1950; Sundquist 1981; Moe and Caldwell 1994). Collective legislative accountability can be a solution to legislative indecisiveness (Gerring, Thacker, and Moreno 2005; Gerring and Thacker 2008). In this sense, decisiveness is central to the question of whether legislative accountability is possible.

1.2. Decisiveness Problems

1.2.1. Bottlenecks and Cycling

Most national legislatures, and many subnational ones, are large assemblies, with diverse members numbering in the hundreds. Size and diversity present a specific challenge. The number of policy options available in any political environment is generally vast. Legislatures are supposed to pare down the potentially infinite number of policy options available to a manageable and coherent set of alternatives, among which a meaningful collective decision can be reached. Failure to solve this decisiveness problem may be the product of either too little legislative action or too much. In either scenario, legislative scholarship envisions parties as a solution.

Cox (2006a) posits a "legislative state of nature" in which all members have equal and unrestricted rights to speak on the floor on any issue, so plenary time is unregulated. This state embodies a strong egalitarian norm that privileges the ability of members to block assembly action over their ability to trigger action, raising the specter of chronic legislative gridlock, even in the face of pressing policy demands (Colomer 2001; Tsebelis 1999). From this point of departure, Cox (2006a) notes that legislatures everywhere resolve the bottleneck problem with internal organization that redistributes agenda powers unequally and that, in modern legislatures, political parties consistently control access to the privileged agenda-setting positions.

In the mirror image of Cox's vision of unlimited filibuster and effective unanimity rule, procedural rights in a legislature may be equally distributed, but rather than any legislator's being able to block a vote on any proposal, any proposal must be voted on. Now the decisiveness problem becomes the potential for chronic instability of choice rather than the inability to make any choice – that is, cycling occurs rather than bottlenecks. The rationale here is well known. Formally, at least, most legislative assemblies rely on simple majority rule for most decisions. Theoretical characteristics of majority rule decision over multiple alternatives suggest that failures of decisiveness could be characterized by general instability of legislative decisions (Condorcet 1785; McKelvey 1976; Riker 1982). Yet, even accounts of legislative politics that take the instability problem as a point of departure frequently point to political parties as the key factors that bring order to the potential chaos of majority rule (Laver and Shepsle 1996; Cox and McCubbins 1993).

In either the bottleneck-based or cycling-based account, parties are credited with providing decisiveness by establishing privileged actors who determine which proposals are debated and voted on and in which order and, in doing so, make it possible for legislators to realize gains unrealizable in unorganized, state-of-nature assemblies. The key point is that, in almost all democratic systems, parties are the gatekeepers of the formal offices that control action within the legislature. Moreover, Carroll, Cox, and Pachon (2006) demonstrate that, as democracies mature, parties expand their control over the offices that determine legislative activity, and the distribution of these offices among parties grows increasingly regular. In short, as party systems stabilize, so do the key partisan elements of legislative organization.

1.2.2. Parties and Legislative Action

How does partisan control over the flow of legislative traffic provide decisiveness? Diverse accounts of legislative politics converge around the idea that parties reduce the potentially infinite number of policy options to a limited set, primarily by establishing platforms or manifestos that advertise party positions to voters and then by disciplining legislators to constrain their voting in line with these party positions (Aldrich 1995). Comparative studies of roll call voting suggest that legislative agendas are strongly limited in ways consistent with the idea that parties produce procedural order (Poole 1998; Cox, Masuyama, and McCubbins 2000; Poole and Rosenthal 2001; Amorim Neto, Cox, and McCubbins 2003; Rosenthal and Voeten 2004).

Because parties so consistently dominate legislative organization, it is difficult to test the extent to which they account for the orderliness of voting patterns. In a pair of ingenious studies, however, Jenkins (1999, 2000) compares voting in the Confederate Congress of 1861–65 with that in the U.S. Congress during the same era. The legislatures were similar in formal structure, in membership (many legislators served in both chambers), and even in the issues on which they voted, but the Confederate Congress was not organized along party lines. Voting patterns of Confederate legislators were far less stable in important ways. First, voting coalitions were more fluid in the Confederate than the U.S. Congress (Jenkins 1999). Second, the ideological positions of Confederate legislators were less stable over time (Jenkins 2000). Overall, the results suggest that political parties impose order on voting in ways that make legislative decisions predictable and stable.

Political parties may play this role in general, but even casual observers will note that not all parties are equivalent. Comparative legislative scholarship has long made much of the difference between strong and weak political parties in controlling legislative outcomes. Yet, apart from abundant analyses of the U.S. Congress, most of the legislative world has yet to be mapped in terms of party voting unity.[1] If parties are highly unified in their voting, then party labels can carry substantial policy content. That is, citizens can observe just the partisanship of a legislator or a candidate and infer what sort of policies she or he will support and oppose in office. If, by contrast, parties are not unified, then this cue about political behavior carries less information. Given that citizens tend to rely on low-cost cues in evaluating politicians and parties, the reliability of party labels is a key component of whether voters can be said to cast informed ballots in legislative elections (Lupia and McCubbins 1998).

1.3. Collective versus Individual Accountability

1.3.1. Competing Visions

The discussion of decisiveness in legislatures implies the outline of a case for collective legislative accountability through party-dominated representation. The key components of the case are as follows. Legislatures are called upon to make decisions on a wide-ranging set of policies. The difficulties of collective decision making mean that no individual legislator can credibly claim credit or responsibility for shaping policy on such a scale. In contrast, political parties can both encompass a broad idea of the public interest and plausibly claim to deliver policies that advance this idea. But legislative parties can do this only if they are unified. Meaningful legislative accountability, therefore, must be collective, through the organization of legislatures by strong parties.

Yet, in the eyes of many political reformers, the idea of party-dominant legislative representation has less appeal, and demands for accountability to citizens at the level of individual legislator predominate. For example, throughout Latin America in recent years a number of political reform efforts have aimed to disconnect legislators from national party leadership

---

[1] Levels and sources of party unity have been extensively examined in the U.S. Congress, where scholarship has been preoccupied for more than a decade with parsing to what extent levels of party voting are due to like-mindedness among copartisans (cohesiveness) versus pressure from party leaders (discipline) (Krehbiel 1998; Cox and Poole 2004). For "unmapped" legislatures, the basic question of how unified parties are is of prior concern to the cohesiveness-versus-discipline matter. Whatever its cause, some measure of voting unity is necessary for party labels to convey information that is useful to voters. I take up the matter of overall level of voting unity in Chapter 5 and the issue of cohesiveness versus discipline in Chapter 6.

when the demands of leaders conflict with responsiveness to local constituencies. Reform advocates describe popular disenchantment with disciplined parties directed by leaders who are insulated from punishment by voters. In many cases, moreover, both the strong discipline and the insulation of the leaders can be traced to a common source: electoral systems in which control over candidate nominations is centralized among party leaders and voters are allowed no means to distinguish among candidates within a given party. The problem is most severe in systems of proportional representation, where multiple seats are awarded in each electoral district.

The accountability dilemma here can be described as follows. As a politician advances within the party leadership, her access to power and perks increases dramatically, but her electoral vulnerability decreases in a corresponding manner because leaders occupy the top positions on closed party electoral lists. This mitigates the leadership's susceptibility to electoral punishment, even if its party as a whole loses electoral ground. As a result, the leaders who stand to gain the most from violating public trust and pillaging state resources stand to suffer the least electoral indignity if their party, collectively, is punished by voters. Rank-and-file politicians, whose heads are the first to roll in any partisan electoral setback, might object to being relegated to the marginal list positions that buffer their leaders, but would-be rebels face a serious collective action problem in revolting against their party leaders, because troublemakers can simply be removed from the lists or demoted to perilous or even hopeless list positions by the leadership.

The individualist dissent from the strong-party ideal implies a case for accountability at the level of each legislator. The core of the argument rests in the critique of party-dominated representation as imbuing the most powerful legislative leaders with a sense of distance from voters that insulates them from public disapproval. Instead, the argument goes, legislators are most responsive to citizen demands when each is responsible for cultivating her or his own support constituency, which in turn can reward and punish its representative directly at the polls. Whereas advocates of collective, partisan representation are primarily concerned with the ideological and policy content of party labels, the decisiveness of legislatures, and the voters' assessments of overall government performance (Powell and Vanberg 2000), advocates of individual-level accountability are more concerned with maximizing virtue – deterring the betrayal of the demands of particular voters who picked an individual legislator as their representative (Persson, Tabellini, and Trebbi 2003).

1.3.2. *Excursus on Electoral Rules: Iraq versus Afghanistan*

The individualist dissent over legislative accountability focuses heavily on the electoral link between citizens and their representatives – specifically, on whether elections that foster collective representation can, or should, be modified to foster individual accountability. Scholars, policymakers, and journalists sometimes mistakenly equate the trade-off between collective and individual representation with the distinction between proportional representation and single-member district systems. Because proposals for institutional design and reform often focus on elections, it is worth considering how electoral rules do, and do not, map onto the matter of collective versus individual representation. A comparison of two contemporaneous, high-stakes cases of institutional design is useful for illustration.

Amid all the debates surrounding the regime changes in Afghanistan and Iraq during the middle years of this decade, one of the less voluble, but nonetheless crucial, was the discussion among both policymakers and academics over how to craft mechanisms to represent diversity in each country's new legislative assembly.[2] U.S.-led invasions of Afghanistan in 2001 and Iraq in 2003 had produced governments commissioned to craft new constitutions and to hold elections to fill the political offices so founded. In both cases, there was widespread acknowledgment that plural societies warranted representation of broad diversity within the legislature. A fundamental challenge in both cases was to identify what sort of diversity ought to be privileged in legislative representation. Various dimensions of representation, including geography, ethnicity, religion, and gender, were prominently on the table in each case. Less widely noted was that the debates over how best to move toward electoral democracy in Afghanistan and Iraq embodied the fundamental trade-off between collective and individualistic representation in contexts relatively unbound by existing precedent.

1.3.2.1. *Iraq.* Iraq elected two legislatures in 2005 – first, in January, a transitional dual-purpose parliament and constituent assembly, the main task of which was to draft a constitution to be ratified in an

---

[2] The brief discussion that follows here of Iraq and Afghanistan is not meant to serve as a thorough review of legislative electoral rules, much less as a comprehensive analysis of the politics of these countries. The former is provided in an impressive literature on comparative electoral systems (Duverger 1954; Taagepera and Shugart 1989; Lijphart 1994; Cox 1997), and the latter is well beyond my capacity.

October plebiscite; then a National Assembly to serve a full four-year term under the new constitution. Notwithstanding some subtle but important modifications to the electoral rules between the two elections, the central characteristic of both Iraqi elections was strong collective representation. The electoral law for January, crafted primarily by the United Nations Electoral Assistance Division and handed down as law by the outgoing, U.S.-led Coalition Provisional Authority, stipulated that the entire country encompassed a single electoral district with 275 seats, the implications of which were far-reaching for the types of legislative representation possible in Iraq (Dawisha and Diamond 2006).[3]

First, the high district magnitude effectively mandated that elections would be based on closed lists. Voters would not have the option of casting preference votes for individual candidates. Second, high magnitude made it possible to award legislative seats to lists that won relatively small vote shares overall, thus allowing for a high degree of proportionality. Third, a nationwide list system like Iraq's does not favor any predetermined concept of representation – for example, geographical, ethnic, or religious – but rather simply rewards lists that can mobilize the most voters. However, because the composition of the assembly is determined as much by the selection of candidates as by the popular vote, such a system also opens up the possibility of adopting measures that might tip legislative representation toward categories of candidates disadvantaged in a more individualistic electoral marketplace. Specifically, in the Iraqi case, gender quotas for candidates mandated that every third candidate must be a woman.

Both of the Iraqi elections in 2005 produced assemblies in which twelve separate lists won representation. The effective number of seat-winning parties was 3.14 in January and 3.45 in December (Laakso and Taagepera 1979), and the elections were marked by a close correspondence between votes cast and seats awarded to each list, with a Gallagher Disproportionality Index of less than 3 percent both times (Gallagher 1991) and substantial representation of ethnic groups previously marginalized in Iraqi politics (Burns and Ives 2005). The guaranteed placement of women at regular intervals on closed lists translated into assemblies with 29 and 26 percent of women overall – almost twice the worldwide

---

[3] One compelling motivation for this choice had to do simply with logistics of electoral administration: Iraq lacked a reliable census by which legislative seats might be apportioned across districts according to population.

average (Inter-Parliamentary Union 2006). In sum, by the benchmarks widely used in legislative studies at least, the Iraqi system realized many of the normative goals associated with the representation of diversity at the collective level.

1.3.2.2. Afghanistan. The Afghan experience with establishing a national assembly was substantially different. An indirectly elected assembly drafted a new Afghan Constitution that was ratified in early 2004 and stipulated the popular election of both a presidency and a bicameral legislature later that year. The presidential election took place on close to the original schedule, in October 2004, but legislative elections were twice postponed, in part because of the logistical challenges of conducting elections that simultaneously honor the determination of the Afghan government to:

- guarantee an element of regional representation via geographical districts;
- avoid a winner-take-all system of elections in which only the top party or candidate in a district wins representation;
- ensure voter choice over individual legislative candidates; and
- guarantee the representation of women (Johnson, Maley, Thier, and Wardak 2003).

Although critics sustained objections, and uncertainty about the electoral system remained into the early months of 2005, Afghan president Hamid Karzai ultimately settled on the single nontransferable vote (SNTV) for the September election (Reynolds 2006). SNTV, currently used only in Taiwan, Jordan, and Vanuatu, but most familiar for its long use in Japanese elections, from 1958 to 1994, is plurality rule in multimember districts. Each voter casts a ballot for her or his first-choice candidate, and the candidates with the most votes are elected in each district, up to the number of seats available. SNTV is attractive in its simplicity, and for its potential to allow minority groups to secure representation while simultaneously holding out the promise of a bond of direct personal accountability between voters and their representatives.

SNTV, however, is subject to at least two severe drawbacks that undermine its potential to provide viable representation in the Afghan context. First, SNTV presents any collective political actor – a party, for example – with a formidable coordination problem in translating electoral support into legislative representation. The problem is a fundamental conflict of interests between the party and its individual politicians.[4] Parties seek to win as many seats as possible. Individual politicians may prefer to be members of strong parties, but their first priority is to win office. Under SNTV, candidates who seek to minimize the risk of individual defeat have incentives to draw votes away from copartisans, undermining the collective goal of translating votes to legislative representation efficiently. By privileging electoral individualism, SNTV presents formidable challenges to parties' ability to foster internal cooperation among politicians and thus to provide collective representation (McCubbins and Rosenbluth 1995; Cox and Thies 1998; Marlowe 2007).

An even more immediate challenge to the feasibility of SNTV in Afghanistan was the incompatibility between individualistic legislative representation and the representation of women. The Afghan Constitution requires that at least two lower-house legislators from each of the country's thirty-four provinces be female (Art. 83). SNTV provides no alternative basis other than individual vote totals for awarding legislative seats, so unless at least two of the top candidates in each province were women, the Afghan system requires bypassing male candidates with more votes in order to seat female candidates with fewer votes. In a society where gender-based inequalities in personal resources, as well as gender bias among voters, constrain the viability of female candidates, this outcome was inevitable. In the September 2005 election, 19 women were elected on the basis of their vote totals alone, but 49 additional women were awarded seats in the Loya Jirga despite having won fewer votes than 422 other male candidates (Reynolds 2006). In sharp contrast to Iraqi gender quotas, the purely personalized and individualized character of legislative voting in Afghanistan throws into stark relief the mechanism by which quotas delivered these women to their seats while male candidates with higher vote totals lost.

The fundamental contrast in the Iraqi and Afghan choices over electoral rules, at this point, is between privileging collective and individualistic representation. For myriad reasons, the system chosen in Iraq leans toward the former. This facilitated the initial, descriptive representation of various collective identities – most notably by party alliance, ethnicity, religion,

---

[4] The problem is also increasingly severe as district magnitude increases. Magnitudes in Japanese SNTV elections ranged from three to five. In Afghanistan, the median district magnitude for parliamentary elections was seven, with a third of districts electing ten or more representatives, and the largest, Kabul, electing thirty-three (Constitution of Afghanistan, Article 82; Reynolds 2006).

and gender. Afghan rules lean toward privileging connections between voters and individual candidates. Trying simultaneously to guarantee representation according to at least one prominent form of collective identity, gender, presents a formidable challenge.

1.3.3. Collectivism versus Individualism, Not Proportional Representation versus Single-Member Districts

The Iraqi and Afghan cases suggest that the distinction between individualistic and collective representation can be more important than the principal characteristic by which electoral systems are more frequently distinguished – whether elections are winner-take-all in single-member districts (SMD) or are based on proportional representation (PR). The characteristics and relative merits of SMD versus PR are central to a long-standing literature on legislative elections, whose predominant conclusion has been that PR elections are normatively superior to SMD elections (Sartori 1976; Lijphart 1994; Huber and Powell 1994; Colomer 2001). This conclusion rests on two key assumptions, however: that political parties are fundamental units of legislative representation and that a left-right spectrum meaningfully describes the ideological arena of party competition. In the long-standing industrialized democracies, where most studies of legislative representation have been conducted, there is solid empirical evidence for these assumptions (Powell and Vanberg 2000). They are open to greater skepticism in other environments, though, particularly where party systems are more volatile or party reputations less stable.

The point here is that the foundation on which the conventional SMD versus PR debate has been conducted is weak in many political environments where the most critical choices about how to organize legislative representation remain open. The Iraqi and Afghan cases, in which established party systems are completely absent, are extreme examples, but it is worth noting that SMD versus PR was not central to the debate in either context; winner-take-all rules gained traction in neither case (Dawisha and Diamond 2006; Reynolds 2006). Rather, the critical distinction in these cases is over whether electoral rules ought to prioritize collective versus individualistic representation. This theme has been central to debates over reforming legislative representation much more widely during recent decades, particularly with respect to mixed-member electoral systems that combine SMD with list PR elections within the same legislative chamber, variants of which were adopted in the 1990s by more than twenty countries

(Shugart and Wattenberg 2001; International Institute for Democracy and Electoral Assistance 1997; Culver and Ferrufino 2000).

Legislatures offer the promise of representing the diversity of the polity, but electoral rules affect the dimensions along which diversity can be translated into representation. Although the differences between SMD and PR elections have traditionally been essential to the study of comparative legislatures, this distinction is growing less central relative to that between individualistic and collective representation, which is quite a different matter, both theoretically and empirically (Carey and Shugart 1995). Whereas the literature on comparative legislative representation tends to favor PR over SMD, there is less academic consensus on the relative merits of individualistic versus collective representation (Golden and Chang 2001; Persson and Tabellini 2003).

1.4. Legislators, Principals, and the Structure of Accountability

1.4.1. Party Leaders and Everyone Else

At the beginning of this chapter, I defined accountability in terms of the relationship between a legislator and a principal or principals who control resources the legislator values and so command loyalty. The discussion of decisiveness that followed illustrates why parties are ubiquitous in legislatures and why they control important resources. Thus, legislators always and everywhere confront, in the leadership of their own party, a key principal in a position to impose demands on their behavior. For legislators in many environments, moreover, party leadership is pretty much the only principal that matters. In electoral systems where voters cast ballots only for the party, and where party leaders control access to their own lists, there is no direct link between legislators and voters. The Iraqi case is an example, but it is far from unique (Lijphart 1999).

In contrast, for a legislator elected by a purely personal vote, the support constituency is clearly a primary principal, but even such a legislator generally confronts two principals – voters and party leaders – because party leaders control resources within the legislature itself even when electoral rules encourage individualism. The extent to which legislative individualism predominates over collective, partisan representation depends on the relative value of the resources that are controlled by either the voters or the party leaders, and the propensity of voters and party leaders to want different things and thus pull "their" legislators in opposite directions.

14

In short, because of the ubiquity of parties, even the individualistic vision of legislative representation tends to involve (potentially) competing principals: voters who pick an individual legislator, and the party (or bloc, or group, or coalition, etc.) with which the legislator aligns in the assembly. Yet the potential for principals to compete for legislator loyalty and the effects of this on legislative individualism go beyond party versus electoral constituency. In many political systems, other actors control at least some resources that affect the legislative process or the ambitions of legislators.

Most prominent here are presidents, who are elected independently from legislators but who are often constitutionally endowed with legislative authorities, such as vetoes, decree- and rule-making powers, or the ability to offer or amend legislative proposals under restrictive rules. Presidents also control appointments to public offices and may have discretion over the release of budgetary funds for public projects. In many democracies, the list of resources controlled by presidents and valued by legislators is extensive. As a result, the possibility for presidents to exert pressure on legislators to act in ways contrary to party, or constituent, demands is substantial.

Though to a lesser extent than presidents, governors in some federal systems control significant resources valued by national legislators. In Argentina, for example, provincial governors often control their parties' nominations, including those for incumbent legislators who aspire to re-election or to election to some other office. In Brazil, governors control appointments to state-level cabinet posts that are widely sought by national legislators. Like presidents, governors may exert pressure on legislators in ways contrary to the demands of the party at the national level.

The list of other principals who potentially compete with party leaders for the loyalty of legislators is not limited and could include interest groups, political activists, those who fund campaigns, and those who use bribery or extortion to induce compliance. My focus in this book is on the most prominent and prevalent principals who exert pressure on legislators in the widest range of contexts: party leaders, voters, and, in systems where the chief executive is directly elected, presidents.

1.4.2. Competing Principals and Individualism

Let us combine the themes discussed in this chapter to consider the relationship between the various principals to which legislators might be accountable and the ideas of collective-versus-individualistic representation. Given the prominence of strong parties as a normative ideal in much of the literature on legislatures, and in light of the empirical fact that democratic legislatures are organized along party lines, I rely on party unity as a touchstone, a fundamental metric. From that conceptual point of departure, I regard legislative behavior in terms of its deviation from party unity.[5]

In terms of legislative principals, representation is party-dominant when the party leadership is the only political actor to which legislators are directly accountable. This occurs when central party leaders control nominations for legislative office and list positions (if more than one legislator is elected from a district). That is, voters are not afforded the opportunity to select from among various legislative candidates within a party. Under these conditions, party leaders control not only resources interior to the legislature but also the key electoral resources on which a legislator's career depends. Voters can reward and punish parties collectively for their positions and performance, and so can be regarded as principals of the parties via elections, but they have no direct say over the fate of individual legislative candidates. Under such conditions, accountability is entirely collective, at the party level. Given the undiluted influence of party leaders over legislators, party unity ought to be high under these conditions. The relationships among legislators, parties, and voters are portrayed in Figure 1.1, where the arrows indicate control by a principal with the political resources to reward and punish.

VOTERS

PARTY

LEGISLATOR

Figure 1.1 Party-dominant representation.

---

[5] In Chapter 6, I also consider broader legislative coalitions – government versus opposition, for example – but parties are the component units of such coalitions, so this is simply a matter of moving to a higher level of aggregation.

Next, consider a political system where voters have the ability to reward and punish individual legislators directly, perhaps because primary elections determine nominations, or because party lists are open and candidates win legislative seats according to their individual preference votes, or because there are no party lists at all and multiple candidates from each party run either in a free-for-all format or under a transferable vote rule.[6] Under any of these circumstances, the voters are a legislator's direct principal. Because party labels are generally attached to the candidates for whom voters vote, and because in the aggregate a party's fortunes depend on the success of its candidates, voters are also indirectly principals to the parties. Meanwhile, party leaders, in all likelihood, remain important principals for legislators, to the extent that they control resources within the assembly itself that legislators value. They may also retain control over electoral resources, such as influence over nominations and financing. Thus, legislators now confront two principals, who may well make competing demands (see Figure 1.2).

We could add a directly elected president to either of these scenarios, as in Figure 1.3. The formal powers of presidents over the legislative process vary enormously, but most control access to coveted appointed posts, and many are endowed with authority to shape the legislative agenda directly, to veto all or parts of bills, and to offer counterproposals to legislative initiatives (Shugart and Carey 1992; Aleman and Tsebelis 2005). The array of powers of most directly elected presidents provides substantial leverage with which to influence legislative behavior. As with a direct electoral

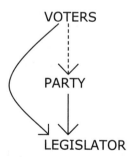

Figure 1.2 Parties and voters as competing principals: Individual-predominant representation.

---

[6] See Carey and Shugart (1995) for more details on the variety of electoral systems and their relationship to the relevance of the personal vote, as well as for empirical examples.

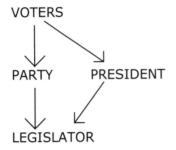

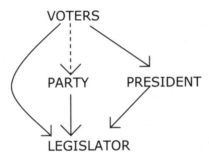

Figure 1.3 Presidents as competing principals with party leaders.

connection to voters, presidential influence adds another, potentially competing, pressure to that exerted by party.

The list of potential principals placing demands on legislators could expand, and some research on legislatures has explored specific examples. Carey and Reinhardt (2004) examine the influence of state governors on their national-level legislative copartisans in Brazil. Unlike presidents, the governors do not exercise direct authority over the national legislative agenda, but they do direct the flow of many resources that are essential to legislative reelection prospects, and they control access to state-level appointed posts that, in Brazil's decentralized system, are attractive to many national legislators. Hix (2002) demonstrates that members of the European Union Parliament experience varying levels of competing pressures from the leadership of their party blocs within the EU Parliament itself and from the national-level parties from which they are elected in

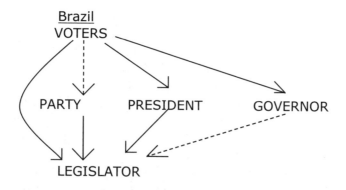

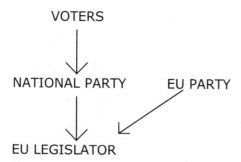

Figure 1.4 Increasingly complex sets of principals.

their countries of origin. Figure 1.4 suggests how such additional principals might map onto the accountability relationships described so far.

As the number of principals grows, the potential for competing pressures to pull legislators away from solidarity with their party increases, and we should expect party unity to drop.

Does the lack of party unity indicate the existence of legislative individualism? I interpret it as such, for a couple of reasons. One is that deviance from the party line often indicates an effort by a legislator to act on behalf of a constituency of citizen supporters, independently from any mediating forces. This story is associated with the idea of the personal vote and of individual-level accountability in the simplest sense (Cain, Ferejohn, and Fiorina 1981; Carey and Shugart 1995). But what if a legislator is pulled away from the national party by another institutional political actor – by the president, for example? Then deviance from party loyalty might not be regarded as simply a matter of individual volition. Yet, as Sophocles' Antigone discovered, cross-pressures, by their nature, turn the decisions individuals make into acts of self-definition. In this light, a legislator who lines up with the president (or governor, or whomever) in contradiction to her legislative party leadership is staking out a position, even if reluctantly, for which she can be held individually accountable. Finally, although the number of potential principals making demands is not limited, legislative decisions almost always come down to binary choices – voting aye or nay. We may sometimes know what side a president is on, or a governor, or an interest group. Less reliably still can we draw any inferences about what the legislator's constituency supporters demand. We can know, however, what side a legislator's party is on by how her copartisans voted.

In short, party unity is the point of reference because legislatures everywhere are partisan, because legislators everywhere answer to party leaders as principals, and because party unity can be identified by the fundamental act of legislative decision making – that is, voting. Where party unity is lacking, there are various stories we can tell about legislative motivation, but they all involve legislators' making decisions to deviate from the game plan of the team – the collective unit – that is the central basis of legislative organization. It is no accident that the term "party line" has entered our vernacular to connote the antithesis of individualism and independent thinking. I contrast party unity and collective representation, then, with disunity, which I associate with legislative individualism. The type of accountability that is possible in any given legislature depends on what sort of representation is provided.

1.5. Plan of the Book

The next chapter discusses collective, party-dominated representation as an ideal, as well as in practice in a range of (mostly) Latin American legislatures. I note the high regard for the idea of collective representation in academic opinion but also the contemporary decline in confidence in political parties among the public. I review various reforms aimed at reducing the influence of central party leaders in Latin America and survey evidence from legislators in fifteen Latin American countries indicating their skepticism about centralized authority in parties and their devotion to the ideal of individualistic representation.

Chapters 3 and 4 explore the conditions under which accountability at the level of individual legislator is possible, focusing on the level of transparency in the fundamental decisive action in all legislatures: voting. Chapter 3 reviews the history of individual accountability through voting records in the United States and then examines the supply of recorded votes throughout Latin America. Chapter 4 shifts the focus to the factors that create, or resist, demand for transparency in legislative voting. Drawing on interviews and primary and secondary documentary sources, I argue that the demand for recorded voting comes most consistently from opposition legislators, dissidents within governing parties and coalitions, and outside groups with an interest in monitoring legislative action. The basic logic is that legislators' most ubiquitous principals, party leaders, have a structural advantage – proximity – in monitoring legislative voting. If other potential principals are to make effective demands on legislators, they need to be able to monitor as well, and that requires externally visible votes. Legislators who want to appeal to outside principals also have an interest in recording votes. Despite resistance from those who control legislative agendas, pressure for transparency from these sources, combined with technological changes that reduce the costs of recording and publishing, is steadily increasing the supply of recorded votes.

The empirical material in Chapters 2, 3, and 4 is drawn overwhelmingly from Latin America for a couple of reasons. First, I am interested in the prospects for individual accountability as a normative rival to collective accountability; individualistic representation is greater in presidential systems than in parliamentary systems; and the greatest concentration of presidential regimes is in the Americas. The political systems of the Americas represent "most likely cases," in that if we are to observe individualistic representation and individual-level accountability anywhere, it is likely to be there. The presidential systems of the Americas may, therefore, exhibit a bias toward legislative individualism, but they should also provide a good window on the variety of ways in which this sort of behavior manifests itself – an attractive property for this mostly qualitative portion of the book. The second reason is purely pragmatic – I am better able to conduct field research in Latin America than in many other parts of the world, because of language and access to sources.

Chapters 5 and 6 turn to the quantitative examination of recorded votes from legislatures in nineteen countries. Here the empirical scope grows broader, in that I draw on recorded vote data from systems beyond the Americas, but also somewhat shallower, in that no recorded votes at all are available for most legislatures, and the records that are available are generally light on context beyond the digital ones and zeros of aye and nay votes. Chapter 5 describes the recorded vote data, as well as the various indices I use to turn the vast matrices of legislators' aye and nay votes into statistics that describe either voting unity at the party or coalition level or the alternative, legislative individualism. That chapter also presents statistics that describe the levels of party unity in the various political systems for which I have collected recorded votes.

Chapter 6 develops and estimates a statistical model of the factors that affect the diversity of principals to which legislators are accountable. The analysis shows that party unity is highest when party leaders are the dominant principal – that is, in parliamentary systems where voters do not cast personal preference votes among candidates. Factors that subject legislators to influences from additional principals can diminish voting unity. Electoral rules that provide for a personal vote among copartisans have this effect. The presence of an independently elected president can also reduce unity, particularly among legislators allied within the president's own party and governing coalition. Presidents, in short, are as much liabilities as assets to their legislative allies.

The final chapter concludes with observations about the distinction between legislative individualism and individual accountability, and the potential for compatibility between the latter and collective accountability.

2

Collective Accountability and Its Discontents

2.1. The Strong-Party Ideal

The normative desirability of strong-party government is often taken as axiomatic among academics. In 1950 the American Political Science Association published a widely read report urging reforms to strengthen the two major U.S. parties in the name of enhancing collective accountability, or what the APSA called "responsible party government." In doing so, the APSA was itself hearkening back to a vision of party-led parliamentary government espoused almost a century earlier by the British journalist and scholar Walter Bagehot (1867). As the APSA (1950:1) put it, "An effective party system requires, first, that the parties are able to bring forth programs to which they commit themselves and, second, that the parties possess sufficient internal cohesion to carry out these programs."

The report, moreover, explicitly linked the party unity that makes possible collective accountability to the ability of the national party organizations to cultivate control over the sort of electoral resources that would make them stronger principals to congressional candidates:

As for party cohesion in Congress, the parties have done little to build up the kind of unity within the congressional party that is now so widely desired. Traditionally congressional candidates are treated as if they were the orphans of the political system, with no truly adequate party mechanism available for the conduct of their campaigns. Enjoying remarkably little national or local party support, congressional candidates have mostly been left to cope with the political hazards of their occupation on their own account. A basis for party cohesion in Congress will be established as soon as the parties interest themselves sufficiently in their congressional candidate to set up strong and active campaign organizations in the constituencies. (1950:21–22)

Current observers might argue that, in the closing decades of the twentieth century, both the Republican and Democratic parties in the United States heeded the APSA's advice in developing formidable candidate recruitment and fundraising organizations at the national level. Indeed, voting unity in both parties rose substantially (Jacobson 2000; Lowry and Shipan 2002). These developments, of course, have been greeted with criticism by many, and calls for reform, much as the looser, midcentury congressional party system did. Yet recent criticism is generally aimed at strategies of campaign finance, whereas the broader ideal of unified parties and collective responsibility retains solid academic support (Corrado 2002; Mann 2003; La Raja 2003).

The norm is even more widely held among academic observers of legislatures outside the United States, according to a recent study of discipline throughout Europe:

The maintenance of a cohesive voting bloc inside a legislative body is a crucially important feature of parliamentary life. Without the existence of a readily identifiable bloc of governing politicians, the accountability of the executive to both legislature and voters falls flat. It can be seen, then, as a necessary condition for the existence of responsible party government. (Bowler, Farrell, and Katz 1999:3)

Wrapping up a broad survey of the state of political parties in Latin America in the 1990s, Mainwaring and Scully (1995:473–74) lament the tendency of presidents to campaign and govern based on personalistic appeals rather than by cultivating stable party support:

As electoral democracy becomes accepted as *the* mode of forming governments in most Latin American countries, and as the enormous costs of weak party systems become apparent, perhaps leaders will pay more attention to the challenge of building democratic institutions and will govern through parties and with them. Without a reasonably institutionalized party system, the future of democracy is bleak.

In short, strong parties have long been held in high academic esteem. In the next section, I describe how legislative parties in a variety of Latin American legislatures where I have conducted research reach and enforce collective decisions. This is a description of the mechanics by which the collective vision of representation through parties might be realized. Political reformers often see things differently. It is not that they aspire to feckless parties. Nor, indeed, would most academics who call for strong parties aspire to Leninist centralism. But whereas academic observers have been inclined, on the whole, to see parties as weaker than they ought to be and needing fortification, the general tide of reform in Latin America has run against the authority of central party leaders, in the name of increasing the accountability of individual legislators.

2.2. Legislative Parties and Discipline in Latin America

2.2.1. How Parties' Positions Are Determined

All legislatures with which I am familiar are organized along party lines, meaning that party units are accorded rights over legislative resources, including representation on the organ that controls the legislative agenda, as well as whatever offices and staff are available. Party groups in Latin American legislatures are variously known as *fracciones*, *bancadas*, or *grupos*.[1]

The norm among legislative party groups in Latin America is to meet at least weekly when the legislature is in session to discuss the upcoming agenda and to establish both whether there is to be a group position on each issue and what those positions will be. Party groups are subordinate to national party organizations and generally can be instructed by them as to how to vote on specific issues.[2] National party congresses invariably occur less frequently than legislative party group meetings, but national party executive committees generally have authority to establish the party line. There is frequently some overlap between members of party executive committees and legislators, particularly among legislative group leaders. Many parties also retain disciplinary bodies, composed of national party leaders, that are authorized to impose sanctions on legislators who break discipline on votes where a party line has been established.

Among the partisan groups from which I have interviewed deputies (see the Appendix for a list), in Bolivia, Colombia, Costa Rica, Ecuador, El Salvador, Mexico, Nicaragua, Peru, and Venezuela, there is remarkable consistency on how decisions are made. Unless consultation is sought

---

[1] Generally, the connection between electoral and legislative parties is straightforward, but it may not be. Party switching in the legislature between elections is common in some countries, particularly where legislators are elected on the basis of personal votes, where volatility in party support is high, or both (Thames 2007). Brazil is notorious on both counts (Desposato 2006b; Samuels 2000). Rules of procedure in many legislatures also require some minimum membership level for registration of a party group, so parties that have insufficient numbers may be forced either to coalesce in the legislature or to forgo whatever resources are allocated to groups.

[2] Venezuela's 1999 constitutional provision (Art. 201) prohibiting such constraints is unusual in this respect.

from, or imposed by, the national party organization, the norm is that decisions are made in party group meetings by majority rule. This applies to the question of whether to require discipline (or, alternatively, to leave a matter open to conscience) and, if so, what the party line should be.

In a few cases, a provisional position for a party group can be set by the group's leaders themselves, although in cases where such an initiative prompts dissent the fallback is to deliberate and vote within the party group. According to Hugo Carvajal, Movimiento Izquierdista Revolucionario deputy and former president of Bolivia's Chamber of Deputies,

> The *bancada* decides [its position] depending on the parliamentary rhythm; the parliament has rhythms. The consultation sometimes gets only as far as a *bancada* leader, and he defines a position and then transmits it to the group – we could say he "socializes" with the members – this decision that he's already made and has adopted in the name of the collegiate body. Sometimes this produces short circuits in the members' reaction.

In the case of such short circuits, the remedy is deliberation and a vote within the *bancada*.

2.2.2. Discipline

Across the overwhelming majority of parties in the countries where I conducted interviews, legislators reported that most votes are matters of discipline. Without estimating precise rates of discipline, Salvadorans concurred that open votes are rare events (A. Alvarenga and Duch interviews). Similarly, Carvajal estimated party-line voting 85 to 90 percent of the time in Bolivia's MIR, Guillermo Landazuri estimated the rate to be 90 percent within Ecuador's Izquierda Democratica, and Xavier Neira reckoned it higher within that country's Social Christian Party (Carvajal, Landazuri, and Neira interviews). In Costa Rica, open votes appear to be slightly more common, as do breaches of the party line on disciplined votes. The chief of staff to the Costa Rican Assembly's *mesa directiva*, Eladio Gonzalez (interview), estimated that across all parties 80 to 85 percent of votes are subject to discipline among all parties.

The most noteworthy exception to regular decision making at the level of the party group was in Colombia, where legislators from both major parties, the Liberals and Conservatives, in both chambers reported that there are infrequent group meetings and that the majority of votes are left open, without any established party decision or direction on how to vote

(Acosta, Devia, García, Gómez Gallo, Navarro, and Holguín interviews).
As Hernán Andrade (interview) put it,

Because . . . practically all the members of our party, as in all of the parties, were
elected thanks to our own efforts, there's no feeling of unity and there's no mechanism in the *bancadas* that allows for prior, coordinated decision making, except in
exceptional cases. . . . Each of us is his own party. Each of us gets here due to our
own effort, with our own financing, with our own friends, without any clear ideology – most of the time *hiding* the party we come from. There's no channel that leads
to the *bancada*, there's no partisan attachment.[3]

In explaining the sources of intrapartisan divisions, interview subjects
concurred that cohesiveness tends to be greater in smaller groups, where
there is more homogeneity of opinion, but that this is offset by economies
of scale that larger groups enjoy in providing benefits that induce loyalty
among legislators. Benefits range from physical resources, like offices and
staff, to committee assignments, to favorable treatment for private member
bills and budgetary funds for individual legislators' chosen projects (de la
Cruz, Hernández, and Hurtado interviews).

2.2.3. How and When Sanctions Are Imposed

Legislators from all parties could cite cases of indiscipline, and they offered
various accounts about how, and how effectively, parties respond. Consistent with academic accounts, pre–Hugo Chavez Venezuela appears to have
produced nearly airtight discipline across the party spectrum (Coppedge
1994). Combellas (interview) affirmed that breaches of party discipline in
legislative voting were rare in all parties, and that every instance – in state
assemblies as well as at the national level – triggered expulsion by the
national party organization. He noted, however, that the "conscience"
provision in the 1999 Constitution (Art. 201) may provide judicial protection for undisciplined politicians.

Legislators in every country except Colombia acknowledged the existence of procedures to provide for expulsion on grounds of indiscipline, but
most emphasized that party leaders prefer to induce loyalty by other means,
if possible, particularly ones that are less public and dramatic. Vicente
Albornoz (interview), of Ecuador's Democracia Popular, for example,

---

[3] Colombia subsequently reformed the extremely individualistic electoral system to which
Andrade refers in this comment, replacing it with one that retains substantial individualism
but increases somewhat the extent to which copartisans' electoral fates are intertwined.

noted that expulsion is used only if a breach of discipline is pivotal to the outcome of a vote, citing a recent tax increase in which votes by renegade deputies had turned the outcome. Nonpivotal defections, on the other hand, tend to be tolerated without formal sanction.

In some countries, including Bolivia, El Salvador, and Nicaragua, electoral party lists assign both a primary legislator (*propietario*) and a substitute (*suplente*) to each legislative seat. When the *propietario* is unwilling to support the party line but willing to recuse himself from a vote, parties summon the corresponding *suplente* (A. Alvarenga, Samper, and Sanchez de Lozada interviews). Only in Mexico, where I interviewed just the president of the lower house and his staff, was there any reluctance to discuss mechanisms by which party discipline is enforced.

The most common theme running through accounts of party discipline, by legislators across parties and systems, was control over career prospects. Not surprisingly, all legislators are acutely aware of party control of this critical resource. According to Alexis Sibaja (interview), Costa Rica's minority party leader,

There is party discipline because political careers in Costa Rica are partisan. My future is in Liberación Nacional (PLN), not outside it. I am disciplined every day because I'm always interested in advancing within the PLN. . . . Desertions on important matters are judged harshly by party militants and supporters. Those who have deserted the party line in the past have effectively been retired from politics because the party is very strict.

Academic accounts, as well as those of other interview subjects (Vargas and Vargas Pagán interviews), suggest that Sibaja overstates the inviolability of party discipline in Costa Rica, but he is unambiguous about the source of what discipline exists. To the extent that legislators are ambitious for political careers and parties can control access to these careers, parties can induce legislative discipline. In August 2000 Mónica Baltodano (interview) described hardball politics within Nicaragua's Frente Sandinista (FSLN) over her breach of discipline two months earlier on an electoral reform bill on which the Frente had agreed to a compromise with the governing Liberals:

Party rules say that on issues of national importance, the party organs decide and the *bancada* is subordinate to these decisions. . . . The Sandinista national assembly decided to go ahead with this reform, and they gave us the chance to express our points of view. Afterward, we [four FSLN legislators] broke discipline. Then, according to the statutes, we could have been sanctioned with expulsion or other measures. This wasn't convenient to them, politically. So they ruled that whoever did not accept party decisions could not aspire to electoral posts. Everyone knew I wanted to run for mayor of Managua, and this way I couldn't be nominated. It's almost certain that they won't permit me to run for reelection as a deputy either. And they took other measures. I was vice president of the Assembly's executive committee, and they took that away, and they won't let me chair any committees.

Baltodano correctly anticipated continued conflicts with party leaders over her aspirations. In December, facing public rebukes from party leaders for failing to support their chosen nominee for the 2001 presidential election, Baltodano noted that if she were in violation of party protocol, the FSLN was bound by its own statutes to expel her, "But they have not done that; therefore they cannot trample on any of my rights" (Latin America Data Base 2001). Although the party's executive committee stopped short of expulsion, it issued a statement formally barring Baltodano from nomination for reelection, citing as the reason her vote in the Assembly against the electoral reform law.

The most consistent theme in the interview responses regarding sources of party discipline is that parties have sanctioning mechanisms on the books, but except for unusual circumstances, less formal measures serve to induce discipline by appealing to legislators' career ambitions.

2.3. Trouble in Paradise: Partisan Representation Falling Short

2.3.1. The Costs of Collective Reputations

Legislative accountability is complicated by a basic tension between party discipline and individual responsiveness. The problem is that unified collective action by its legislators is necessary for a party to pursue its collective goals, whether the goal is to implement policy or to capture state resources, but the discipline required for effective collective action can undermine individual legislators' responsiveness to their constituents. There is a trade-off between demanding that legislators follow the party line and allowing them flexibility to cultivate support by responding to diverse interests.

Parliamentary systems of government are widely held to resolve the tension between collective and individual accountability in favor of the former. So long as legislators value the stream of future benefits associated with sustaining the government, the collective responsibility of governing entities from cabinets to assemblies places a premium on party and coalition discipline over individualism (Cox 1987; Huber 1996; Diermeier and Feddersen 1998).

Whether in parliamentary or presidential systems, coherent party labels and the legislative efficiency achieved by discipline are both public goods shared among supporters of the party that provides for them. Breaching discipline may serve the particular interests of a given legislator's supporters, but it degrades the public good shared by copartisans. To wit, the fundamental dilemma of party discipline, and the root of the tension between discipline and individual responsiveness, is that "My own discipline to the party is in my interest only when it is in my interest, but your discipline is in my interest generally."

In Chapter 6, I present cross-national evidence confirming that governing parties in parliamentary systems are more unified in legislative voting than those in presidential systems. For now, I simply note that even observers of European parliamentary systems document that breaches of discipline occur and are products of demands for direct responsiveness by representatives to their electoral constituencies when these run counter to collective partisan objectives (Lanfranchi and Luchi 1999; Whitely and Seyd 1999). Studies of European public opinion have noted a general decline in trust in political parties over the past few decades (Pharr, Putnam, and Dalton 2000). Scarrow (2001a) attributes a rise in provisions for direct election of executives and local officials, as well as in initiatives and referenda, in Organisation for Economic Co-operation and Development (OECD) countries to citizens' decreasing trust in parties. Similar trends are evident among the presidential democracies of the Americas. Although public opinion survey data do not extend back so far as in Europe, the Latinobarómetro (2003) annual survey picks up declining trust in political parties regionwide from the mid-1990s to the early years of this decade. Barczak (2001) documents an increase in provisions for, and the use of, direct democracy throughout Latin America, which she attributes to widespread popular dissatisfaction with political parties and the promise to increase the responsiveness of political institutions to popular demands.

In short, there is a widely acknowledged tension between collective and individualized accountability, and some scholars have noted signs of dissatisfaction with party-dominated representation. For the most part, however, studies of legislatures in presidential systems, and in Latin America in particular, have been critical of individualized representation, demonstrating a normative bent toward strong parties capable of coordinating legislative actions. This position reflects a preoccupation among Latin Americanists about the marginalization of legislatures by powerful executives, but it is also rooted in a preference for collective partisan accountability behind a broad program of government (Linz 1994; Valenzuela 1994). A central idea here, as in the literature on accountability in parliamentary systems, is that strength in these aspects is necessary for parties to be able to offer citizens coherent choices over policy and, in turn, be judged by citizens in elections on the basis of past performance and the credibility and appeal of their promises for the future (Luna and Zechmeister 2005; Rosas 2005).

2.3.2. Political Reform and Individual Accountability: Mixed-Member Electoral Systems

Political reformers appear little concerned with currents in academic opinion – in this case, with the normative emphasis on strong parties. Throughout Latin America, a number of reform measures in recent years have aimed to disconnect legislators from national party leadership when this conflicts with responsiveness to local constituencies. A prime example is the adoption in Bolivia, Guatemala, Panama, Venezuela, and Mexico in the past two decades of mixed electoral systems, combining single-member districts (SMDs) with proportional representation (PR) in over-arching districts.[4] The explicit goal of such reforms is most often to tighten the local constituent-legislator bond, even at the expense of discipline among national parties.[5] As part of an effort to resuscitate support for a discredited party system in the early 1990s, for example, the President's Commission on State Reform (COPRE) in Venezuela advocated the shift from closed-list PR to SMD-PR elections on the grounds that the previous system

> strengthened the party line, which is defined by the top party leaders and the tribunals of discipline responsible for its application. As a result, the legislators vote as the party dictates without attending to the demands and interests of voters in their regions . . . [whereas legislators elected under the proposed SMDs] ought to act in the interests of their electors, ought to attend to their demands, ought to respond to their mail, and will have to explain to their electors why they vote as they do in the deliberative body. (Rachadell 1991:207–8)

---

[4] Ecuador, meanwhile, combines personal voting in two-seat districts with closed-list proportional representation in an upper tier.

[5] Mexico used a straight SMD plurality until the 1970s, approaching the mixed system from the opposite direction, adding PR seats gradually from the late 1970s to the early 1990s, to allow for minority-party representation while maintaining the advantage that SMD plurality tends to provide for the largest party (Molinar Horcacitas and Weldon 2001).

The same motivation spurred the shift from pure closed-list PR election to SMD-PR in Bolivia in 1994 where the plummeting stature of political parties, evident in street protests as well as opinion polls, was understood as a demand from voters "that deputies should be known and acknowledged representatives of their constituencies and not anonymous representatives of party leaders. Direct connections between deputies and voters would therefore enhance the legitimacy and representativeness of the parliament, making possible the responsiveness and accountability of deputies to their constituencies" (Mayorga 2001). Precisely the same arguments were made by advocates of a proposal for SMD-PR in Costa Rica in 2000 (Sibaja interview).

Whether these reforms deliver enhanced individualistic representation and accountability remains an open question. In Bolivia, an early review of the local responsiveness of SMD deputies (called *uninominales*) found only modest improvements (Culver and Ferrufino 2000). In Venezuela, electoral reform in the late 1980s proved insufficient to salvage public support for the traditional parties and avert their complete collapse in the 1990s. Yet the COPRE's recommended SMD-PR format survived even President Chavez's constitutional overhaul of 1999; indeed, the champions of Chavez's reforms echoed the COPRE's calls for strengthened electoral ties to local constituencies (Combellas, Tarek Saab, and Fernández interviews).

Finally, although the empirical focus of this book is primarily Latin America, it is worth noting that the arguments made in that region resonate as well among SMD-PR advocates in Europe and elsewhere. In the past decade and a half, Italy, Japan, New Zealand, the Philippines, Russia, and Ukraine have adopted mixed SMD-PR electoral systems.[6] Richard Katz describes the Italian electoral reform of 1994 as motivated by popular demands for alternation in government and for "direct accountability of individual members of parliament to their electors. There was a desire to free the electorate from the confines of party labels and ideologies, and to allow electors to take into account the character, qualifications, and performance in office of individual candidates when casting their votes" (Katz 1994:103). Historically, the "mother of mixed systems," in Germany, was distinguished by its advocates from the prewar Weimar system of closed-list PR by its virtue of strengthening the connection between voters and individual representatives. As noted by Susan Scarrow (2001b:63),

---

[6] Germany has used such a system since 1949.

German advocates of mixed-member rules argued that such rules would "personalize" voters' choices by letting them choose individual representatives from small districts – indeed, Germans still refer to their system as being an example of "personalized PR," a label that is meant to distinguish it from proportional systems that lack a nominal tier.

2.3.3. Venezuela's Constitution of 1999

Perhaps the most controversial institutional reform in recent decades in Latin America was the adoption, at the behest of President Hugo Chavez, of a new constitution for Venezuela in 1999. Chavez's critics decry him as an autocrat who has systematically removed or enfeebled any meaningful checks on his own power (McCoy 1999; Gunson 2006). His admirers tout his reforms as improving the quality of democracy in a system long dominated by an entrenched and unaccountable oligarchy of parties – a "partyarchy." Without attempting to arbitrate this debate, which promises to endure well beyond Chavez's presidency, I note here only that the 1999 constitution includes a number of new measures aimed specifically to foster personal responsibility by legislators to their district constituencies.

There is a four-year residency requirement for eligibility to run for the legislature from any given district or state, designed to ensure that representatives know firsthand the needs and preferences of district voters (Art. 188). Legislators are obliged to "render accounts" of their activities each year in public forums (*rendiciones de cuentas*) in their districts and to explain and defend their behavior and their votes (Arts. 197, 199). All legislative votes are explicitly deemed matters of individual conscience for representatives, rather than matters of partisan obligation (Art. 201). Finally, all elected officials are subject to recall elections, which can be initiated by a petition of 10 percent of the voters in their districts (Art. 72, 197).

To the extent that forcing legislators to render accounts to their districts produces additional information for constituents about legislators' actions, its connection to the idea of accountability established in Chapter 1 is straightforward. More broadly, game-theoretical analysis suggests that requiring individual representatives to explain votes increases the efficiency of electoral punishment for legislators otherwise inclined to ignore constituents' wishes and, in doing so, enhances responsiveness at the individual level (Austen-Smith 1994). All these anticipated effects were articulated – albeit, without the game theory – by Venezuelan legislators in interviews. Ricardo Combellas, a constituent assembly delegate and opponent of President Chavez, describes the motivation behind the reforms:

We wanted to eliminate partyarchy – not to eliminate it constitutionally, but in terms of norms, for the representative to respond more directly to the wants and needs of his constituents. His responsibility in parliament is personal – the Constitution says so – not to respond to a party but to his constituents. We established a rendering of accounts that didn't exist before . . . [and] a vote of conscience that wasn't there either. . . . [In the past], the parties overwhelmed their representatives. They imposed the line, imposed the vote, imposed attitudes. We have tried to relax this and create a more fluid relationship between legislators and their constituents. Besides, a legislator now has to have lived at least the past four years in the region where he is elected. And we have recall elections. All this is to say that there are innovative constitutional reforms, very different from what we had before, but that we don't know how they're going to work. That much will require a cultural change, but what we did with the Constitution was important.

Referring to the same set of provisions, *chavista* constitutional delegate and later deputy William Tarek Saab is even more unrestrained in his interview: "A big space is opened where the parties used to have complete control, and power is completely realigned. I think that we have put organized society above the parties – that the organized people, the organized popular movement will have a chance now because these constitutional measures give them a chance." Whatever effect, if any, these provisions have on legislative representation in Venezuela in the long run, Chavez supporters, and at least some skeptics, justify their intent as increasing the personal accountability of politicians, even if this loosens the bonds of party.

2.3.4. Citizen Demand for Legislative Individualism

Measuring overall citizen opinion about the proper balance between party control and individual legislative responsiveness is difficult. Nevertheless, some surveys tap into the issue, as do data from elections in countries where ballots offer voters the choice of casting a party or an individual preference vote. Again, these eclectic sources support the proposition that there is a deeper reservoir of public support for individual-level accountability than is reflected in most of the academic literature.

In a rare public opinion poll addressing the matter of legislative individualism directly, 1,505 Chileans were asked in 2007 whether, in general, deputies and senators in Congress ought to vote according to their own preferences or the preferences of their parties. Nearly twice as many respondents wanted legislators to vote their own preferences rather than with their parties – 50 to 28 percent (Centro de Estudios Públicos 2007).[7]

A 2006 survey in Bolivia tapped into the same sentiment, albeit indirectly, during the lead-up to elections for a constituent assembly, which was widely expected to declare itself sovereign and appropriate the powers of the existing legislature. In this context, 3,013 Bolivians were asked how members of such an assembly should be elected: by political parties, by citizen groups, by indigenous groups, by labor unions, by municipal committees, in single-member districts, or none of the above.[8] The two alternatives with which survey respondents were most familiar were by parties and in SMDs, because Bolivian democracy used closed-party-list PR elections up through the mid-1990s, and a mixed-member system combining SMDs with closed-list PR thereafter. Of these two options, SMDs are widely associated with individual-level accountability and election by parties with collective accountability. More than twice as many survey respondents preferred election in SMDs to election by political parties – 19 to 7 percent (Seligson et al. 2007:106–7).[9]

Finally, consider that, in the current decade, both the Dominican Republic and Colombia adopted ballots that allow voters the option of casting a preference vote for an individual candidate or endorsing a single slate presented by their party.[10] Given the choice, voters overwhelmingly used the individual-candidate preference vote. In the Dominican Republic's 2006 election, its first with the preference vote, 80 percent of voters exercised that option (Morgan, Espinal, and Seligson 2006:135). Colombian ballots first offered the preference vote in 2005, and 80 percent of voters used it there as well (Shugart, Moreno, and Fajardo 2006, table 7.9). In Brazil, which has offered the list-versus-preference option longer, between 82 and 92 percent of voters exercised the preference vote option in elections from 1990 to 2002 (Nicolau 2007:108).

---

[7] Another 11 percent each said it depended on the circumstances, or offered no opinion.

[8] The menu is, admittedly, a bit ambiguous, in that the details of selection within these groups were not spelled out.

[9] The plurality choice was by citizen groups (34%), with other responses including municipal committees (11%), indigenous groups (6%), unions (5%), and no opinion (15%).

[10] The Dominican Republic previously used closed-list PR. Colombian lists were also closed, although each party was allowed to present multiple lists, injecting substantial individualism into Colombian elections.

2.3.5. The Move toward Individualism

The reforms discussed here were developed independently, and the opinions and behaviors cited are drawn from various legislative environments, but a common thread running through them is the stated intention to strengthen the accountability of individual legislators to voters. At least in their rhetoric, contemporary Latin American political reformers are critical of legislative party discipline because it conflicts with the individual accountability that they endorse and that citizens apparently desire. In the next chapter, I discuss a reform I regard as integral to any shift toward individual legislative accountability – recorded voting. For now, I turn to some survey evidence that the expressed preference for greater legislative individualism is widespread among legislators themselves.

2.4. The View from the Chamber

During the late 1990s, and again during the first half of this decade, the Proyecto de Elites Latinoamericanas project conducted surveys of legislators throughout Latin America on an array of issues, including the principals to whom they are responsive and their disposition toward party leaders. Some of the questions were repeated across the two rounds of surveys, and attitudes toward party leadership and discipline in these cases show remarkable stability over time (Alcántara 1994–2000; Proyecto Élites Parlamentarias Latinoamericanas 2006). In most cases, the team was able to get responses from well over half the membership of the lower chamber (or only chamber, in unicameral systems) and across the full range of parties. Of course, one must take into consideration that the survey respondents, the legislators themselves, might answer according to what they regard to be norms of acceptable behavior. To put it less delicately, survey responses could be self-serving. Nevertheless, there are good reasons to expect that the surveys contain useful information, especially for the purposes of comparison across countries.

Most important, the surveys are anonymous, so from a legislator's perspective there is nothing to be gained from self-promotion. Contrast this with the legislator interviews on which I draw throughout this book. I introduced the interviews purely for the purposes of academic research, but I did not present anonymity as the default condition, and almost no interview subject requested it. Subjects frequently described their own actions as based on personal ambition, political deal making, and compromise of principles (not to mention how they depict the machinations of their colleagues). If interviewees are willing to portray their behavior in a manner that might be regarded as unseemly despite the lack of anonymity, then it is reasonable to expect a greater level of candor in the surveys.

The next three figures present the relative influence of three potentially important principals – national party leaders, voters in their district, and the government – on the decisions legislators make. Respondents were asked whether they take the opinion of each principal into consideration "a lot," "somewhat," "a little," or "not at all" when making political decisions. In the interest of simplicity, Figure 2.1 presents the results with respect to our universal principals, party leaders, with the combined percentage of "a little" and "not at all" responses subtracted from the percentage of "a lot" and "somewhat" responses.

The first thing to note is that a plurality of legislators in every country, and big majorities in most, acknowledge paying substantial attention to party leaders. Note that if 70 percent say "a lot" and "somewhat" while 30 percent say "a little" and "not at all," the net score will still be 40 percent, as in Chile, for example. Venezuelan and Peruvian respondents profess the most independence from party leaders, although this could be at least in part a product of the specific cohorts of legislators

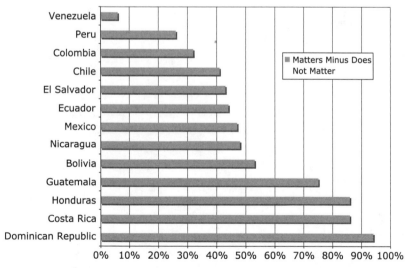

Figure 2.1 How much do you take the opinion of national party leaders into consideration when making political decisions?

to which the surveys in these countries were administered. The Venezuelan survey was administered in 2000, following directly on the ratification of the new constitution, which repeatedly professes its commitment to legislative independence from partisan control. The Peruvian survey was administered in 2001, following the downfall of President Alberto Fujimori's government on corruption charges, in a context where the principle of party discipline was tarred with the brush of corruption (Carey 2003). On the whole, however, legislators acknowledge substantial deference to party leaders. Colombian legislators are generally regarded as dismissive of party leaders, as the interview responses suggested, but even here only a little more than 30 percent say they pay little or no attention to this principal, whereas twice as many professed some allegiance.

On the other hand, in twelve of the thirteen countries for which I have survey data, more legislators say they pay "some" rather than "a lot" of attention to party leaders (not visible in Figure 2.1). Although legislators take party leaders into consideration, they reserve a higher level of deference for another principal, voters in their district, as indicated by Figure 2.2.

In every country surveyed, more legislators claimed to pay greater attention to voters in their district than to any other factor when making

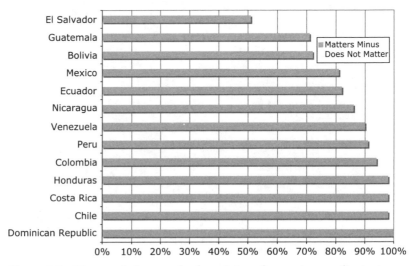

Figure 2.2 How much do you take the opinion of voters in your district into consideration when making political decisions?

political decisions. Other potential sources of influence in the survey, but not discussed in detail here, included national public opinion, voters from within the legislator's party, the media, and interest groups. According to the surveys, none warranted such deference as district voters. This is noteworthy, particularly because most of the legislators surveyed were elected from closed party lists in which the direct link between district voters and their representatives is tenuous at best.

Figure 2.3 shows the amount of attention legislators claim to pay to the government in forming their decisions. Within each country, responses separate according to whether the legislator's party is allied with the president or not, with the former indicating greater levels of deference to this principal and the latter, lower levels. Even among presidents' allies, however, the levels of stated deference do not approach those legislators' claim to voters in their districts.

As a final indication of this tendency, consider the survey question, "Do you think the national party leadership should have more power over legislators, less power, or maintain the same?" Figure 2.4 shows the percentage responding "more" minus that responding "less," such that negative

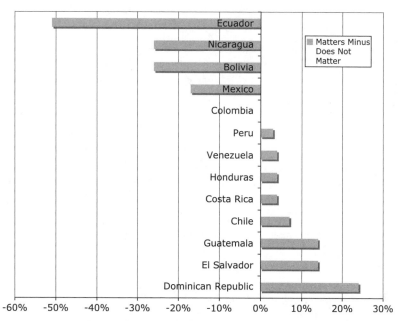

Figure 2.3 How much do you take the opinion of the government into consideration when making political decisions?

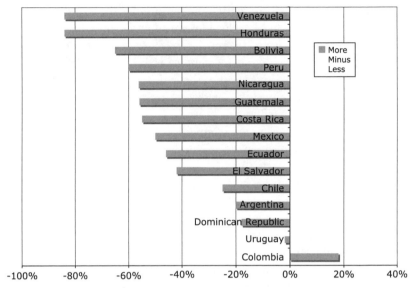

Figure 2.4 Do you think the national party leadership should have more power over legislators or less?

numbers favor decreasing party leader control overall. In every country but Colombia, more respondents said "less" than "more," generally many times more. In ten of fifteen countries, an outright majority of respondents indicated a preference for less central party control. Across countries, the mean level of support for increased party control is 13 percent, whereas the mean support for decreased control is 56 percent.

According to the surveys, legislators claim they prefer more of their own discretion, and less control from their parties, toward the expressed priority of representing the interests of voters from their districts. All this may be posturing, of course, if legislators for some reason felt obliged to dissemble on the surveys. Even if the relative commitment professed for district voters versus party leaders or presidents is not sincere, it indicates a professed commitment to the sort of representation generally associated with legislative individualism rather than collectivism.

2.5. The Shift toward Individual Accountability

In this chapter, I suggest that over the past decade various factors have increased the sensitivity among legislators in Latin America to pressures other than the demands of national party leaders. It is important to acknowledge that even party leaders should not necessarily demand blind responsiveness to the national command on the part of their troops. Total failure by legislators to attend to local, sectoral, and even individual constituent demands can leave national leaders sitting atop organizations with no electoral support. This calculus by national leaders was responsible for the adoption of mixed-member electoral systems in Venezuela and Bolivia (Crisp and Rey 2001). National party leaders pursuing such a strategy may parcel out reforms providing a modicum of individual flexibility while retaining other powers and resources that ensure discipline. Thus, for example, leaders of most Bolivian, Mexican, and Venezuelan parties have maintained centralized control over candidate nominations, seriously limiting the extent to which district pressures induce even SMD legislators to buck party discipline (Mayorga 2001).

Despite these constraints, however, the overall trend is toward the exposure of legislators to increasing pressures from sources in addition to their parties. In the mixed-member systems, SMDs induce individual legislative entrepreneurship and constituency service. Moreover, other electoral reforms aimed at increasing voter discretion among candidates within parties, such as preference voting within lists and primary elections for candidate nominations, have been advanced in Costa Rica, Mexico, and Venezuela. These reforms are expected to increase the willingness of legislators to break party discipline in legislative voting (Kulischeck and Crisp 2001; Mayorga 2001; Weldon 2001; E. Vargas interview).

Even the Colombian electoral reform of 2003, which aimed to enhance collective accountability by requiring that each party present a unified list of candidates in each district rather than multiple lists, affords parties the option of presenting open or closed lists to voters. It is noteworthy that, in the 2006 congressional elections, the first to employ this new system, more than 80 percent of parties competing opted to present open lists and that more than 80 percent of voters seized the opportunity to cast a preference vote for an individual candidate rather than simply to indicate a choice for a party's list as a whole (Shugart, Moreno, and Fajardo 2006). In short, among reformers of late – and among voters – there is a strong attraction toward individual accountability as a normative priority in legislative elections.

Have institutional reforms enhanced legislative individualism in Latin America? This is a hard question to answer. The Proyecto de Elites Latinoamericanas data provide snapshots of legislative attitudes, but we lack survey data over long time periods. In taking stock of specific reforms, one confronts similar challenges. The 1999 Venezuelan Constitution is still relatively young, and Venezuelan politics during its first few years has been punctuated with government crises (Gunson 2006; Pérez-Liñán 2007). With respect to Latin America's mixed electoral systems, early case studies suggest some impact. Even before Chavez's overhaul of the Venezuelan Constitution, SMD-PR elections generated legislators with distinctive perceptions of accountability. A majority of SMD deputies surveyed in 1997 claimed that citizens' votes are based on the personal characteristics of candidates, whereas more than 90 percent of PR list deputies contended that voters "think of politics in terms of parties" (Kulischek and Crisp 2001). In Bolivia, similarly, one observer judged the mixed system to have "produced two classes of deputies and two different parliamentary roles. Overall, a trend toward locality-centered politics, constituency-serving 'retail politics' (and perhaps also corporative politics) has been strengthened at the expense of national politics" (Mayorga 2001).

Systematic cross-national comparisons are more difficult, and I do not offer a definitive judgment on the reforms discussed in this chapter and their effect on individualism. In Chapters 5 and 6, I propose various indices of party unity that measure the willingness of individual legislators to buck party unity and evaluate the factors that generate high levels of unity or, conversely, more legislative individualism. The indices are based on legislative votes recorded at the level of the individual legislators. But the entire project of studying individual voting behavior confronts a fundamental and serious problem – namely, that in many legislatures recorded votes are scarce or unavailable altogether. In the next chapters, therefore, I explore the prior phenomenon of recorded legislative votes themselves, describing where they exist, where they do not, why, and what the practice of recording legislative votes implies for legislative accountability at the individual level.

3

The Supply of Visible Votes

Let us make public the names of those who voted in favor, so our children will know whom they should curse.

Russian legislator Yuli Rybakov, on a proposal to accept nuclear waste from other countries in exchange for cash (National Public Radio 2001)

3.1. Visible Votes and Accountability

3.1.1. Questions about Visible Votes

Whatever else voters in the United States know or do not know, they can count on being alerted as to whom they should curse for any decision Congress makes. Interest groups publish widely cited "report cards" based on legislative voting records, challengers comb through their incumbent opponents' records, and incumbents whose voting records are out of sync with their districts' interests pay an electoral price (Canes-Wrone, Brady, and Cogan 2002). It is sometimes held that elected representatives generally operate according to a calculus familiar to U.S. legislators. In her cross-national study of corruption, for example, Susan Rose-Ackerman (1999:127) offers as axiomatic that, "If politicians vote against the interests of their constituents, they can expect to suffer at the polls." But is this true? In many legislatures, who voted for and against a given proposal is almost never revealed, and proposals to record votes at all are contentious.

The conditions that foster, or undermine, political accountability are increasingly central to students of comparative democracies (Adserá, Boix, and Payne 2003; Cleary and Stokes 2006; Johnson and Crisp 2003; Stokes 2001).

43

The broad question motivating this chapter, and the next, is whether the information necessary to make individual accountability possible is available from legislatures. Why tie the transparency of information about legislative votes so tightly to individual but not collective accountability? This chapter argues that the responsiveness of individual legislators depends heavily on which of their potential principals can easily monitor their actions. Party leaders can monitor voting in the legislature relatively easily, regardless of whether the votes are published and transparent. A lack of transparency, therefore, fosters asymmetry between party leaders and constituents. Voting transparency is less relevant to citizen monitoring of parties as wholes. Even when individual voting records are unavailable, those outside the legislature can get access to information about the policy positions and actions of major collective actors – parties, unions, business associations – at relatively low cost through newspapers and broadcast media. This chapter emphasizes the connection between transparency and individual accountability, contending that, when votes are not readily visible, the costs of information about individual legislative behavior are prohibitive for legislative outsiders.

To make the case, I address a number of specific questions: What information about votes is available? What factors generate change in the revealed information about votes? What conditions are necessary for voting records to be politically salient? What effect does public voting have on the relationship between individual representatives and their parties? As the chapter discusses, the amount of information revealed about votes varies tremendously across legislatures. Vote records are potentially salient in all legislatures, although more in single-member-district than multi-member-district electoral systems. Lawmakers disagree on whether public voting is desirable, with those who control the agenda generally opposed. Pressures from opposition and dissident lawmakers and from pro-transparency actors outside legislatures, as well as technological advances, all encourage publication of legislative voting records. Finally, there is a tension between public voting by individual legislators and disciplined voting among political parties.

3.1.2. Looking for Visible Votes in the Americas

I bring to bear on these issues evidence from Latin American legislatures, as well as observations about the genesis of public voting in the United States. The country cases included in this examination of legislative transparency are described in Table 3.1.

Table 3.1. *Data Included in Analysis of Legislative Transparency*

Country	Data on the Number of Visible Votes	Archival and Interview Data Based on Field Work	Archival Data Based on Research Assistance and Correspondence
Argentina	X		X
Bolivia	X	X	X
Brazil	X		X
Chile	X		X
Colombia	X	X	X
Costa Rica	X	X	
Ecuador	X	X	
El Salvador	X	X	
Guatemala	X		X
Mexico	X	X	X
Nicaragua	X	X	
Panama	X		X
Peru	X	X	
United States	X		X
Uruguay	X		
Venezuela	X	X	X

What are the implications of examining this particular set of cases? First, all these cases are presidential, and together they constitute most of the pure presidential democracies in the world. In these regimes, the separation of powers allows legislative performance to be evaluated independently from executive performance (Cox 1987; Diermeier and Feddersen 1998; Samuels 2004). Because legislative votes on individual policy proposals do not directly affect the survival of the executive in office, as they may under parliamentary and hybrid regimes, accountability for individual voting decisions ought to be more pronounced under presidentialism. If public voting is politically salient anywhere, then it should be so in the Americas. In this sense, the countries examined in Chapters 3 and 4 may be biased toward high demand for legislative transparency. Amplified demand could facilitate the job of detecting conditions that encourage transparency – for example, by heightening sensitivity to whether particular electoral rules or procedural rules favoring the opposition favor transparency of individual legislators' behavior. If this is the case, it may be that in parliamentary and hybrid regimes the effect of similar conditions on transparency should be muted.

The exclusive concentration on presidential regimes in the next two chapters is largely a product of resource constraints.[1] As an initial examination of legislative voting transparency, it focuses on the "most likely suspects." The U.S. case is a benchmark in assessing the importance of public voting because that is where the practice is most firmly established and most widely recognized to be politically consequential. In Latin America, demands for individual-level legislative accountability have increased in recent years, and the availability of reliable electronic voting equipment has dramatically reduced the logistical barriers to public voting (Barczack 2001; Mayorga 2001; Rachadell 1991). The interview and archival evidence presented in these chapters suggests that voting transparency can be central to legislative accountability – at least under presidentialism, an institutional format expected to favor scrutiny of individual legislators – and the evidence sheds light on the specific conditions that foster such transparency.

3.1.3. Why Focus on Legislative Votes?

This book rests on the premise that voting records provide important information about the actions of parties and of individual legislators and that it is worthwhile to compare this information cross-nationally. Is this a sensible way to proceed? It is important to acknowledge that voting on the floor is far from the only consequential action that takes place in most legislatures. Much of the policymaking and bargaining action in any legislature takes place before proposals reach the voting stage – in public pronouncements and debate, in legislative committees and party caucuses, or during negotiations between executive and legislative actors or between party leaders and rank-and-file legislators. Transcripts of legislators' speeches and floor debates, for example, which generally fill volumes of published records (variously called *Boletines, Gacetas, Hansards, Records, Proceedings,* etc.) from assemblies around the world, are a staple of legislative behavior. In a remarkable recent innovation, Quinn et al. (2006) have developed software to scan text records of legislative debate for rhetorical content that can then be used to locate speakers' ideological positions in a multidimensional ideological space in

---

[1] The discussion in Section 5.4 of data included in the analysis of recorded voting in Chapters 5 and 6, which extends beyond the Americas and beyond pure presidential regimes, elaborates further on how research resources affect access to data on legislative voting, and with what implications.

a manner analogous to methods based on recorded vote data that are common currency in scholarship on the U.S. Congress (Poole and Rosenthal 1985, 1997). An advantage of the Quinn et al. method is that it does not require access to voting records, so it can be applied anywhere politicians go on record doing what they do best (or most, at any rate), which is to speak. Once applied comparatively, this method will provide a fine-grained ideological map of legislatures. Yet it will not indicate directly whether legislative copartisans act in such a way as to pass the policies they profess to support. This is not just because legislators might say one thing but do another when it comes time to vote; it is also because rhetorical ideological proximity does not identify the dividing lines between support and opposition for a given proposal, much less whether breaches in voting unity cause parties or coalitions to lose votes they might otherwise have won.[2]

It is also important to acknowledge that there are good reasons for caution in interpreting analyses of recorded votes as complete portraits of legislators' support for the proposals with which they are confronted, and for the authors of those initiatives. Consider, for example, the prospect of drawing inferences about the legislative effectiveness of executives based on the success rate of executive-sponsored bills in legislative votes (Figueiredo and Limongi 2000; Siavelis 2000; Cheibub, Przeworski, and Saiegh 2004; Calvo 2007). Ames (2002) sounds a cautionary note by documenting the incidence of executive policy initiatives in Brazil that are delayed, are modified, or die outright before ever reaching the point of a recorded vote. Such action is clearly critical to the legislative process but is effectively invisible to analyses that are limited to recorded votes taken on the legislative floor.

The general point that much important legislative action never shows up in floor votes is indisputable, but it does not imply that the information contained in floor votes is unimportant. Indeed, many crucial policy choices in most democracies – like those on annual budgets, the appointment of government officials, or international agreements – are constitutionally required to be voted on the floor of the legislature.

A related rationale for skepticism about the relevance of floor votes is that, if party leaders have good information about legislators' preferences,

---

[2] This is not meant as a criticism of rhetorical ideal point estimation, which is a groundbreaking innovation, but merely to note that it is a distinct, and complementary, endeavor from measuring voting unity.

voting outcomes themselves may be foregone conclusions. In the extreme case, the information available in floor votes might not be inconsequential but rather unrepresentative of what goes on within legislatures. In a majority party or coalition, for example, the leadership may dictate the legislative agenda and have perfect information about how all legislators will vote on any proposal. If those leaders hate to lose, they may allow no votes on any proposals where their side will lose. The votes we observe, then, will tell us something about where legislators stand, and probably about what they fight for and against in other aspects of their legislative duties, but the picture will be incomplete and biased.

It is undeniable that parties and governing coalitions – and particularly their leadership – work constantly to turn the legislative agenda to their advantage. When the task at hand is to infer from floor votes the preferences of legislators or the unity of parties and coalitions, the implications of agenda control should always be kept in mind. Yet the potential distortions in the information contained in floor votes implied by agenda control should be examined rather than assumed. Leadership information about legislators' preferences is never perfect. Legislative rules sometimes allow qualified minorities to demand votes, and so challenge majority agenda control. Some votes, as noted earlier, are mandatory. Control over the agenda is generally less than absolute, and how it is distributed depends on institutional and political factors in ways that can often be theorized, measured, and tested. In subsequent chapters, I show that floor voting is generally not just a string of faits accompli. Records almost always include votes that are divisive within the assembly, and often within legislative parties and coalitions themselves, and vote outcomes turn on these divisions.

For now, it is sufficient to note that floor voting is a critical procedural element of all democratic legislatures. There are theoretical and empirical reasons to expect that floor voting patterns can provide relevant information about what it is that legislators value, and about how effectively they, and the groups into which they organize themselves, pursue those values. This presents us with a puzzle, however; in many legislatures, most of the information contained in voting records is invisible to all but those present for the votes themselves.

The remainder of this chapter examines how much information about legislative votes is visible to those outside the legislature. First, I present a typology of legislative voting methods according to whether they can be monitored by observers inside the legislature, outside, both, or neither, and develop propositions regarding the politics of public voting based on these conditions. Next, I review the historical trajectory of public legislative voting, and its political salience, in the United States, and then turn attention to Latin America, surveying the extent of public voting, and the process by which it was adopted in some recent cases. The empirical basis for much of this chapter, and the next, is a series of interviews conducted by the author with fifty-six legislators, party leaders, and legislative staff, during 2000–1, in Bolivia, Colombia, Costa Rica, Ecuador, El Salvador, Nicaragua, Peru, and Venezuela.

3.2. Who Can Monitor Votes?

Table 3.2 distinguishes voting procedures by the relative ability of actors inside and outside the chamber to monitor individual legislators' votes

Table 3.2 *Monitoring Legislative Votes*

	Internal (e.g., party leaders)	
	No	Yes
External (e.g., citizens)		
No	Secret voting • U.S. House officer elections, pre-1839	Signal voting • Latin America standard operating procedure in lieu of electronic voting
	• Peru, at request of one-third of legislators, or Panama at request of one-half • Italian final passage votes, pre-1988	• U.S. House voice votes
Yes	NA	Public voting • U.S. Congress roll call and teller votes • Latin America *nominales* • Latin America with electronic voting when records are made available

and illustrates the three relevant configurations, along with examples of each type of procedure that is discussed in the text. Under *secret voting*, legislators cast anonymous ballots such that the position of each is unknown by any monitor. Under *public voting*, the position of each legislator (most commonly, "aye," "nay," "abstain," or "not voting") is generally published in some official journal of the legislature and often available on a legislative Web site. Under both secret voting and public voting, the ability of actors internal and external to the legislature to monitor individual votes is symmetrical. *Signal voting* refers to procedures by which individual legislators' positions are visible to those physically present in the chamber, but no individual-level record is available to outside actors, introducing asymmetry in the capacity of internal and external actors to monitor individual votes. Most votes in most Latin American legislatures – and almost all votes in many – are signal votes. The mechanics generally involve hand raising ("All in favor . . .") or standing up to be counted.

An example from Argentina illustrates the difficulties of monitoring legislator behavior when signal voting is used. On April 26, 2000, the Argentine Senate approved sweeping reforms to the country's labor code in a series of signal votes. Subsequently, allegations raised in the press, then by the administrative secretary of the Senate, held that the government of new president Fernando de la Rua had bribed some senators for their votes, triggering a scandal that prompted the resignation of Argentina's vice president and gravely wounded de la Rua's presidency. Yet determining which votes were allegedly bought proved impossible. Of fifty-nine senators present for the vote on final passage of the Labor Code, eleven spoke in favor of it on the floor, four spoke against, and the rest left no trace (Gonzalez Bertomeu 2004:39–40).

Senator José Luis Gioja was singled out as having allegedly betrayed his Peronist copartisans in opposition to de la Rua and sold his affirmative vote to the government, but there was no way to determine whether Gioja's vote was registered in support of the administration's reform in the first place. The video record of that session showed Gioja, during what became known as the "grooming vote," run his hand through his hair, touch his face, adjust his glasses, then turn to talk to his colleague (*Clarín* 2004a, 2004b). In short, in a case where an explosive charge of vote selling was at stake, signal voting made it impossible even to evaluate the premise of the charge. Most signal votes are, of course, less quirky in their execution and less consequential in their impact on policy and politics, but they produce official records equally inscrutable in terms of individual accountability.

The rules of procedure in all Latin American legislatures include provisions for public voting. These votes are usually called *nominales*, or named votes, in which the roll is called and each legislator's position is recorded. Requirements for demanding a *nominal* range from requests by a handful of legislators to petition by a majority of those present. Apart from these thresholds, traditional *nominal* procedures are inevitably time-consuming and procedurally costly. Electronic voting machines, in contrast, generate individual-level voting records automatically, so that, when they are used, the procedural costs of public voting plummets, regardless of whether electronic votes are formally deemed *nominales* (Congreso del Perú 1998).

3.3. The U.S. Experience

3.3.1. Voting Records as the Currency of Individual Accountability

I rely on the U.S. Congress as a point of reference for my examination of recorded voting, not because it necessarily represents a normative ideal for legislative organization, much less because it is empirically representative of legislatures more generally, but rather because recorded voting is more ubiquitous, and has been for much longer, than anywhere else. The sustained centrality of voting records to U.S. politics allows for scholarly examination of how visible votes have been perceived by various political actors and how they are connected to legislative accountability. My brief discussion of the United States highlights four points. First, public voting encourages legislators to be responsive to constituent interests. Second, this has been the case since the early days of the republic. Third, public voting imposes a strain on party discipline by exposing representatives to pressures from outside the legislature. Fourth, technological advances that reduce the procedural costs of recording votes increase their salience as tools for dissident and opposition legislators. These themes are echoed in subsequent discussion of public voting in Latin America, although somewhat more faintly than in the United States, because in Latin America the conditions for voting records to serve as tools of accountability are, and have long been, less propitious.

The first point is uncontroversial. The centrality of voting records to campaign strategies is apparent to any observer of U.S. legislative politics. Incumbents try to avoid casting votes that potential challengers could trot out as evidence that constituent interests have been betrayed. The connection is also established in academic research, both qualitative and quantitative (Erickson 1971; Fenno 1978). In Mayhew's seminal account of the electoral connection, roll call voting records are an essential component of legislators' position-taking strategies (Mayhew 1974:69–73). In a recent analysis of recorded votes across four decades, from 1956 to 1996, Canes-Wrone, Brady, and Cogan (2002) demonstrate that U.S. House members whose floor votes prioritize the demands of their parties over their constituents win lower shares of the popular vote and face higher probability of defeat than do members whose votes are more in line with the estimated preferences of voters in their districts. The results suggest that constituents are aware of their representatives' voting behavior and that electoral ambition induces responsiveness to constituent preferences.

3.3.2. Punishment at the Polls

Modern campaigns and communications media facilitate dissemination of information on voting but also raise the question whether legislative politics in the United States has always been characterized by accountability of this sort. The historical record suggests that it has. Consider, for example, the controversy surrounding the Compensation Act of 1816, in which a Republican-controlled Congress voted to switch from per diem compensation to a considerably larger salary for its members. Federalist newspaper editor William Coleman decided to attack the bill in print on the grounds that his readers would blame the majority party but would never bother to inquire how individual Federalist legislators voted. On the other side of the partisan divide, Thomas Jefferson shared the expectation that individuals' votes would not be monitored, predicting that "almost the entire mass [of Congressmen] will go out, not only those who supported the law or voted for it, or skulked from the vote, but those who voted against it or opposed it actively, if they took the money" (White 1951:401).

Both Coleman and Jefferson proved mistaken, however, as Republican newspapers were quick to point out that a greater proportion of Federalist than Republican members voted for the pay raise, as well as to publish the names of the guilty parties (Skeen 1986; Bianco, Spence, and Wilkerson 1996). Public outrage fell more heavily on supporters of the act than on opponents: 19 percent of supporters were reelected against 46 percent of its opponents (Skeen 1986). Recent research, moreover, strongly suggests that the members of the Fourteenth Congress themselves perceived better than Coleman or Jefferson the salience of their individual positions on the act to voters in their districts, both before and after the vote. Legislators who had won their previous election by smaller margins were systematically less likely to support the act, and those who supported it were subsequently much less likely to seek reelection (Bianco, Spence, and Wilkerson 1996). The controversy surrounding votes on the Compensation Act included intense newspaper coverage and public meetings in various communities. According to Skeen (1986), the episode undermined the idea of deference by citizens to representatives in the new republic and established the norm of deference by legislators to public opinion instead.

3.3.3. Objections to Secret Voting

If the practice of recording and making public individual votes is as old as the U.S. Congress, one critical nineteenth-century episode sheds light on how public voting affects relations between legislators, party leaders, and their constituents. At issue was the procedure for electing officers of the House of Representatives, including the Speaker. Prior to 1839, internal House elections were conducted by secret ballot. During the 1830s, battles over patronage controlled by these offices incited moves by leaders of the Democratic majority to push for public voting in House officer elections.

It is important to highlight that the impetus to record votes in this case came from party leaders, who otherwise could not monitor the votes of their rank and file, not from actors outside Congress. Yet, right away, the discussion incorporated the assumptions that, if votes were recorded, they would be made public, and that if they were made public, citizens would take note. Fierce debates ensued between advocates of "the right of constituents to know all the public acts of their representative" and "the democratic principle of accountability to the constituent body" and defenders of a legislator's right to "express the convictions of his heart, separate from party ties and party allegiance," fearing "that the power of party can condescend to the smallest, most unimportant, and contemptible matters" (Jenkins and Stewart 2003:494, 495, 497).

The Democratic leaders prevailed in this initial battle, winning the ability to monitor their members' votes and putting a stop to the subterfuge by majority party dissidents and cross-party coalitions that had characterized many House officer elections early in the century. Yet, the effect of public voting on party discipline, particularly for the highly salient votes to elect House Speakers, was "exactly the opposite in the long term . . . [because] the daylight that shone on speakership elections highlighted regional animosities just as much as partisanship. It became more difficult to elect Speakers and organize the House than before the onset of *viva voce* voting" (Jenkins and Stewart 2003:504–5). The *viva voce* episode illustrates that, in the U.S. context, the move away from unmonitored votes initially strengthened the influence of national party leaders over rank-and-file legislators, but universal monitoring ultimately strengthened an even greater force, countervailing that of party – constituents, with their diverse regional demands.

3.3.4. Interest Group Monitoring

Subsequent historical accounts demonstrate that organized interest groups systematically monitored voting records in the early twentieth century and that legislators feared the influence of these records on voters. In his account of the rise of Prohibition, Peter Odegard (1928:90) quotes correspondence between a state legislator and a local Anti-Saloon League's chapter, which sums up the politician's simple calculus:

> While I am no more of a Christian than I was last year, while I drink as much as I did before, you have demonstrated to me that . . . there are more Anti-Saloon votes in my district than there are saloon votes; therefore I will stand with you both with my influence and my vote if you will give me your support.

The league, moreover, was not satisfied with fair-sounding pledges and relied on methods of monitoring recorded votes that echo those of modern interest groups. "Elaborate indexes of politicians and their records were kept at Washington and in most of the states, and professions of sympathy were matched with deeds. The voters were constantly apprised of the doings of their representatives" (Odegard 1928:91). The Farm Bureau, the American Legion, the American Medical Association, and the National Rifle Association engaged in similar activities during this same era (Kile 1948; Mayhew 1974:66–67).

3.3.5. Electronic Voting

An important jump in the salience of recorded votes in the United States came in 1973 with the adoption of electronic voting technology in the

House. Sponsors of the Legislative Reorganization Act of 1970 reduced the requirements for members to demand that a vote be recorded on the grounds that this would improve accountability of members to their constituents. Shortly thereafter, to accommodate the increased demand for recorded votes within time constraints, the House installed electronic voting machines. These changes produced a gigantic increase in the number of recorded votes in the House, particularly on amendments to bills, and a concurrent increase in the relative importance of voting records to legislators' relations with their constituents. One additional property of the shift to electronic voting in the United States is worth noting. Minority-party members – those most likely to be dissatisfied with overall legislative outcomes – were inclined to push amendments that, when subject to recorded votes, would be politically uncomfortable for the governing majority (Smith 1989:29–34).

3.3.6. Lessons from the United States

Recorded voting has been integrally connected to legislative accountability throughout the history of the U.S. Congress. Since at least the early nineteenth century, members expected voting records to be available and salient to constituents, and relevant to their own electoral success. Party leaders, too, have a keen interest in monitoring votes but, except under unusual procedural circumstances (e.g., secret voting in House officer elections), leaders face minimal obstacles to monitoring votes, so asymmetries in monitoring costs generally favor party leaders over other competitors for legislators' loyalties. Interest groups have long treated voting records as the currency of legislators' performance. Finally, the reduced procedural costs of publicizing votes that accompanied electronic voting in the House increased their importance and amplified their relevance as a tool of the legislative opposition.

3.4. The Supply of Recorded Votes in Latin America

In contrast to the U.S. Congress, Latin American legislatures generally record very few votes. Beyond this straightforward observation, I want to highlight three key points in this section. First, the supply of visible votes in the Americas directly reflects the technological and procedural obstacles to recording and publishing votes. Second, declining technological barriers have prompted procedural reforms in some cases that facilitate the recording and publication of votes, which in turn increases their supply. Third, this has not been so in all cases, however; some legislatures in which the technology is available still do not record, or else record but do not publish, which means that votes remain invisible and effectively impossible to monitor for actors outside the legislature. The Appendix to this chapter recounts an episode from my own field research that illustrates how difficult it can be to gain access to vote records, even for a persistent and reasonably well-connected investigator.

3.4.1. Procedures for Recording Votes

Rules of procedure in Latin American legislatures often require recorded votes under specific circumstances – for example, on votes to override presidential vetos in Uruguay, on the vote to select a president in the absence of a popular-vote majority in Bolivia, and on constitutional amendments in various systems – but these circumstances tend to be unusual. In every Latin American legislature, members may also request recorded votes. The procedural barriers to such requests vary from requiring a majority vote in Costa Rica and Bolivia, to a one-third threshold in Peru, to petition by ten legislators in Ecuador or six in Guatemala. Literally calling the roll in order to take votes, however, is always a time-consuming and impractical process. Moreover, rules of procedure for *nominales* often require that each legislator, in casting a vote, be allowed floor time to justify her position. In short, logistics alone are sufficient to rule out the traditional *nominal* as a means of legislative voting throughout Latin America under all but exceptional circumstances.

The procedures for taking standard votes (sometimes referred to as *económicos*) vary. In chambers with smaller memberships, such as the Central American assemblies and senates in bicameral legislatures, individuals generally cast votes by either standing or hand raising, with a head or hand count conducted from the *mesa directiva*. This procedure is impractical when membership rises much more than 100, however, and larger chambers such as Mexico's and Venezuela's have conventionally expedited matters by allowing party leaders to cast votes for their entire blocs. Legislators who are present and do not explicitly state their opposition are counted as having voted as the leadership declares.

3.4.2. The Frequency of Recorded Votes

Table 3.3 shows the incidence of recorded votes across twenty-four legislative chambers in the Americas, plus the joint sessions of the Uruguayan Congress. The Panamanian Assembly is included twice, under separate voting regimes, both before the advent of electronic voting and after. The cases are grouped according to the procedural barriers to recording – whether an electronic voting system is used, and the threshold for requiring a recorded vote. These two elements are connected, both logically and empirically. Modern electronic voting systems automatically and instantly generate individual-level records of votes, reducing the cost of recording, in terms of legislative staff labor and session time, to near zero. Where the cost of recording votes is negligible, in turn, there is less reason to maintain rules that discourage recording.

Of twelve chambers with electronic voting systems, the rules of four establish electronic voting as the default procedure for floor votes and another five set request thresholds at 10 percent of members or less. Of twelve chambers without electronic systems, only the U.S. Senate records as standard operating procedure, two more set low barriers, and seven set a majority request threshold to record. The mean number of recorded votes per year is derived from collection of data from parliamentary Web sites in those cases where complete transcripts of all legislative sessions (or, more rarely, the votes themselves) are systematically posted and from field research or consultation with legislative staff or academic experts in each country otherwise.

Average number of votes per year is a fairly raw statistic, to be consumed with some caution. The averages are derived from across thirty-three years for Costa Rica, ten for the United States, seven for Guatemala, four-year legislative periods for Colombia and Ecuador, and a mere nine months in Nicaragua's dawning electronic era. Although most of the figures are the result of comprehensive archival searches, some of the vote totals reported are estimates based on incomplete data (see, e.g., notes *e*, *i*, and *j* to Table 3.3).

Specialists in the legislative politics of each country might also reasonably argue that legislative floor votes can have distinctive meanings in different settings. Where most legislative work takes place in committees, for example, floor votes may be less frequent and less central to the policymaking process than when more of the action is on the floor. Even if we acknowledge such qualifications, however, these votes are critical to legislative decision making in every chamber. Floor votes are where statutes, budgets, treaties, veto

Table 3.3. *Effects of Procedure on the Availability of Public Voting Records*

Country	Chamber	Members	Request Threshold	Votes[a]
Standard operating procedure, electric				
Chile	House	120	Art. 9	328
Chile	Senate	47	Art. 157	45
Nicaragua	Unicameral	90	Rules do not yet reflect adoption of electronic voting (Arts. 104–10)	924[b]
Peru	Unicameral	120	Art. 57	540
Standard operating procedure, manual				
United States	Senate	100	Rule XII	350
By request, electric				
Mexico	House	500	6 legislators (Art. 148)	155
Mexico	Senate	128	6 senators (Art. 148)	156[c]
Panama (2004)	Unicameral	71	Majority of those present (Art. 196)	144[d]
Brazil	House	513	6%, or party leaders representing 6% of members (Art. 185)	>68[e]
Argentina	House	257	10% of deputies present (Art. 190)	17[f]
United States	House	434	20% of quorum (Rule XX)	559
Brazil	Senate	81	Majority of those present (Art. 294)	125[g]
Venezuela	Unicameral	165	Majority of those present (Arts. 120, 125)	0[b]
By request, manual				
Guatemala	Unicameral	140	6 legislators (Art. 95)	8.4
Ecuador	Unicameral	100	10% of legislators (Art. 70)	4.5
Bolivia	House	130	Majority of those voting (Art. 107)	0
Bolivia	Senate	27	Majority of those voting (Art. 116)	0
Uruguay	House	99	One-third of those present (Art. 93)	<1.0[i]
Argentina	Senate	72	Majority of those present (Art. 205)	21[j]
Colombia	House	161	Majority of those present (Art. 146)	2.5
Colombia	Senate	102	Majority of those present (Art. 146)	2.0

The Supply of Recorded Votes in Latin America

Country	Chamber	Members	Request Threshold	Votes[a]
Costa Rica	Unicameral	56	Majority of those present (Art. 101)	0.5
El Salvador	Unicameral	84	Majority of those present (Art. 37)	0
Panama (1991–2003)	Unicameral	71	Majority of those present (Art. 196)	1.9[k]
Uruguay	Senate	31	Rules allow, but do not specify procedure to request, recorded vote (Art. 100)	<1.0[i]
Constitutional requirement, manual				
Uruguay	Joint session	130	Recorded vote required on motion to override presidential veto (Art. 141)	6.3[i]

[a] Recorded-votes-per-year averages are based on the time periods listed in Table 5.3, which describes data included in the analysis of voting unity in Chapters 5 and 6. Cases without recorded votes (i.e., votes/year = 0) are based on the author's observation at the time field research was conducted, during the early years of the 2000 decade.

[b] An electronic voting system installed in 2000 was immediately put into regular use for all votes. The vote records, however, are not published.

[c] The Mexican Senate Web site currently publishes all recorded votes, but leaves only those from the most recent session on the Web site, continually replacing records of previous votes. As a result, only a handful of votes are available at any given time, and any actor who seeks to monitor Senate voting must be vigilant and assiduous in harvesting votes as soon as they are "ripe."

[d] As of September 2004, the National Assembly began to use its electronic voting system and to post electronic votes on its Web site (http://www.asamblea.gob.pa/portada.asp). During the last three months of 2004, 36 votes were recorded, a rate of 144 per year.

[e] Actual number is somewhat higher. Figueiredo and Limongi's (2000) data included 678 votes over a ten-year period, but excludes votes in which less than 10 percent of deputies voted on the losing side.

[f] Source: Asociación pro los Derechos Civiles, Buenos Aires.

[g] Source: Scott Desposato, personal communication.

[h] Art. 125 states that a single deputy may solicit a recorded vote, but does not stipulate a requirement for the approval of such a request. Art. 120 states that Assembly decisions are to be made by vote of a majority of those present. The transcripts of floor debates available in the *Diarios de Debates* online report only aggregate vote totals, not individual-level voting records, even for votes said to be taken by the *nominal* method. Thus, no records are public.

[i] Extensive search of *Diarios de Sesiones*, 1985–94, turned up only a handful of recorded votes in either chamber, beyond 63 from joint sessions on votes to override presidential vetoes, per constitutional requirement. Method of archiving makes it difficult to determine whether any other recorded votes exist. Sources: Scott Morgenstern, Daniel Buquet, and Daniel Chasquetti.

[j] The Asociación por los Derechos Civiles reports that the Argentine Chamber produced 17 recorded votes in 2003, and *Clarín* (2004a) reports that the Chamber recorded votes in a total of nine sessions. The same article reports that the Argentine Senate recorded votes in a total of eleven sessions. The estimate of 21 votes is based on an assumption that the Senate recorded votes with the same frequency per session, given that records were produced.

[k] Source: Harry Brown Araúz, personal communication.

overrides, and constitutional amendments are ultimately approved or rejected, and the availability of vote records indicates how much hard information citizens have about the most consequential actions of their representatives.

The connection between the procedural obstacles to recording votes and the amount of such information available is not surprising, but it is striking nonetheless. Those chambers where electronic voting is standard operating procedure average 459 recorded votes per year; the U.S. Senate (standard operating procedure, manual) averages 350; chambers with electronic systems but where recorded votes must be requested by some subset of legislators average 153 votes; and those where voting is manual and recorded votes must be requested average about 2.

3.4.3. From Electronic Voting to Visible Voting

The experiences of individual countries that have adopted electronic voting suggest that, once systems are in place, demands grow to alter rules of procedure to facilitate recorded voting, and that where these demands are successful, the numbers of recorded votes will rise, and pressure to make votes visible increases. Electronic voting systems were adopted in the lower legislative chambers more or less concurrently with the return to democracy in the mid-1980s in Argentina and Brazil and in the 1990s in Chile. They have been in use in Mexico and Peru since 1998, Nicaragua beginning in 2000, and in Panama since late 2004. A system has been in place in Venezuela since 1997 but has not yet been used. The same is true for Costa Rica's first-generation system, installed in the mid-1970s, and for the systems in both chambers of the Colombian Congress, in place since the late 1990s. See Table 3.4.

There are purely pragmatic reasons to adopt electronic voting. It yields a faster, more accurate count than hand raising. It is a concrete manifestation of modernization, an ideal widely embraced in the abstract by governments and legislative leaders (Cevasco Piedra 2000). The impact of electronic voting, however, is potentially more substantial than the logistics alone imply. Electronic voting generates records of individual legislators' votes. If the records are available to the public, this effectively transforms all votes into *nominales* – matters of record that individual legislators could be called upon to defend.

There is no guarantee that journalists, interest group leaders, activists, and the like will register how legislators vote or that constituents will pay

The Supply of Recorded Votes in Latin America

Table 3.4. *Electronic Voting Systems in Latin American Legislatures (lower chambers or unicameral systems)*

Country	Installed	In Use?	Availability of Electronic Vote Records
Argentina	Prior to redemocratization, 1983[a]	Yes	Retained in congressional archives, not published
Brazil	Prior to constitutional assembly,1987 [b]	Yes	Camara dos Deputados *Plenario*[c]
Chile	With construction of new Congress, 1990	Yes	In text of *Boletin de Sesiones*[d]
Colombia	1999	No	NA
Costa Rica	Mid-1970s[e]	No	NA
Mexico	1998	Yes	*Gaceta Parlamentaria*[f]
Nicaragua	2000	Yes	Retained by Assembly clerk, not published
Panama	Late 1990s[g]	No	Asamblea Nacional Panama[h]
Peru	1998	Yes	Congreso de la Republica[i]
Venezuela	1997	No	NA

[a] Personal communication with Mark P. Jones (Michigan State University).
[b] Personal communication with Octavio Amorim Neto (Instituto Universitário de Pesquisas do Rio de Janeiro).
[c] http://www.camara.gov.br/Indice.asp?Endereco=Intranet/Plenario/Plenario.htm.
[d] http://www.camara.cl/, on line since 1996.
[e] Interview with Fernando Castillo.
[f] http://gaceta.cddhcu.gob.mx/.
[g] Personal communication with Harry Brown Araúz.
[h] http://www.asamblea.gob.pa/portada.asp, on line since 2004.
[i] http://www.congreso.gob.pe/index.htm.

attention. Without a record, however, the prospect is moot, and until recently there was no record most of the time. The adoption of electronic voting means that records are being created in many places, and the existence of records opens the possibility that the information will enter into political discourse.

What rough data are available suggest a positive relationship between visible votes and legislative individualism. The surveys of legislators in Latin America discussed in Chapter 2 included a question on whether party leaders should always impose discipline on rank-and-file legislators or never impose discipline (i.e., the discretion on how to vote should always remain with the individual), or whether discipline should depend on what issue is at hand (Proyecto Élites Parlamentarias Latinoamericanas 2006).

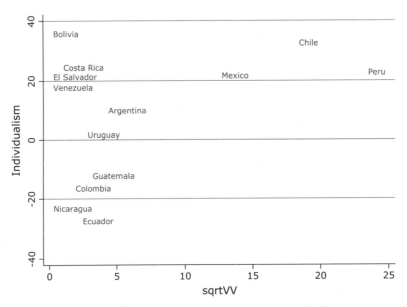

Figure 3.1 Recorded votes (square root) and preferences for legislative individualism.

I constructed an index of overall preference for individualism in each country by subtracting the percentage preferring "Always discipline" from that preferring "Always individual discretion" (assuming the "Depends" response to be neutral). Figure 3.1 plots this index against the square root of the average number of votes recorded and made public each year (based on the data in Table 3.3) for those lower chambers for which both recorded vote and survey data were available.

The figure shows an overall positive correlation (.29) between recorded votes and legislators' expressed preferences for individualism. This result is consistent with the cross-national pattern by which legislatures with plentiful recorded (and, generally, visible) votes are also those in which legislators express more support for individual autonomy from party leaders. The correlation by itself does not demonstrate which way causality runs between visible voting and individualism – that is, whether individualism (whatever the source) encourages the adoption of visible voting procedures, or visible votes (adopted for whatever reason) increase individualism – or whether the phenomena are mutually reinforcing. The next sections describe the link between the adoption of electronic voting and visible voting in two legislatures where the move was contentious, and the next chapter explores the sources of support for, and opposition to, visible voting more generally.

3.4.3.1. Peru. The prospect that visible voting would increase the premium on individual legislator accountability was explicitly on the minds of Peruvian legislators on both sides of the reform debate in 1998, as they considered the implications of switching from the traditional hand-raising method of voting to the electronic system, which had recently been installed as part of a broader government modernization plan. On September 24, in an effort to embarrass the pro-Fujimori majority on a motion related to a corruption investigation, the opposition demanded that the electronic voting machines be incorporated into standard legislative procedure:

> The whole reason for electronic voting is so citizens know how their representatives voted, so [votes] can be publicly justified. It's an instrument of democracy and transparency, which is why Congress spent as much as it did [to have it installed], not so we can use it on some votes and not on others. . . . What the country is going to notice is that the parliamentary majority is afraid that, through the Internet and other mechanisms, its votes on some matters will be made visible. (Congreso del Perú 1998)

The opposition threatened procedural maneuvers designed to grind progress on all matters to a halt if the electronic system were not employed. The majority eventually broke ranks, with one of its members concurring on the matter of transparency and accountability: "One reason for this system is that it leaves a record of votes for current political analysts and for history, so that how each one of us voted is known; and those congresspersons that run for reelection, when they face the voters, they'll have to explain how it is that on each of the issues they voted as they did" (Congreso del Perú 1998). Soon after the old system was breached, the Peruvian Congress began posting records of all electronic votes on its Web site, at a rate of more than 500 per year.

3.4.3.2. Panama. A similar dynamic appears to have played out in the Panamanian National Assembly in 2004. Early that year, during the waning months of a legislative term, opposition deputies won initial committee approval for a reform of chamber procedures to facilitate use of electronic voting and to eliminate altogether the practice of voting by legislators' banging on their desks (loudest group wins). Supporters of the proposal outside the assembly echoed the pro-transparency arguments of Peruvian opposition legislators that signal

63

voting diluted accountability and allowed legislators to dissemble about their positions on unpopular initiatives. As in Peru, the leadership of the majority coalition initially resisted using the electronic system (Tapia G. 2004). By September of that year, however, after an intervening election, the new National Assembly, now controlled by a former opposition party that had campaigned on an anticorruption, pro-transparency platform, had adopted electronic voting and begun to post votes on its official Web site.

Panama is the only case for which I have systematic data for the rate of recorded votes both before and after adoption of electronic voting, and the difference is dramatic. In the seven years from 1991 to 1997, without electronic voting, the Assembly recorded 11 votes, at a rate of 1.6 per year. During the last three months of 2004, it recorded 36 votes, an annual rate of 144.

3.4.4. Why More Votes Are Not Recorded, and Why Recorded Votes Are Not Always Visible

Even if we take technological and procedural barriers into account, the Latin American legislatures generally record fewer votes than the U.S. Congress. After all, the U.S. Senate has no electronic voting, and House rules impose a significant request threshold, yet both record hundreds of votes per year. One obvious explanation is a lack of staff resources in Latin American legislatures without electronic systems. Legislatures in the region are chronically and notoriously underfunded, and recording votes by hand is labor-intensive and time-consuming.

Procedural costs cannot be the whole story, however. Even where electronic systems are in place in Latin American legislatures, their use is not a given. Electronic systems are in place in the Costa Rican and Venezuelan assemblies, but they are never used, just as in Panama until 2004, and the electronic systems in the Argentine and Colombian lower chambers are very rarely employed. In other cases, the systems are used regularly, but voting records are not systematically published. The Nicaraguan Assembly, for example, records all votes, but does not publish the records. The Argentine Chamber's Web site puts up the aggregate (yes, no, abstain, absent) results for votes taken electronically but includes the lists of individual deputies' voting decisions only sporadically. The Mexican Senate's Web site, curiously, publishes its recorded votes the evening of each given session but then removes the records when the votes from the next session are put on line. The Mexican Chamber's Web site has changed its policies for making recorded voting data available various times during the early years of the 2000 decade before settling on putting up complete records of electronic votes.[3]

Public access to information about electronically recorded votes may be partly attributable to technical capacity. Maintaining a comprehensive Web site taxes the resources of many assemblies. On the other hand, party leaders and the members of dominant coalitions sometimes prefer not to make voting records public even when they are kept and not to use electronic voting systems even when they are in place. For now, it is worth noting that, although the point of departure is different, the relationship between electronic systems and recorded voting in Latin America runs in the same direction as that in the United States, albeit starting from a different point. In the United States recorded voting is common even in the absence of electronic voting, and it became more prolific with the adoption of an electronic system in the House of Representatives. In Latin America, recorded voting is negligible in the absence of electronic voting. It is increasingly common – but not a given – where electronic systems reduce procedural costs.

The experiences of individual countries that have adopted electronic voting systems affirm the pattern evident in the cross-national data: electronic voting and minimizing procedural barriers to recorded voting boost the amount of information available to those outside the legislature about legislative decision making.

3.5. Conclusion

Legislative voting can be an element of accountability only if votes are publicly known. They can be known, in turn, only if they are recorded and the records are available. Voting records are so essential to how legislative accountability is conceived in the United States, and have been for so long, that it is easy to forget that there is nothing automatic about their relevance, or even their existence and availability. Beyond the United States, essential components of the legislative voting–legislative accountability relationship are often missing.

---

[3] The practices described in this paragraph refer either to convention at the time field research was conducted for this project, during the first years of the 2000 decade or, in the references to Web site content, to practice up through the middle years of the decade.

In the Latin American context, systematic voting records never exist in the absence of electronic voting. Given this empirical fact, it is important that reliable electronic voting equipment be more easily accessible than ever before. The technical obstacles to keeping and maintaining legislative voting records are rapidly diminishing. This, in turn, makes it increasingly feasible for advocates of visible voting to push their case, and difficult for opponents to resist demands to record and publicize legislative votes. Diminishing technological barriers do not, however, mean recorded voting and public voting have been, or will be, welcomed into all legislatures as standard operating procedure, as the next chapter makes clear.

Chapter 3 Appendix: Stalking the Elusive Recorded Vote

During field research in Bogota, Colombia, in May 2001, various legislators assured me that the office of the secretary-general of the House of Representatives maintained computerized records of all electronic votes from the previous five years or so and that these could be made public. The aide to one of these legislators managed to deliver me all the way to the secretary-general himself, who listened uneasily to my request, but assured me that all information is public, and handed me off to his technical assistant, who, as I initially understood it, would produce for me computerized files of the votes.

The technical assistant took me to the House chamber itself to show me the voting machines, which are used regularly to take attendance but less frequently to record votes. The machines are modern and recognize the representative's hand, rather than fingerprint. (The assistant noted that the larger hand recognition slots are more trouble than the smaller fingerprint recognition type because when legislators eat lunch at their desks, they tend to get pieces of food stuck in there, which are difficult to get out. He looks forward to the day they can be replaced with a fingerprint recognition system.) The assistant also told me that the electronic system had originally been installed in the House chamber in the 1980s but was modernized in the late 1990s. He said that the Senate had installed the exact same system shortly after the House, but that the senators never use it. He did not know why.

Gradually, it became clear to me that the technical assistant had not been instructed that his task was to provide me with computerized files of votes. When I asked him directly, he told me he did not think the office of the secretary-general even had complete records of votes, in part because some of the more Luddite legislators did not like to use the electronic machines, even when *nominales* are taken, and instead write down their votes and pass them forward. The complete record of any *nominal*, therefore, is actually assembled by the chamber's Division of Recording and Dissemination.

Having established exactly what I was seeking, the technical assistant to the secretary-general took me to the director of the Division of Recording and Dissemination. This director listened to my request for electronic records of votes, and then sent me, with *his* assistant, to the deputy secretary of the House chamber, who, I was assured, was the guy who knows where the computer files containing votes are, and how they are organized.

The deputy secretary listened to my request and told me that records of all *nominales* are published in the *Gaceta* (the official published record of legislative proceedings), which I already knew. I explained that I hoped to avoid having to go through every page of every *Gaceta* to find the rare *nominales*, make photocopies, and then transcribe each vote to a spread-sheet. I told him that I had assumed electronic records must exist – perhaps even of more votes than the formal *nominales* – given the existence of an electronic voting system. I noted that even the records published in the *Gaceta* are written up on computers prior to printing, that electronic copies would be far more convenient than print versions. And I pointed out that various sources – legislators and staff – within the House of Representatives itself had confirmed the public availability of these resources. The deputy secretary countered that the electronic voting system does *not* produce a record of the votes; then clarified that the system does produce a record, but that the record is deleted from the system immediately after each vote is taken and the result of it is printed up. Subsequently, he explained, the Division of Recording and Dissemination transcribes from these printouts a new list of who voted how, which is inserted in the *Gaceta*. The sub-secretary explicitly did not offer to make electronic records of the *Gaceta* available. Rather, he reiterated his offer to let me – or anyone, because this information is public, after all – leaf through the hard copies page by page to find the votes and make photocopies.

After leaving the deputy secretary's office, the assistant from the Division of Recording and Dissemination (still with me) told me that the director of the Legislative Archive, or possibly director of the *Gaceta*, would likely be more cooperative, and that I should check with them. I took this advice, but with results that should, by now, be predictable. Pursuit of legis-lative voting records in many other countries, including Bolivia, Ecuador, and El Salvador, yielded similar results.

4

![horizontal bar]

Demand for Visible Votes

4.1. Is Transparency Desirable?

Democratic legislatures are forums for debate and collective decision over the diverse values their members represent, and their internal workings are generally meant to be subject to monitoring from outside actors. By forcing debate into an open setting, legislatures may limit admissible arguments on behalf of interests or policy positions to those that can be defended in public. Transparency in voting, moreover, opens the possibility that individual representatives can be held accountable for their votes by those they represent.

The argument for transparency in legislative voting rests on twin ideas. One is that political elites and ordinary citizens differ in their claims to anonymity in political action. The other is that information about legislative voting actually gets to voters. According to the conventional logic, anonymity is necessary for voters, through the secret ballot, to free them from intimidation in elections, but in legislative voting it undermines democratic accountability. In effect, legislators ought to be subject to pressure on their votes, but citizens should not (United States Supreme Court 1958).[1]

The distinction between legislative voting as public and elections as private is not universally shared. Jean Jacques Rousseau, for example, did not advocate public voting in legislatures but nevertheless makes a case for public voting in elections. Rousseau regarded individual legislative votes as of less interest than the collective result. Whether the latter was consonant

---

[1] For a contrary argument, that even citizen voting at the polls should be public, see Brennan and Pettit (1990).

with the general will, according to Rousseau, could be determined only through popular election, and in this forum Rousseau prioritized the accountability of citizens to each other, holding that the requirement to state one's vote publicly could encourage citizens to support only proposals that are in the general interest (Rousseau 1763).

Neither is the principle that information regarding legislative votes ought to be available to voters a given. As Chapter 3 demonstrates, empirically the supply of voting information is spotty at best in many legislatures. Moreover, at around the same time as Rousseau, but drawing on an altogether different conception of representation, Edmund Burke rejected the idea that legislative representation ought to consist of legislators' faithfully reflecting their constituents' preferences or answering to voters for failing to do so. Burkean representation, as famously depicted in his *Speech to the Electors of Bristol* (1774), has no place for legislative transparency and the monitoring of votes by those outside parliament. Burke pointed out to his constituents the narrowness of their own political vision and demanded that they trust their representative's (i.e., his) judgment as to the common good and forgo demands for responsiveness to their own wishes.

In short, political theory can supply normative arguments against legislative transparency, but this book subscribes to the belief, mainstream to much modern political theory, that transparency makes accountability possible and that accountability of representatives to citizens is desirable.[2] All the evidence in this chapter suggests that the normative commitment to transparency is widely shared, or at least outwardly acknowledged, among legislative insiders and outsiders alike. Advocates of visible voting regularly echo this normative argument, and even those who are reluctant about visible voting do not directly challenge it. The main obstacles to visible voting in modern legislatures are not normative arguments but other factors. In order to understand the empirical pattern of recorded and signal voting described in Chapter 3, it is necessary to examine the political forces and preferences on the matter at play in legislative politics.

---

[2] For example, Snyder and Ting (2005) offer a formal model to explain why public voting in legislatures ought to be appealing both to legislators and to citizens. The outcome depends on symmetrical monitoring of legislators' voting behavior by both their constituents and some other principal – say, a powerful interest group or a political party leader – whose preferences may be at odds with constituents'. Symmetrical monitoring is necessary for legislators to make binding electoral contracts with their constituents – to commit credibly to be faithful representatives and to expect any reward for doing so. A critical assumption of the model is that information about legislators' votes gets to constituents.

This chapter advances a series of propositions regarding differences across political systems that shape the electoral salience of voting records and differences among actors within political systems in their preferences for making votes public. Then I examine these propositions in light of evidence from field research, interviews with legislators, and archival and secondary sources.

4.2. Incentives to Monitor and Publicize Votes

I distinguish between two types of factors that affect the impetus toward visible voting. The first operates at the level of the political system – specifically, the manner in which legislators are elected – and shapes the incentives legislative candidates have to emphasize voting records in campaigns. The second distinguishes among political actors within a given political system according to their inherent ability to monitor votes even in lieu of recording and publication (i.e., signal votes, which are the procedural default in most legislatures), as well as their relative inclination to answer to principals whether inside or outside the legislature.

4.2.1. SMD versus MMD Elections

Citizens cannot be expected to keep track of voting records on their own, even where votes are published regularly in places easily accessible to citizens. Common sense dictates that all but the most peculiar have better things to do than to comb through records of legislative proceedings on a regular basis.[3] Without relying on the initiative of citizens themselves, then, how might information about the quality of representation delivered via legislative votes get into the hands of voters so that it can contribute to accountability? In the U.S. context, it is clear that politicians are motivated to deliver information about legislative voting records to voters, but this is less obvious for many legislatures elsewhere.

---

[3] Although Burke would eventually prove to be among the most sympathetic members of the British Parliament to American grievances against the crown, many of the colonists did not share his views about deference to legislators. One particularly un-Burkean reform advanced by reformers in Pennsylvania around the eve of independence would have required any proposed law to be posted in public houses for a year before the colonial legislature could vote on it, to ensure citizens could monitor their representatives in *advance* of acting (Morone 1990:40). The Internet notwithstanding, these Founders appear to have had a keener sense than we do at present of how to use available technology to foster accountability.

Candidates in single-member-district (SMD) elections dominated by two parties have strong incentives to provide voters with bad news about their opponents' records because any candidate is the primary residual claimant of whatever popular vote loss her opponent suffers as a result. In the context of U.S. elections, challenging candidates are key vehicles by which information on legislative voting records are delivered to voters in a legislator's district.

In multimember-district (MMD) electoral systems, which predominate in Latin America, the incentives for candidates to deliver news about their opponents' voting records are weaker. In closed-list systems, such as those of Argentina, Costa Rica, Ecuador, El Salvador, and Nicaragua, ballots do not afford voters the opportunity to indicate a preference for individual legislators, so any punishment for bad voting behavior (or reward for good behavior) is spread across all of a party's candidates, and any benefit to the lists of other parties accruing from such punishment may be spread across the other parties' running lists. Within each of these lists, any gain in electoral support benefits the candidate highest in the list who would otherwise not be elected. The identity of this marginal candidate, however, is unlikely to be known with certainty before the election.

Systems that allow for personal preference voting over candidates within parties, such as the open lists in Brazil, Peru, Chile, and Colombia,[4] provide stronger incentives for the delivery of information about voting records but still not as strong as under SMD because of the diffusion across multiple candidates of any gains to be had from exposing flaws in a given legislator's record. In the concrete sense, a candidate in a Peruvian district with eight incumbent legislators has multiple voting records to criticize but cannot expect to monopolize whatever electoral support she dislodges from incumbents by publicizing their negligent voting behavior. Instead, this support may be spread across the other challengers for the eight seats at stake.

In short, even in personal vote systems, the potential gains to be had from publicizing "bad" voting by an opponent depends on how widely any votes shaken loose by such publicity will be dispersed among other candidates. How many candidates there are in the district will likely depend, in turn, on the district magnitude, the fragmentation of the party system, and how may candidates each party nominates. By and large, the incentives of

---

[4] Open lists were used in Colombia beginning with the 2006 election, but the previous system of multiple lists was at least equally personalistic (Cox and Shugart 1995).

campaigns in large-magnitude districts are to undersupply information about individual legislative behavior (Desposato 2004a, 2006a). Generally speaking, the smaller the pool of candidates chasing votes in a district, the greater the incentive for candidates to emphasize their opponents' individual voting records in campaigns.

The incentives for candidates to make voting records central to campaigns are strongest under the electoral rules and party structure that characterize U.S. legislative elections. Purely electoral incentives for candidates to publicize their opponents' voting records are not altogether absent in other electoral environments – and citizens may well come to monitor legislators' votes for other reasons – but the structure of electoral competition in MMD systems provides less incentive than in SMD systems to make voting records central to political debate. Legislative voting procedures may determine who has the *ability* to monitor legislators' actions, but electoral rules and the nature of party competition shape the incentives for politicians to deliver this information.

4.2.2. Legislative Insiders versus Outsiders

Recording and publishing votes provide less marginal benefit to actors who enjoy natural advantages in monitoring signal votes (call these "insiders") than to those who are relatively disadvantaged ("outsiders"). To the extent that insiders and outsiders compete with each other for influence over legislators, then insiders should oppose making votes visible while outsiders should support visible votes. With respect to legislators themselves, they know that insiders will be able to monitor their behavior, rewarding and punishing accordingly; the question at stake in recording and making votes public is whether outsiders will be able to do so as well. Thus, those who seek to appeal to outside audiences and constituencies – and particularly those inclined to resist coercion from insiders – should support visible voting, whereas legislators whose foremost principals are insiders should oppose visible voting, or at least be indifferent (Snyder and Ting 2005).

The political actors with the greatest monitoring advantages are legislative party leaders – particularly those from majority parties or coalitions that control legislative agendas. Interest groups with substantial resources, including lobbyists or staff poised to oversee legislative activity, may also be able to monitor signal votes on the assembly floor. Actors motivated to monitor, but with disadvantages in doing so, include nongovernmental and watchdog organizations with constrained resources, journalists, and academics. The actors most resistant to coercion from legislative leaders are opposition legislators and dissidents within majority parties and coalitions. Interviews and documentary evidence confirm that the politics of recording votes and making records transparent conforms to these expectations.

4.2.3. Friends and Enemies of Visible Voting

Three propositions follow from the discussion of visible voting in this section. First, the purely electoral incentive to emphasize an opponent's legislative voting record should be stronger in SMD than in MMD systems, contributing to somewhat greater salience of visible votes in the former than in the latter. Second, various sorts of political actors may be inclined to monitor legislative votes – for example, constituents, political party leaders, and interest groups. Among these actors, those inside the legislature (e.g., party leaders) for whom monitoring votes is relatively cost-efficient have little interest in formally recording votes relative to those outside the legislature, for whom monitoring costs are higher (e.g., constituents, interest groups). Third, among legislators themselves, visible voting should be favored by those inclined to resist pressure from inside actors and opposed by those in a position to apply it.

In light of the last proposition, consider the relative attraction of visible voting and the common alternative, signal voting, for legislative party leaders and for rank-and-file legislators, respectively. A variety of factors might come into play here, including the mundane procedural costs of recording a vote, the value of signaling loyalty to (or independence from) one's party, and the value of being on the winning side. In traditional, low-tech legislatures, signal voting imposes lower procedural costs than does recording and publishing individual votes. These time and labor savings are salient especially to party leaders, who generally manage the administration of their chambers. However, technological changes that make electronic voting technology cheaper and easier are erasing the procedural advantage of signal over visible voting.

Next, consider the signaling value of individual votes among insiders. Within the legislature itself, signal and visible votes are equally visible to other legislative actors. Leaders can monitor, and rank-and-file members can express fealty, or dissent, to their leaders under either format. The situation is different with respect to signaling outsiders, however. For leaders who bear primary responsibility for maintaining their party's collective reputation, responsiveness to outside actors whose demands might conflict with the party line is a liability. Signal voting protects legislators from such demands, so it is preferable to visible voting. For rank-and-file legislators, the situation is less clear-cut. The anonymity of signal voting, and the protection it affords from pressure by legislative outsiders, may be attractive in some instances. But so may be the flexibility visible voting allows to signal individual vote positions (even dissent from the party line) to an array of potential principals, including voters, interest groups, governors, or presidents.

Finally, particular policy questions aside, consider the value of winning itself. The positions of parties, and their legislative leaders, are generally known to journalists and disseminated in the media, so whether a party is seen to be on the winning side does not depend on whether a vote is visible or not. However, if a party loses *because its members split* on a given vote, visible voting will expose the split to audiences outside the legislature, compromising leaders' reputations for authority and competence, a matter of less concern to rank-and-file legislators. The consistent pattern here is that visible voting presents a potential liability to party leaders – the consummate legislative insiders – whereas its costs to rank-and-file legislators are less and its appeal is considerable.

4.3. How the Political Actors See Things

The discussion in Chapter 3 demonstrates that visible legislative votes have long been ubiquitous, and politically important, in the United States. The availability of individual voting records far surpasses that of any Latin American legislature. This situation, together with the demonstrated centrality of legislative votes to electoral accountability, supports the proposition that visible votes are more salient in the United States, where elections are exclusively SMD, than in Latin America, where MMDs prevail. In this section, I consider the varying demand for visible votes among actors in legislative politics within Latin American systems, where field research for this project was conducted. This research confirms the intuition that insiders, for whom the opportunity costs of monitoring are low to begin with, tend to oppose voting transparency, whereas outsiders and legislative dissidents support it. Legislative party leaders – the ultimate insiders – are reluctant to use institutional resources to eliminate the very monitoring asymmetries that signal voting implies. Actors outside legislatures, for whom costs of monitoring are otherwise high, favor public voting. Among legislators, members of majority parties or coalitions – and most vehemently their leaders – tend to oppose public voting, whereas opposition legislators and dissidents within majority coalitions support it.

4.3.1. Legislative Leaders

In enforcing party discipline, legislative party leaders have an inherent interest in monitoring votes.[5] However, they are best off if they can monitor effectively without formally recording, insofar as the absence of an official record that can be examined by outside actors shields their rank-and-file legislators from competing pressures. Party leaders' interest in recording votes, if it were to exist at all, would stem from their inability to keep track of how their groups vote by other means (Cárdenas interview; Jenkins and Stewart 2003).

Most legislators interviewed suggested that formally recording individual votes is not necessary for leaders to monitor their troops, and all the party leaders interviewed found informal methods of monitoring votes to be sufficient for their needs, consistent with the proposition that the monitoring advantages are a valuable resource for legislative insiders under signal voting. Former Salvadoran Assembly president Juan Duch (ARENA) explained that "we don't count with an electronic system, but it is still easy to know how a party group voted, and therefore one can know with near certainty whether there is a majority, and whether it is a simple or extraordinary majority."

Other party leaders pointed to the ergonomics of how seating and voting in their chambers operate. Carlos Vallejo Lopez, former president of the Ecuadorian Congress, for example, noted that, "Because the party group is almost all in a line – they are physically together – one can observe how the bloc moves. Ten deputies raise their hands, five deputies, whatever." Legislators from that and other chambers – party leaders and back-benchers, governing coalition and opposition – made similar points about party leaders' ability to monitor voting (Lucero, Sibaja, and Vargas Pagán interviews).

It may be that such low-tech monitoring is more feasible in smaller than in larger legislatures. Most Latin American legislative chambers have fewer than 150 members. The lower houses of Argentina, Brazil, and Mexico, on

---

[5] Legislative parties in Latin America are referred to variously as *bloques, fracciones, bancadas, grupos,* or *partidos.* For simplicity, I refer to such units generically as party groups.

the other hand, have 250 to more than 500 members, and all three have electronic voting systems installed. Chamber membership is positively correlated (.45) with use of electronic voting, but the correlation between membership and frequency of recorded votes is much smaller (.15), and not significant. Party leaders in all chambers where interviews were conducted emphasized that discipline is expected in voting, so recording individual legislators' votes would be redundant (R. Alvarenga and Duch interviews). According to Gonzalo Sánchez de Lozada, former president of Bolivia, "Here it's not like the United States where you say 'I voted this way or that.' . . . Here, people presuppose and expect legislators to be loyal to their party."

Overall, party leaders interviewed were consistently dismissive of the need to record and publish legislative votes. Press reports from other legislatures confirm this pattern. The president of the Panamanian National Assembly dismissed a proposal by opposition deputies to adopt electronic voting on the grounds of unspecified technical problems with the system and the lack of training in its use among the deputies themselves (Tapia G. 2004). After an intervening election, however, the next Panamanian Assembly saw fit to begin recording and publishing votes (Asamblea Nacional de Panamá 2005). Similarly, in 2003 party leaders in the Texas House of Representatives initially resisted demands to record and publish votes on the grounds that to do so would be too costly in terms of time, despite the fact that an electronic voting system was already in place, and in terms of the extra paper required to include the voting rolls in the published *House Journal* (*Dallas Morning News* 2003a). Neither factor proved pivotal in the longer run, however; by 2005 Texas votes were available on the state legislative Web site (Texas Legislature Online 2005). In contrast to leaders, legislators further removed from positions of control over the agenda express consistent support for recorded voting. Many of these also suggested that party leaders are actively hostile, rather than indifferent, toward recorded voting.

4.3.2. Opposition and Dissident Legislators

Legislators from opposition parties, as well as occasional dissident legislators from within governing parties or coalitions, are dependable supporters of the idea of recorded voting, whether or not recorded voting was the standard procedure in their chamber. Their motivations fall into four categories: to obstruct the legislative process, to prevent the manipulation of voting results, to hold their adversaries' feet to the fire on votes that are unpopular, or to publicize dissidence within the majority party or coalition.

4.3.2.1. Obstructionism.

The first motivation, obstruction, is relevant only in chambers that lack electronic voting systems. Where recording a vote literally means that the roll must be called – and, in some cases, where legislators are allowed to explain their position, however briefly – the effect can be to grind progress on the legislative agenda to a halt (Cárdenas interview).

4.3.2.2. Honest Tallies.

The second motivation is simply that recorded votes prevent outright manipulation of voting results by those who control legislative procedures. One Ecuadorian legislator, who asked for anonymity with regard to this one comment, said:

The truth is the following: the president of the Congress often manipulates the votes. So, when you don't have a *nominativa* . . . if the secretary says there are sixty-four votes out of the 110 delegates who are present in the hall, the article is passed. [My party] usually has two of its assistants in the Congress at the front, on both sides of the plenary hall. . . . It's a warning for the secretary, because on more than one occasion we've demonstrated with the accounting that we have brought with us that they are giving a result that's incorrect. [See also Lucero interview.]

Salvadoran deputy Aristides Alvarenga (Partido Democrata Cristiana) also complained of manipulation of vote outcomes under the hand-raising method of voting, but in an interview he described a conscious decision to tolerate such abuse during the tumultuous 1980s:

[Electronic voting] has already been considered [in El Salvador]. This was many years ago, around 1985. A committee studied the possibility, and at that time USAID offered to pay for it, but at that time issues were so complicated – we were in the war, at times it was necessary to contrive votes, to find a way, in order to move forward, and it was said that [electronic voting] was not appropriate at the time and we should wait a while.

By Alvarenga's estimation, sufficient time has now passed that the Salvadoran Assembly should adopt electronic voting, but to this point it has not. It is worth noting that Alvarenga's PDC was a majority party during the period when he found "contriving votes" acceptable practice, but currently it is much smaller and outside government.

Legislators interviewed in every chamber that lacked electronic voting asserted that outcomes were altered when signal votes, which generally involve standing, hand raising, or banging on the table (*el pupitrazo*), were

77

used, and they generally expected that electronic voting would remedy the problem (interviews with Landazuri and Lucero in Ecuador, Sánchez Bezraín in Bolivia, Navarro in Colombia, and Guido in Costa Rica). Nicaraguan deputy María Lourdes Bolaños (FSLN) confirmed the improvement under electronic voting on the basis of recent experience:

I think the change is transcendental. Members of the Salvadoran opposition have told me they want to acquire an electronic system because they regard transparency as very weak in El Salvador, to the point where the Junta Directiva manipulates votes. They always overcount, they're never satisfied. In contrast, we are satisfied with the votes. We believe there is transparency, we believe there's efficiency. That's important. With manual voting, for all the time it would cost us, now we have agility. It's not just about transparency, but agility.

4.3.2.3. Putting Adversaries on Record.

Procedural concerns with obstruction and accurate vote counting aside, the most common motivation behind demands for recorded voting among opposition legislators is transparency. The practice forces those who control the legislative agenda to go on the public record with specific votes to which citizens might object and whose publication might benefit the opposition (Jones and Hwang 2005). Statements along these lines from opposition legislators were abundant (e.g., the Bedregal and Sibaja interviews). Former Bolivian deputy Alfonso Ferrufino (Movimiento Bolivia Libre) describes the reason majority coalition legislators resist electronic voting as "the intention and the will of the representative *not* to be transparent in his job – to say one thing in public and do another inside the Congress."

A staff member (personal communication) for an opposition COPEI (Comité de Organización Política Electoral Independiente) deputy in Venezuela's National Assembly portrayed the governing party's resistance to electronic recorded voting as less subtle, claiming that state-of-the-art voting equipment installed with support from a foreign aid program was vandalized by members of the majority party to avoid having to take responsibility for their votes. In Panama, an opposition-led proposal to force the chamber leadership to use the existing electronic voting system was justified on the grounds that majority-party legislators ducked responsibility for votes in favor of unpopular tax legislation and motions to grant immunity from prosecution to government officials charged with wrongdoing (Tapia G. 2004).

Members of majority parties or coalitions were inclined to dismiss the importance of electronic voting on the grounds that recorded votes can be requested in any instances either where there is doubt about the outcome or where enough legislators want to insist on a public record (Acosta, Carvajal, and Lucero interviews). Yet opposition legislators objected that those who control the flow of legislative traffic fail to handle such requests evenhandedly (Devia, García Valencia, and Holguín interviews). According to Colombian senator Rafael Orduz,

Orduz: Sometimes, if a group of senators opposes a project and is in the minority, but it's in our interest that how everyone voted is known, we can demand a recorded vote, if we are recognized to speak.
Author: How many do you need to make the demand?
Orduz: One – and it has to be approved by the chamber.
Author: By majority?
Orduz: Of course, and this too can be voted by *pupitrazo!*

4.3.2.4. Party Mavericks.

Making votes public makes it easier for legislators to stake out positions independent from those of their parties. Recorded votes can serve as means for maverick legislators to "go public" over the heads of party leaders and, in so doing, to establish reputations either among a target audience of supporters or perhaps nationally. The rare decisions to hold *nominales* in systems where anonymous legislative voting is the norm can illustrate this. According to Costa Rican minority leader Sibaja (interview),

One sign that there's going to be a *nominal* isn't that the opposition is divided – that's no problem. The problem is when the governing party is divided. There was a famous case here in the early 1970s, having to do with student protests over an agreement that permitted a transnational company to mine [in a wilderness area]. It was called the Alcoa Agreement. At that time, the PLN controlled the presidency and had a big parliamentary majority. One government deputy started the fight. That deputy himself later became president, but not as a member of the PLN – don Rodrigo Carazo Odio, who founded the Unity Party, which is governing currently. He led a group of PLN deputies to break the party line. I think that was the last time they used a *nominal* on an important issue, precisely because the government's *fracción* divided at that moment. That was thirty years ago. It's not common.

By Sibaja's account, public voting on the Alcoa Agreement provided a mechanism for a deputy with national ambitions, Rodrigo Carazo, to draw a line in the sand between himself and his party's leadership. This suggests that electronic voting, and visible votes more generally, should encourage independence in legislative voting both insofar as they provide

79

party mavericks with a forum for position taking and insofar as they open legislators to demands of accountability for their votes from actors outside the chamber (Bolaños interview).[6]

In the first years of this century, a similar story was unfolding in Nicaragua, where a group of FSLN deputies objected to a deal cut between their leaders and those of the president's Liberal Party on a package of constitutional and electoral system reforms. The FSLN dissidents took advantage of the recently adopted electronic voting system to publicize their rebellion, drawing the ire of loyalists, such as Deputy Maria Lourdes Bolaños: "[The voting records] have been used to make public the divisions within coalitions. Not for transparency, but to the advantage of those four deputies who are against the pact. That's what it has come to" (Bolaños and Urbina interviews). Bolaños evidently saw no boost to transparency inherent in making votes visible. One of the dissidents, Deputy Mónica Baltodano, however, was becoming acutely aware of the costs of going public with her breech of voting unity: "We broke discipline. . . . So [the party leadership] ruled that whoever did not accept party decisions could not aspire to electoral posts. Everyone knew I wanted to run for mayor of Managua, and this way I couldn't be nominated. It's almost certain that they won't permit me to run for reelection as a deputy either." As anticipated, Baltodano was subsequently barred from nomination for reelection as deputy, citing as the reason her vote in the Assembly against the electoral reform law. By 2002 she was out of elected office.

4.3.3. Outside Actors

Other sources of demand for recorded voting are outside the state. By and large, the public clamor for voting records is modest in the countries where records are not regularly kept. Legislators in Bolivia and Colombia – even those who strongly favored recorded voting themselves – described a general lack of public attention to individual legislators' voting behavior (Carvajal, Cárdenas, and Holguín interviews). Nevertheless, there are pockets of interest. Organized interest groups – unions, business organizations, and

---

[6] Testing this proposition empirically – for example, by comparing party unity levels in legislatures with electronic voting against levels on recorded votes in legislatures without electronic voting – is problematic, because votes that get recorded in the latter may be biased toward disunity. In the Alcoa vote described by Alexis Sibaja, for example, both major parties split.

farmers' groups – sometimes monitor legislative voting, even in systems where no records are kept, and lobby legislators and party leaders to support their demands (Navarro and Sánchez de Lozada interviews).

More general demand for recorded votes comes from the media, from academics, and sometimes from watchdog nongovernmental organizations. During Colombian elections since the late 1990s, Congreso Visible/Candidatos Visibles, based at the Universidad de los Andes in Bogota, has solicited background information and policy position statements from all legislative candidates and published all responses on its Web site, supplementing this material between elections with information on partisanship and committee assignments, policy proposals, the status of legislation, and public statements by legislators. The organization also collects the few votes recorded at the individual level in the Colombian Congress and has been aggressive in lobbying for the adoption of recorded public voting as a matter of standard procedure (Ungar Bleier 2002).

In Argentina, the Asociación por los Derechos Civiles has pursued a judicial strategy, filing suit in Buenos Aires municipal court demanding full public disclosure of all municipal council votes while simultaneously lobbying at the national level for recorded voting by publicizing controversial legislation on which the public records produced by Congress do not make it possible to determine how individual legislators voted (Gonzalez Bertomeu 2004; *Clarín* 2004a). In Panama, the local branch of Transparency International supported opposition-led efforts within the Legislative Assembly to require that the electronic voting system be used (Tapia G. 2004). In Mexico, as well, persistent pressure from academics at the Instituto Tecnologico Autonomo de Mexico (ITAM) during the late 1990s and early years of this decade appears to have hastened the systematic dissemination of voting records via the Congress's Web site.

4.3.4. Presidents

Presidential commitment to recorded voting is a product of the specific political conditions at hand and the goals of a particular president. The rare circumstances that land the issue at the top of a presidential agenda, however, may be sufficient to establish recorded voting as standard practice.

As with party leaders, interview subjects dismissed the need for executives to rely on recorded voting to monitor their legislative allies, on the grounds that informal networks within legislatures themselves were sufficient for these purposes (Guerra and Holguín interviews). Nevertheless, presidents may demand recorded voting for other reasons – as a gambit to enfranchise third-party monitors to offset the inherent advantages of legislative party leaders, or even out of a genuine desire to increase transparency in the policymaking process.

Many presidents express a generic interest in modernization and efficiency and a willingness to push such demands on a reluctant legislature. An ironic example is the case of Alberto Fujimori, whose administration is not generally associated with transparency. Yet Fujimori's campaign to modernize the state included an initiative to computerize the Peruvian Congress, which in turn included the installation of electronic voting machines (Cevasco Piedra 2000). Although Fujimori's legislative allies initially refused to use the equipment, the legislative opposition eventually succeeded, through the aggressive use of obstructionist tactics, in forcing the adoption of electronic voting as standard operating procedure (Carey 2003). Thus, Fujimori's modernizing drive appears, unintentionally, to have produced the regular practice of recorded voting in Peru.

Less inadvertently, and also less successfully, Colombian President Alvaro Uribe's first act as president in 2002 was to introduce a broad package of political reforms, the first element of which was a requirement that all votes taken in the Colombian Congress be recorded and made public (*El Tiempo* 2002). The priority Uribe gave to this procedural detail is remarkable given that he assumed the Colombian presidency in the midst of a civil war.[7] His stated rationale was that lack of confidence in government institutions was responsible for the crisis of the Colombian state and that transparency was needed to produce greater accountability among elected officials.[8] Facing congressional resistance to his proposal in 2002, Uribe put his reform package directly to voters in a fifteen-point referendum the next year. The public voting provision received 94 percent support among votes cast, but only 24.7 percent of eligible voters participated. In Colombia, referenda require 25 percent participation to be valid, so Uribe's proposal failed, and most votes in Colombia remain invisible to those outside the Congress.

---

[7] Uribe's inauguration ceremony itself was subject to a mortar attack.

[8] It is worth noting that Colombia's previous president, Andres Pastrana, in the name of transparency, had also tried to pass a package of reforms that included the requirement of public voting. The proposal died in the face of legislative opposition.

4.4. Effects of Recorded Voting

Are the motivations and concerns of these actors who care about the move to recorded voting justified? What impact does recorded voting have on legislative representation? The most obvious effect is an increase in transparency and greater opportunities for actors outside the legislature to exert pressure on elected representatives. The discussion of monitoring also suggests that publicizing votes should weaken party leaders' influence over legislators. This section presents evidence confirming both of these propositions.

4.4.1. Transparency

When asked the open-ended question, "What effects, if any, does recorded voting have on legislative representation?" most legislators mentioned an increase in transparency.[9] The term, however, is sufficiently general (and such talk is sufficiently cheap) that it is worth spelling out more explicitly what it entails. In its crudest sense, the transparency afforded by recorded voting is a check against the ability of legislators to lie outright about the policies they have supported or opposed inside the chamber. None of my interview subjects confessed to having perjured themselves in this manner, but claims that their colleagues had were common.[10] Colombian senator Rafael Orduz (interview) was willing to name names:

I'll give you an example, having to do with a particular part of a recent tax reform. In public – I'm talking about on television – the president of the Liberal Party, Luis Guillermo Veles, said he was against it. In the vote, inside the Senate, he voted in favor. There was no TV and no recorded vote, but nobody has called him on it in public. So publicly, he continues to position himself as if he had opposed the article I'm talking about.

Orduz's point was that a recorded vote on the tax measure in question would have offered a deterrent against the obfuscation of which he accuses Senator Veles, or else have provided incontrovertible evidence with which any of Veles's opponents (presumably including Orduz) could expose his perfidy.

Another Colombian senator offered a similar assessment with respect to why the Colombian Senate never used an electronic voting system that been installed two years before: "They say it has technical problems, but

---

[9] In legislatures that do not regularly record votes, I asked, "What effects, if any, do you expect recorded voting would have on legislative representation?"

[10] I am still not sure how I managed to overselect honest politicians to such an extreme.

this is just an excuse because they don't want votes to be public. Too many senators are afraid they will lose votes if they are all made public" (Blum interview). I pursued the same issue later, at a meeting attended by a group of senators and representatives, asking why neither chamber of the Colombian Congress used its electronic voting system:

Anonymous senator:	"There were problems. They didn't work."
Author:	"Why not? Technical problems?"
Anonymous senator:	"Well, *politico*-technical problems."
All legislators:	[Big laughs all around the table.]

Beyond their jaded perspective, these Colombian examples reflect the belief that the transparency provided by visible votes acts as a deterrent to bad behavior – to lying about votes or voting against constituent interests – by legislators. Most of those interviewed for this project also mentioned more general positive effects of transparency, suggesting that voting records are a basic mechanism for transmitting information about legislative decision making and that this information is a public good. Without rehearsing each such statement, Ecuadorian Alexandra Vela (Democracia y Progreso) provides the general flavor:

The mechanism for rendering accounts doesn't function if there's no way to verify the votes. Why? Because from this election we have the obligation to present a legislative program. So, we notarize, we go to the notary and we publicly say this is the program. But citizens request accounts from their delegates as to whether this is the program that was presented and you don't know how each one voted. So, the process of rendering accounts demands that there be voting of this kind. Also, for knowledge and for learning, as a pedagogical matter for citizens who don't understand and can't see how the mechanisms of a democracy function. It's important for them to see it.

4.4.2. Direct Effects on Policy Decisions

Some of the general claims about transparency point to education and information (Ferrufino interview). Others suggest that the threat of sanction from voters deters legislators from shirking constituents' interests in their voting behavior, which in turn suggests the stronger claim that recorded voting can change actual policy outcomes (Blanco Oropeza interview). Testing such a claim systematically is inherently difficult, of course, because in any given case the outcome realized must be compared against the counterfactual – the outcome that *would have been* realized in the absence or presence of recorded voting.

84

One example, drawn from the Texas state legislature, suggests such an effect for recorded voting. In April 2003 the state House of Representatives was considering a motion to kill a widely popular proposal to require legislative candidates to disclose the sources of their campaign contributions. The motion was initially put to a nonrecorded vote and appeared to be headed toward passage (which would have killed the bill); however, "When a recorded vote was requested, the scoreboard changed completely and the motion to kill the bill failed" (*Dallas Morning News* 2003b).

Multiple independent interviews conducted in Peru pointed toward another case where recorded voting changed an important policy outcome (Masías, Pease, De Althaus, and Ortiz de Zevallos interviews). At issue was a proposed change in the electoral system for the 2001 election. Incumbent legislators had been elected from a single national district. The proposed reform would divide Peru into multiple electoral districts (*circunscripciones*) defined by departmental boundaries. Despite popular support for the idea, many legislators were skeptical about altering the rules under which they had, by definition, been successful. Congressman Henry Pease (Union por el Peru) provided the most compelling account of recorded voting's effect on the outcome:

[This reform] obviously was not good for small parties, or for those that knew that, after the way they had governed, they were going to be small parties. There was a lot of tension when this issue was put to debate, with strong public opinion in favor, and a bunch of legislators demanded, based on an article of the rules, that the vote should be secret. I wasn't in Congress at the moment because I was sick in the medical clinic, so I saw on television the impact, above all, of public opinion. I was in the clinic at least from 6:00 or 7:00 P.M. on, in a room watching the TV, and the nurses were coming in – not to look after me, but to watch the TV and express their indignation at what was happening, because as soon as they saw that it was going to be a secret vote they said "It's going to lose" and in fact, they didn't get enough votes to get rid of the national district. This led to a mobilization and to demands of all sorts and criticisms of all sorts and allowed us to force, a month later, another proposal, and vote on it . . . and finally, even though it was a much more radical bill, it was accepted because of public pressure.

4.4.3. Do Citizens Pay Attention?

Pease's comments suggest a critical issue with respect to the prospects for recorded votes to act as mechanisms for legislative accountability in the manner that they do in the United States – whether voting records find their way into the mainstream of political discourse. To put the matter more bluntly, even if votes are visible, does anyone look? The Peruvian fieldwork for this project was conducted in May 2001 – a period of intense politicization in that country, after the fall of the Fujimori regime, and in between the two rounds of the election that produced the presidency of Alejandro Toledo. Congress, which had produced the interim president Valentín Paniagua, and which was conducting investigations into the spectacular corruption charges against members of the Fujimori administration, was in the national spotlight. In this context, the Peruvian media reported intensively on congressional voting records. Newspaper articles reproduced roll calls (Diez Canseco 2001; *La Gaceta* 2001), and television talk shows focused on motivations (De Althaus interview). Recorded voting in Peru appeared to have, in very short order, established itself at the core of political discourse.

One should be cautious, however, about generalizing too quickly from the experience of Peru in 2001, which was extraordinary on a number of counts. The early experience of Nicaragua with recorded voting stands in contrast to Peru. Field research in Nicaragua was conducted in August 2000, and electronic voting had been adopted as standard operating procedure only eight months earlier, in January. Deputy Carlos Hurtado (Accion Conservador) described the status of the voting records this way:

Hurtado: Despite the fact that votes are recorded, they aren't widely known among the people, except when a particular issue becomes decisive at election time.

Author: Is this a process that is beginning?

Hurtado: Yes, it's happening. It requires that the electorate, the political analysts, have the record. It's not so simple to create this record because it requires a certain infrastructure, a certain culture, a certain systematization. There's no independent center that keeps a record of the votes. In the United States, there is – there are lots that keep complete records of the details. That's more sophisticated. I think eventually we'll get there, but certainly as of now it's not so easy. At least it's known when a certain deputy takes a certain position.

Individual votes are, indeed, known within the Nicaraguan Assembly because its electronic voting system includes a large screen indicating each deputy's position on each motion, yet they are not widely known beyond the Assembly hall because the records are not published, nor is it easy for would-be observers from outside the Assembly to obtain them. Deputy Jorge Samper (Movimiento Renovacion Sandinismo) pointed toward the status of legislative staff – and specifically of civil service protection of government employees – in explaining the obstructed flow of information about what goes on inside the legislature to sources on the outside. In Nicaragua, according to Samper, legislative employees, lacking civil service protection, are reluctant to release voting records out of fear that any discomfort those published records generate among powerful politicians could cost the staff members their jobs:

Right now some [members of the legislative staff] still resist publishing things without someone giving them orders to do it. Sometimes they're a bit afraid. . . . It's important that there be career officials who will be the institutional memory who attest to what's done and that it be published – that there be a guarantee, a nonpartisan guarantee, independent of who's in the government or who has the majority in the parliament, in order to provide real, effective, and concrete information, without of any sort of fears.

4.4.4. Visible Votes and the Quality of Representation

Beyond the accounts of legislators themselves, it is difficult to estimate the effect on transparency of recording and publishing legislative votes. The Corruption Perceptions Index (CPI), calculated by Transparency International for most countries in the world, measures perceptions of corruption generally. The CPI is not legislature-specific, but it is a widely recognized measure of political transparency and allows cross-national comparison. Figure 4.1 plots the square root of the average number of votes recorded and made public per year, by country, against the 2004 CPI. I use the square root of the number of votes per year on the logic that there are diminishing returns to the information conveyed through visible votes (positive correlation .55, or .37 when dropping the United States and retaining just the Latin American cases) between the log of public votes per year and the CPI.

Whether because legislative transparency reduces corruption, or because some combination of factors that produces legislative transparency also contributes to cleaner government in general (or, more likely, some combination of these effects), perceptions of corruption tend to be lower in countries where legislative votes are visible.[11]

---

[11] I found no relationship between public votes and "confidence in Congress," as measured by the Latinobarómetro during the late 1990s through early 2000s. To the extent that the crafting of legislation resembles sausage making, per Bismarck's famous observation, visibility may enhance accountability and deter corruption without necessarily increasing public affection for Congress.

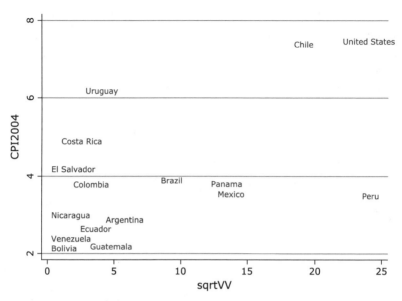

Figure 4.1 Recorded votes per year (square root), by country, and 2004 Transparency International Corruption Perceptions Index.

The experiences of specific countries demonstrate that individual legislators' voting records can attain political salience in Latin America and can do so relatively quickly, as in Peru. The broader pattern is confirmed as well by Brazil and Chile, with longer experiences with recording votes. On the other hand, it is not automatic that "If you record it, they will come." MMD elections in Latin America mitigate incentives to monitor individual voting behavior, and resistance to recorded voting from powerful legislative actors also discourages forces otherwise inclined to publicize voting records.

4.4.5. Partisan versus Individualized Legislative Representation

Much of the discussion so far has suggested that recorded voting can undermine discipline in legislative parties and coalitions. Discipline implies the ability on the part of party leaders to compel legislators to vote contrary to their immediate preferences or contrary to preferences induced through their electoral connection with constituents. Recording votes and making them public increase the costs to legislators of voting that is disciplined in this sense. The fact that party leaders, in interviews, supported recorded voting less than other legislators is consistent with this interpretation.

This analysis cannot test the hypothesis that recorded voting weakens discipline, for the obvious reason that no data exist and no levels of party voting unity can be measured when voting records do not exist, but the interviews support this proposition. Deputy Mónica Baltodano, the FSLN dissident sanctioned for voting against the party, described strong public support for independence from absolute party discipline: "There is a great tolerance [of indiscipline] among citizens and Nicaraguan society, which can be demonstrated in polls and studies. But within the political institutions, there's great intolerance, above all within the party." A vignette provided by Peruvian congressman Carlos Blanco Oropeza (Cambio 90 – Nueva Mayoria) illustrates the expected effect among party leaders of recorded voting on discipline in more colorful terms:

I'll never forget when, in 1998, I was vice president of the Congress, and we hosted some German legislators, and naturally one of the things we did was to visit the facilities of the Congress. I accompanied them to the chamber, the place where we meet, and right there is the screen for the public votes, and I'll never forget the German legislator – who was a leader of his party – and he said to me, "Is the vote public?" So I explained, and he said, "You guys are crazy. How can you control the members of your party? Everyone has to vote how the party votes."

Blanco's German colleague was referring to the practice of signal voting in the Bundesrat, a practice with which Blanco himself was familiar because the Peruvian Congress had relied almost exclusively on signal voting until modernization, including the installation of electronic voting equipment, in the late 1990s ushered in recorded voting. Blanco confirmed that recorded voting increased the willingness of individual legislators to resist leadership directives (Blanco Oropeza interview).

Whether the potential for recorded voting to undermine party discipline is realized depends on whether citizens come to regard voting records as salient in evaluating legislator performance, whether they are willing to reward independence from parties in the pursuit of some other conception of constituent interests, and whether these forces supersede whatever other tools party leaders retain to enforce discipline. Interview subjects contended that voting records encourage responsiveness to citizens in legislators' immediate electoral constituencies, even at the cost of loyalty to the national party, because voters are prepared to weigh either regional interests against those of the national party (A. Alvarenga interview) or sectoral interests (Masías interview).

The priority of individual over partisan accountability to the electorate was a theme repeated in interviews in one country after another, even where recorded voting has made no progress toward adoption. In Venezuela, for example, the same antiparty chorus was echoed by both opponents and supporters of President Hugo Chavez. Former Constituent Assembly deputy Ricardo Combellas described the philosophy behind the new constitution adopted in 1999: "We wanted to eliminate partyarchy – to eliminate it constitutionally, but in terms of norms, for the representative to respond more directly to the wants and needs of his constituents. Responsibility in parliament is personal – the Constitution says so – not to respond to a party but to one's constituents." William Tarek Saab (Movimiento Quinta Republica), a leading member of President Hugo Chavez's party in both the Constituent Assembly and the current legislature, concurred: "I think that here you have to listen to the voice of the people. One of the requirements for this is the vote of conscience. You pay attention only to your conscience." To this point, of course, whether votes in the Venezuelan National Assembly are regularly being cast according to the demands of conscience – perhaps even independently from party lines – must remain a matter of faith, because of the failure of the Assembly's leadership to use the electronic voting system that is in place.

4.5. The Trend toward Visible Votes and Its Limits

Recorded voting is a controversial reform, resisted by powerful legislative actors. Its principal advocates are opposition legislators and dissidents within governing coalitions, as well as nongovernmental organizations and journalists for whom government transparency is a priority, and the odd academic. Its main opponents are the leaders of governing parties. In short, those inclined to oppose recorded voting determine who sets rules of legislative procedure. On the other hand, the gradual spread of electronic voting in many Latin American legislatures over the past decade or so indicates that the barriers are not insurmountable and that demand for visible votes sometimes prevails. Procedural rights granted to legislative minorities may provide some leverage for those demanding the regular use of recorded voting, as was the case in Peru. In Panama, and in the state of Texas, pressure from the media preceded the adoption of visible voting in legislatures. The Colombian case suggests that supporters of recorded voting might occasionally find allies with clout in the executive branch, and in Argentina, transparency advocates are looking to the courts.

Perhaps most important to the overall trend is that recorded voting as standard practice appears to be subject to a sort of ratchet effect. Once the practice is adopted, it is difficult to backslide. According to Peruvian congressman Blanco Oropeza, "Once it's done, you're not going to change it. It's not going to change because even if the general public doesn't pay much attention, the journalists do. The journalists and the other politicians, too, because they are the ones who get accustomed to using this information." In another interview, political commentator Jaime De Althaus, also from Peru, summed up the matter even more categorically: "[Recorded public voting] has had its own inertia. . . . It's an almost inevitable consequence that runs according to its own logic."

The point is that, although opponents of visible voting may be able to keep the issue off the reform agenda quietly for extended periods of time, once the practice is established, a move to eliminate it would be difficult to defend publicly. In this sense, the empirical evidence from this chapter suggests that the case for visible voting, as well as the conception of legislative accountability that goes with it, resonates widely. In spite of scholarly appeals for responsible party government, or even the arguments of Rousseau and Burke about legislative detachment, citizens want to know how their representatives vote – or at least representatives are reluctant to suggest otherwise.

This is not to say we should necessarily expect legislative voting records to assume in other political contexts the central role they play in U.S. legislative politics. In particular, MMD elections dilute the incentives for individual politicians to use incumbents' voting records as ammunition in electoral battles. Nevertheless, many actors *are* motivated to promote voting records, technological advances are on their side, and backsliding on this matter is improbable. Recorded voting, therefore, should become more common, and voting records should grow increasingly salient to political debate and increasingly central to the accountability relationships between legislators and voters, even if they never attain the prominence they have in the United States.

5

Counting Votes

5.1. Party Voting Unity and Collective Accountability

When votes are visible, what can we learn from them about legislative accountability? Citizens can learn whether specific representatives have pursued their interests in motions put to a vote on the floor – information that can provide a basis for individual legislative accountability. Even apart from the policy substance of the votes themselves, voting patterns can tell us about prospects for collective accountability, because collective accountability requires that groups of legislators vote in a unified manner to shape outcomes on the floor.

I propose various measures of voting unity and success among groups of legislators. Because parties are the ubiquitous organizers of legislative work, the groups on which I focus primarily are parties, so unless otherwise noted, voting unity and related terms refer to unity among members of the same party. The measures of unity, however, can be equally well applied to any other group, such as coalitions that encompass more than one party or legislators from a particular region, sex, race, or religion – any characteristic of interest for analysis.

Why should we care about party unity in legislative voting? First, legislative votes are the means by which major public policy decisions are ratified in all democracies. Voting behavior is of intrinsic interest because the stakes are high. Second, political parties are potentially important information conduits to citizens. Parties can pledge to support comprehensive policy platforms on which individual politicians cannot credibly claim to have much impact. Whether voters can know what they are getting in elections depends partly on legislative voting unity. If the voting behavior of a party's legislators is unrelated to the positions in its national platform, then the party's label has no informational value. Third, unity affects the ability of parties to win votes and shape policy. Unity determines whether governments can act decisively or, by contrast, whether each legislative decision requires separate deliberation and the construction of a distinct support coalition. In this sense, party unity is linked to the ability of parties and governments to deliver the promises in their platforms (Bowler, Farrell, and Katz 1999).

I focus on three main characteristics of how parties vote: how consistently their members take the same position on the motions on which they vote, how much they win, and how frequently their losses might have been avoided but for breaches of voting unity. Voting together matters not just because mobilizing its full voting capacity can help a party win floor votes and so promote its supporters' interests. Voting together (or failing to do so) also sends information to citizens about the party's policy positions and its level of commitment to them. When votes are visible, cross-voting within a party or failure to mobilize its members on a given measure blurs the party's brand name. A party that mobilizes its potential and votes in a unified manner, by contrast, fortifies and clarifies its reputation. Thus, the degree to which copartisans vote together is relevant to accountability both through the delivery of wins and losses and through its communicative content.

The indices developed in this chapter measure raw levels of party unity and are agnostic as to whether the source of unity is like-mindedness among legislators (cohesiveness) or pressure from party leaders (discipline). Raw levels of party unity matter in their own right. Low unity reduces the communicative value of party labels to voters, and high party unity increases it, regardless of whether the source is cohesiveness or discipline. Low unity reduces the ability of parties to deliver their policy promises through legislation, and high party unity increases it, regardless of whether the source is cohesiveness or discipline. Indices of party unity that can be deployed across systems and across parties describe variance in a common metric that makes cross-national comparison possible. As this chapter demonstrates, party unity varies a lot, both across political systems and among parties within systems. The next chapter uses the indices developed here to shed some light on the relative importance of cohesiveness versus discipline in accounting for the levels of party unity observed empirically and to test propositions about the sources of high and low party unity.

Party unity is a necessary condition for collective accountability, not its guarantee. As Chapter 2 highlights, when voters are unable to demand accountability from national party leaders, highly unified parties can be turned into cartels to monopolize state resources on behalf of narrow sets of beneficiaries or to pursue policies contrary to those advertised in electoral campaigns, to voters' widespread chagrin (Coppedge 1994; Stokes 2001). Yet without unity, parties can neither communicate a coherent collective reputation to voters nor credibly claim to deliver on policy platforms that reflect that reputation. As long as party unity is a condition for collective accountability, even if not its equivalent, it is important to develop a common metric to compare unity across political systems.

The first part of this chapter develops some indices I use to measure voting unity, discusses their properties, and illustrates them by applying them to votes in hypothetical legislatures as well as to some empirical examples. Then I present recorded vote data collected for this project from legislatures in nineteen countries and apply the measures to describe partisan voting unity across these chambers statistically and graphically.

5.2. Measures of Voting Unity and Success

5.2.1. RICE and UNITY Scores

I rely on a variety of indices built from the voting record. The indices are summaries of information from across multiple votes. Their most basic building blocks are the aye and nay votes, abstentions, and nonvotes cast by individual legislators. These are used to construct party voting unity scores for individual votes, which in turn are aggregated into indices that describe patterns across sets of votes.

The first measure is familiar to legislative scholars and is based on the measure of unity developed by Stuart Rice (1925) more than eighty years ago. RICE scores reflect levels of cross-voting among members of the same party on a given vote and are calculated as:

$$RICE_{ij} = |AYE_{ij} - NAY_{ij}| \text{ for party } i \text{ on vote } j,$$

where aye and nay are calculated as proportions of those voting either aye or nay, and so sum to 1.0. The RICE score can range from zero (equal numbers vote aye and nay) to one (all members who cast votes vote together).

One limitation of RICE is that it does not account for nonvoting, levels of which are substantial in most legislatures. For example, if a party has 100 members, 60 of whom cast affirmative votes on a measure and 40 of whom abstain or otherwise do not vote, RICE regards this event as perfect unity (RICE = 1.0), equivalent to if all 100 members of the party voted aye (or nay). Intuitively, these are two fundamentally different events, the difference between which could obviously affect the vote outcome. This suggests some type of measure that is sensitive to *whether* copartisans vote, as well as to how they vote. For this, I propose UNITY, which captures the extent to which a party exercises its decisive capacity on a given vote:

$$UNITY_{ij} = |AYE_{ij} - NAY_{ij}| \text{ for party } i \text{ on vote } j,$$

where the proportions are calculated as shares of *all* members of party i in the legislature.

Like RICE, UNITY can range from zero to one, but it "dips" more easily than RICE, taking the minimum value either if those legislators who do vote split evenly between aye and nay (like RICE) or if no members cast decisive votes. It takes the maximum value if all members cast decisive (i.e., aye or nay) votes in the same direction, and it falls between these extremes when either decisive voters within the party divide against each other, or some members vote while others do not, or both. In effect, UNITY is a cousin to RICE, but it is discounted according to the rate of nonvoting in the group. For an illustration of RICE and UNITY scores from a hypothetical assembly, see Appendix 1 at the end of this chapter.

5.2.2. RICE and UNITY Indices

Because I am aiming to discern general characteristics of party groups, it is convenient to aggregate the vote-specific measures of voting unity into indices that summarize, for each party, the overall tendency toward unity across all the recorded votes in a given legislature. I aggregate at the level of legislatures because this is the largest period for which some important characteristics of party groups (e.g., share of seats, government or opposition status) are constant.

One problem with simply averaging voting scores to create indices is that many votes in most legislatures are lopsided, either because they are taken on matters of consensus across parties or on matters unimportant enough to attract any opposition, or because their outcome is obvious ahead of time and the losers may choose not to register their opposition formally through their votes. To correct this problem, when aggregating parties' RICE and UNITY scores across votes into indices, I weight the score from each vote according to how closely the vote was contested. The procedure for calculating weighted RICE (WRICE) and UNITY (WUNITY) indices is described in Appendix 2.

5.2.3. Winning, Losing, and Voting Unity

Mobilizing legislators and voting together matter to parties' collective reputations and may also matter to whether parties win or lose votes, but winning and losing can also be observed directly, along with the relationship between mobilizing votes, cross-voting, and voting success rates. I calculate for each party, i, on each vote, j, whether it wins, WIN_{ij}, which is simply an indicator of whether the plurality of party i's members voted on the winning side. The details of how this legislative success index is created are described in Appendix 3.

Finally, whereas $RICE_i$ and $UNITY_i$ reflect the extent to which parties project, through legislative voting, collective reputations, my last pair of measures is based on the intuition that unified parties more effectively influence policy than disunified ones. $RLOSER_{ij}$ and $ULOSER_{ij}$ reflect whether a party suffers a loss on a given legislative vote because, respectively, of cross-voting or of a failure to mobilize its full voting capacity. $RLOSER_{ij}$ takes a value of 1 if party i loses on vote j even though, *given how all other legislators voted*, party i could have won had all its voting members voted together. $ULOSER_{ij}$ takes a value of 1 if party i loses on vote j even though, *given how all other legislators voted*, party i could have won had it mobilized its full voting capacity behind its preferred outcome. Details on the calculation of these indices, as well as illustrations from a hypothetical legislature, are in Appendix 4.

5.3. The Silence of Nonvotes

5.3.1. What Do Nonvotes Mean?

Because they take account of nonvoting, and so capture the degree to which a party mobilizes its full potential vote behind its preferred positions, $UNITY_i$ and its cousin, $ULOSER_i$, might appear to be more comprehensive and reliable reflections of the extent to which a party translates its legislative representation into influence over legislative decisions than $RICE_i$ and $RLOSER_i$. Yet there is a serious potential shortcoming with these indices because how one interprets nonvoting is more complex, both mechanically and strategically, than how one interprets cross-voting.

Some studies of recorded votes seek to interpret the *motivation* behind nonvotes, in order to infer whether they likely represent breaks with party discipline – for example, if legislators were present for some votes in a session but not others (Haspel, Remington, and Smith 1998; Ames 2002). This approach implicitly attributes analogous meaning to nonvoting and to voting, regarding each as an equivalent action for the purposes of measuring party voting unity. Under most conditions, however such an approach can mismeasure the *effects* of nonvoting (Jones and Hwang 2005).

On most votes in most assemblies, threshold for approval is set in relative terms, as a proportion of votes cast (subject to a quorum). But for some votes – and in a handful of assemblies, for all votes – the threshold for approval is set in absolute terms, as a proportion of the full membership. The effect of nonvoting on outcomes depends directly on such rules, and absolute thresholds create particular challenges for the voting unity indices developed in this chapter. These issues are discussed in Appendix 5. Going forward, my default approach is to treat nonvotes according to their effects on vote outcomes. Because of the ambiguity absolute-threshold rules generate, however, I replicate all the quantitative analyses in the book dropping the absolute-majority cases: Nicaragua, Guatemala, and Russia. Where doing so affects results, I report both specifications and discuss the differences in interpretation.

5.3.2. Nonvoting Equilibria

Beyond the different mechanical implications of nonvotes under absolute-versus relative-majority threshold voting rules, nonvoting also carries potentially important strategic ambiguities under either type of rule. Parties may tolerate nonvoting by members who *could have* been mobilized, if necessary. Leaders may strike agreements with rank-and-file members within their own parties to tolerate nonvoting as long as preliminary head counts suggest nonvotes will not be pivotal (King and Zeckhauser 2003). Alternatively, they might strike agreements with leaders of other parties to "match" nonvotes that offset each other across party lines, so as not to affect the overall outcome. A nonvoting equilibrium arrangement might be advantageous both to party leaders, as a means of hiding displays of internal dissent, and to individual legislators, both when they prefer not to support their party's line and when they are merely beholden to other commitments besides attendance and voting on the floor – for example, to committee work, to constituency service, or even to professional or personal obligations outside the legislature. The existence of such agreements is asserted in various Latin American legislatures in interviews conducted during the course of research for this project. To the extent that such agreements represent equilibria within or across parties not to mobilize their full voting potential, and that leaders *could* mobilize their legislators if necessary, then their party is *potentially* more unified than the observed voting record suggests, and the validity of $UNITY_{ij}$ and $ULOSER_{ij}$ as measures of party voting unity are dubious.

Consider the illustrations of party voting unity in Argentina and New Zealand in Figures 5.1 and 5.2. In the figures, $WRICE_i$ indices are represented by the height of each bar on the y axis. Each party's share of seats is represented by its width on the x axis. In each case, $WRICE_i$ is quite high, whereas $WUNITY_i$ is substantially lower, with the decline of similar magnitude across parties, indicating little cross-voting, but suggesting the possibility of matched nonvoting equilibria. The implications for the win-loss-based indices are striking. For example, Argentina's governing Peronist Party (PJ, or Partido Justicialista) was on the winning side in 95 percent of recorded floor votes, but in all of its losses it suffered cross-voting that, if reversed, would have flipped the outcome in the Peronists' favor ($RLOSER_i = 5$ percent). The main opposition Radical Party (UCR), by contrast, lost 85 percent of recorded votes. None of these defeats is attributable to cross-voting ($RLOSER_i = 0$), but the $ULOSER_i$ measure suggests that 30 percent could have been reversed had the UCR mobilized its full cohort behind the party's position. Could the opposition have prevailed in this manner? More likely, had the UCR increased mobilization, the Peronists could and would have countermobilized, summoning more votes to the floor (raising $WUNITY_i$ for both, and driving the UCR's $ULOSER_i$ index down). The UCR's inflated $ULOSER_i$, that is, might well be a mere reflection of a nonvoting equilibrium across parties – an equilibrium also reflected in the even drop-off from $WRICE_i$ to $WUNITY_i$ indices. The data from New Zealand's parliament of 1993–94 suggests a very similar potential relationship between the National and Labour parties, with an even larger spike in the latter's $ULOSER_i$ index.

The patterns from Argentina and New Zealand suggest equilibria across governing and opposition parties whereby the former tolerate nonvoting provided that less-than-full mobilization does not cost them victories, and the latter tolerate nonvoting, aware that full mobilization would only trigger countermobilization by governing parties. But not all legislatures exhibit similar patterns. Consider the pattern in the early months of Alejandro Toledo's administration in Peru, from August to October 2001, shown in

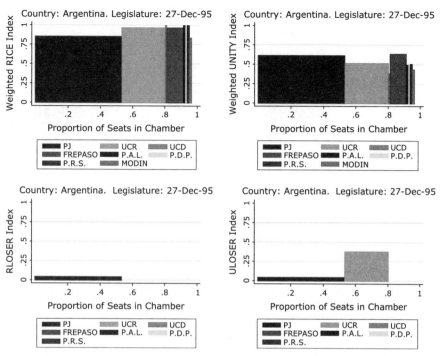

Figure 5.1   WRICE, WUNITY, RLOSER, and ULOSER indices for Argentina, 1995–97.

Figure 5.3. The drop-off from $WRICE_i$ to $WUNITY_i$ was more pronounced for President Toledo's Peru Posible (PP) party than for others, and it cost the government party victories on about 3 percent of all recorded votes – a higher rate than for any other party.

Along the same lines, consider the voting record of the Czech Republic's parliament during its 1996–98 term. In Figure 5.4, the parties of the governing coalition are white and all others shaded various hues of gray. There is the familiar drop-off from $WRICE_i$ to $WUNITY_i$ indices, and the rise from $RLOSER_i$ to $ULOSER_i$, as the latter capture nonvoting as well as cross-voting. But the rise in $ULOSER_i$ is spread across all parties and is more pronounced within the governing coalition than outside it. In short, patterns of these indices across countries suggest that nonvoting equilibria are possible but not uniform. Moreover, the combined patterns of $WRICE_i$, $WUNITY_i$, $RLOSER_i$, and $ULOSER_i$ across parties can detect signs of such equilibria in some cases and help rule them out in others.

Figure 5.2 WRICE, WUNITY, RLOSER, and ULOSER indices for New Zealand, 1993–94.

Furthermore, even where nonvoting equilibria exist, it is not obvious that these ought to be regarded as cases of party unity on par with those in which votes are fully mobilized. When rank-and-file legislators have other, more pressing, priorities than getting to the floor to cast votes in line with their copartisans, the observed level of mobilization represents an intrinsic level of support for the party's position. Leaders might be able to increase mobilization beyond that point in a pinch, but to do so they might also have to twist arms and otherwise expend political resources. By this interpretation, the very existence of nonvoting equilibria can reflect a lack of common purpose within parties.

Voting records tell us, among other things, who does not vote, but nonvoting is a more ambiguous act than casting an aye or a nay. In part, this is because the mechanics of voting can vary across legislatures. Where the threshold to approve a measure is set in absolute terms, the effect of nonvoting is substantively different from where the threshold is relative.

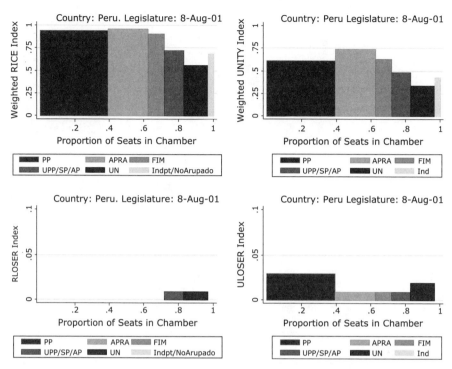

Figure 5.3 WRICE, WUNITY, RLOSER, and ULOSER indices for Peru, 2001.

Under absolute-threshold rules, I treat nonvotes as nay votes, but I also replicate all analyses dropping the absolute-majority cases, and the results reported in this book do not change. In part, nonvotes are ambiguous because nonvoting may reflect strategic behavior that reflects layers of agreements among party leaders and between leaders and their rank-and-file members. The mobilization-based indices, $WUNITY_i$ and $ULOSER_i$, are particularly sensitive to nonvoting and, therefore, to nonvoting-equilibria.

5.3.3. Small Parties

One last set of issues associated with the voting unity measures employed in this book focuses on applying the measures to very small parties. WRICE and ULOSER are not calculated for single-member parties, and RLOSER is not calculated for parties with fewer than three members. These matters,

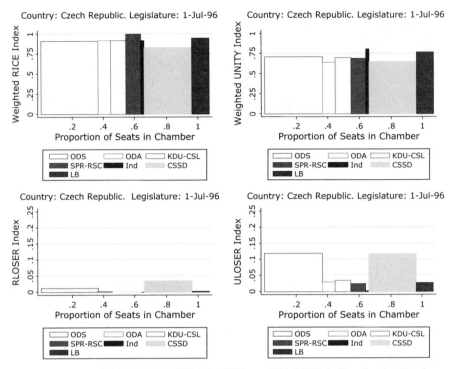

Figure 5.4 WRICE, WUNITY, RLOSER, and ULOSER indices for the Czech Republic, 1996–98.

as well as corrections for bias inherent in RICE and UNITY scores for small parties, are discussed in Appendix 6.

5.4. Data on Recorded Votes

As discussed in Chapter 3, the availability of recorded votes in many legislatures, particularly in quantities that facilitate quantitative analysis, is limited. My main criterion for including recorded votes from a given legislature in this study was simply whether I could get data. In this sense, data collection resembled a Drunkard's Search, with the most energy devoted toward legislatures where there was sufficient transparency (enough light) that I might collect some recorded votes. This includes all the cases from the analysis of transparency (see Table 3.1) that yielded usable recorded vote data, plus all others from which I was able to collect data. Some further background on data availability and collection is in order here.

Data on Recorded Votes

The study of recorded legislative votes is well established in the United States, and every recorded vote taken in the U.S. Congress throughout its history is publicly available in machine-readable format.[1] Studies of recorded votes outside the United States are rare, in part because most legislatures record very few votes, or none, at the level of the individual legislator. Where votes are recorded, collecting data often requires traveling to the country, navigating bureaucratic and political hurdles, and transcribing hard copy documents into machine-readable format. This is an extremely labor-intensive proposition (see the Chapter 3 Appendix). Scholars focusing on a variety of countries have undertaken this work, generally in piecemeal fashion, producing legislative voting studies for a single country or just a few countries at most.

Research for this book entailed determining, for Western Hemisphere democracies, whether recorded votes are available and collecting samples of votes large enough to allow for quantitative analysis wherever possible. In most cases, this required field research to collect the data, or at least to determine that no recorded votes exist. In some cases, I was able to hire in-country research assistants. Outside the Americas, data collection confronted bigger obstacles. Language barriers; limited contacts among politicians, academics, and legislative staff; and finite time and travel budgets prohibited original data collection for the most part.[2] To acquire data under these constraints, I identified academics from other countries who had recorded vote data and who might be willing to share or trade. This approach yielded datasets from Australia, Canada, the Czech Republic, the French Fourth Republic, New Zealand, Poland, and Russia.

The data included in my analysis of voting unity, then, are not drawn from a random sample of legislatures in the sense of being generated by some stochastic process from among all democratic regimes worldwide. Rather, the sample of national legislatures examined in this chapter and the

[1] For this, legislative scholars owe gratitude to sustained effort and a commitment to data sharing by Professor Keith Poole of the University of California, San Diego.

[2] One exception was Israel, where an Israeli colleague put me in contact with a Knesset staffer who had access to archives and was willing to transcribe hard copy records of votes into spreadsheet format. Meanwhile, legislative scholars with diverse language skills and institutional contacts should make it a priority to determine where any yet-untapped archives of recorded legislative votes are, and to collect and disseminate those data. To facilitate this effort, *VoteWorld: The International Legislative Roll-Call Voting Website* (http://ucdata.berkeley .edu:7101/new_web/VoteWorld/voteworld/) is a data clearinghouse established in collaboration by scholars committed to open access. All the data for this project are available either via *VoteWorld* or at http://www.dartmouth.edu/~jcarey.

next includes all those where I know data to exist, making this, to my knowledge, the broadest cross-national study of legislative voting undertaken to date.

The samples of votes from these legislatures are shaped by vote availability and resource constraints, such as the labor to transfer each vote to machine-readable format. Some assemblies post vote records on line as lists of names that, with some work, can be prepared for analysis. In other cases, my travel to the assemblies themselves aimed at locating and collecting hard copies of whatever votes were recorded, or else contracting with local assistants to collect the information. Scholars who had collected vote data in similarly painstaking fashion were, by and large, generous in making those available. In some cases (e.g., United States, Uruguay), my sample of votes represents all recorded votes during complete legislatures; in others (e.g., Chile, Israel, Peru), it includes all votes between specified dates; and in still others (e.g., Canada, Czech Republic, Russia) the sample includes those votes that colleagues made available.

What are the implications for how we interpret measures of voting unity? If unity is fundamentally different in legislatures where recorded votes are unavailable, then the measures reported here may be unrepresentative of the whole population of legislatures. If the factors correlated with higher and lower levels of unity are different in legislatures where recorded votes are unavailable, then the explanations offered here for levels of voting unity are limited to environments where votes are visible. Time spent observing legislative behavior in legislatures both where votes are visible and where they are not leads me to only a modest conjecture on the possibility of differences in the power of presidential patronage to sway votes in visible-versus invisible-vote systems. I discuss these in the following chapter. That said, it must be noted that where recorded votes are unavailable, we cannot know for sure what levels of voting unity are and what explains them.

I draw on recorded vote data from lower legislative chambers across nineteen countries. The unit of analysis is the party group during a given legislature. I calculated voting indices for each party in each legislature that it enjoyed representation ($\%WON_i$ and $WUNITY_i$), or where its group consisted of two or more legislators ($WRICE_i$ and $ULOSER_i$), or three or more legislators ($RLOSER_i$). The dates, the total number of votes, and properties of the corresponding mean $CLOSE_j$ scores for the cases examined in this chapter are shown in Table 5.1.[3]

[3] For an explanation of $CLOSE_j$ scores, see Appendix 2.

Data on Recorded Votes

Table 5.1. *Recorded Vote Data*

Country	Dates of Assemblies	No. of Votes	Sum CLOSE	Mean CLOSE
Argentina	December 1984–December 1986	20	12	0.62
	December 1987–September 1989	20	14	0.71
	December 1989–December 1991	65	39	0.6
	December 1991–December 1993	27	14	0.53
	December 1993–December 1995	64	35	0.55
	December 1995–November 1997	21	16	0.77
Australia	May 1996–July 1998	457	308	0.67
Brazil	January 1989–December 1990	57	33	0.57
	March 1991–January 1995	166	104	0.63
	March 1995–December 1998	452	291	0.64
Canada	May 1994–April 1997	735	398	0.54
Chile	May 1997–January 1998	215	59	0.27
	October 1998–May 2000	522	167	0.32
Czech Republic	January 1993–June 1996	5,067	2,149	0.42
	July 1996 – December 1998	4,741	2,075	0.44
Ecuador	July 1998–June 2002	22	5	0.25
France IV Republic	July 1946–June 1951	365	175	0.48
	July 1951–June 1956	352	246	0.7
	June 1956–June 1958	172	109	0.63
Guatemala	December 1994–November 1995	10	6	0.58
	February 1996–January 1999	42	21	0.51
	January 1999–April 2000	7	5	0.75

(continued)

Table 5.1 *(continued)*

Country	Dates of Assemblies	No. of Votes	Sum CLOSE	Mean CLOSE
Israel	October 1999–November 2000	598	205	0.34
Mexico	October 1998–April 2000	299	113	0.38
New Zealand	November 1990–August 1993	592	384	0.65
	December 1993–November 1994	185	145	0.78
Nicaragua	January 2000–September 2000	693	417	0.62
Peru	March 1999–June 2000	689	430	0.33
	August 2000–December 2000	332	227	0.26
	August 2001–October 2001	103	129	0.09
Philippines	July 1995–April 1997	147	3	0.02
Poland	October 1997–May 1999	3,045	1,226	0.4
Russia	January 1996–May 1997	356	197	0.55
United States	January 1991–December 1992	901	495	0.55
	January 1993–December 1994	1,094	666	0.61
	January 1995–December 1996	1,321	836	0.63
	January 1997–December 1998	1,157	622	0.54
Uruguay	October 1985–November 1989	41	28	0.68
	December 1990–August 1994	22	10	0.47

There is tremendous variance across the legislatures for which I have voting data in how many votes are recorded and thus available for analysis of party unity. There is also variance in what information is available about each vote (e.g., origin of the initiative, issue area, whether final passage). The only information available for every vote in every chamber is date, threshold for approval, and how each member of the assembly voted (e.g., aye, nay, abstain, or no vote). Finally, there is variance in the overall tendency toward consensus or contestation in votes. Mean $CLOSE_j$ summarizes the extent to which an average vote was contested for each case. Votes were most narrowly won in New Zealand, Argentina, the French Fourth Republic, and Guatemala, less so in Ecuador, Chile, Peru, and especially the Philippines. In all legislatures, some votes are consensual, but in most there are deep divisions on many votes as well – enough that we can be confident that the real fights over policy have not all ended before votes come to the floor.

5.5. Describing Voting Unity

5.5.1. Cross-National Patterns

I calculated the various voting unity indices described in this chapter for each party within every legislative period from which I obtained data. Across all the periods in all the legislatures, this amounts to more than 300 observations on each of the indices.[4] Each index, in turn, summarizes a large amount of information about individual legislators' actions, and these descriptive statistics could be summarized and examined in myriad ways.

Table 5.2 presents the four main indices aggregated at the level of country, along with the standard deviation across parties within each country.[5] The highest average $WRICE_i$ is found in Australia and New Zealand while the lowest are in Nicaragua, Poland, and Russia. Recall, however, that the extremely low indices for Nicaragua and Russia reflect the decision to treat nonvotes as nay votes in these legislatures. When nonvotes are discarded in calculating $WRICE_i$, the indices shoot up in both cases.

$WUNITY_i$ does not track $WRICE_i$ perfectly. The two are correlated at .55 across all parties, and although Australia is highest on $WUNITY_i$ as well, the French Fourth Republic, the United States, and Uruguay are close behind. Meanwhile, along with Nicaragua and Russia (again, owing largely to the coding decision), Canada, Israel, Peru, the Philippines, and Poland

---

[4] There are the fewest observations on $RLOSER_i$, because it is not calculated for parties with fewer than three members. There are more observations on the other indices.

[5] Table 5.2 summarizes information on four voting unity indices across all the countries examined. It is useful as a reference source, but the format does not facilitate comparison across cases. Figures 6.2 and 6.3 illustrate more clearly the patterns of $WRICE_i$ and $RLOSER_i$ and their variance cross-nationally.

Table 5.2. *Voting Unity Index Averages and Standard Deviations by Country*

Country	WRICE Mean	WRICE s.d.	WUNITY Mean	WUNITY s.d.	RLOSER Mean	RLOSER s.d.	ULOSER Mean	ULOSER s.d.
Argentina	0.86	0.17	0.51	0.21	0.003	0.011	0.020	0.095
Australia	0.99	0.02	0.69	0.26	0.000	0.000	0.000	0.000
Brazil	0.75	0.17	0.59	0.15	0.008	0.019	0.014	0.025
Canada	0.82	0.25	0.42	0.24	0.001	0.002	0.002	0.003
Chile	0.82	0.15	0.48	0.12	0.003	0.006	0.022	0.020
Czech Republic	0.87	0.08	0.53	0.16	0.006	0.008	0.049	0.037
Ecuador	0.92	0.09	0.71	0.16	0.006	0.016	0.006	0.016
France	0.85	0.14	0.68	0.18	0.011	0.015	0.021	0.020
Guatemala	0.83	0.21	0.65	0.22	0.000	0.000	0.001	0.005
Israel	0.88	0.23	0.44	0.14	0.002	0.002	0.048	0.040
Mexico	0.84	0.16	0.63	0.21	0.011	0.010	0.025	0.015
New Zealand	0.96	0.02	0.59	0.21	0.018	0.022	0.108	0.239
Nicaragua	0.36	0.1	0.36	0.10	0.038	0.023	0.038	0.023
Nicaragua NV~ = nay	0.95	0.01	0.6	0.04	0.038	0.023	0.057	0.030
Peru	0.8	0.14	0.45	0.14	0.006	0.008	0.013	0.017
Philippines	0.70	0.28	0.45	0.14	0.000	0.000	0.000	0.000
Poland	0.42	0.2	0.35	0.17	0.026	0.027	0.027	0.027
Russia	0.55	0.14	0.55	0.14	0.010	0.009	0.132	0.045
Russia NV~ = nay	0.94	0.05	0.66	0.16	0.010	0.009	0.018	0.012
United States	0.70	0.06	0.68	0.06	0.119	0.038	0.133	0.045
Uruguay	0.79	0.25	0.67	0.25	0.037	0.034	0.037	0.034

all exhibit low values. Parties in the United States average the highest rates of losses because of both cross-voting (RLOSER) and failure to mobilize fully (ULOSER), although relatively high rates on RLOSER are also present in Nicaragua, Poland, and Uruguay, and on the latter in various countries, although the preceding discussion of nonvoting equilibria suggests wariness toward that statistic. A few countries, including Australia again plus Canada, Guatemala, and the Philippines, show no – or almost no – vote losses due to breaches in voting unity.

5.5.2. *Looking at Legislatures*

The next chapter focuses on explaining levels of voting unity according to these various measures. Before closing, it will be useful merely to demonstrate, with a few more graphs like those already presented, that the indices allow us to visualize legislatures in ways that illustrate key characteristics of

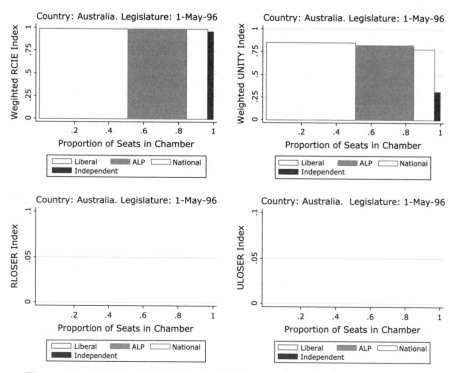

Figure 5.5 WRICE, WUNITY, RLOSER, and ULOSER indices for Australia, 1996–98.

their party systems. The statistics presented in Table 5.2, for example, suggest Australia as the prototype of a highly unified legislative party system. Figure 5.5 illustrates this uniformity by juxtaposing its WRICE$_i$, WUNITY$_i$, RLOSER$_i$, and ULOSER$_i$ indices during the 1996–98 period. Again, government parties are white and opposition shaded various gray hues. The relative simplicity of Australia's coalition structure during this period and the regularity of legislative voting behavior are clear.

Compare this with the structure of the Israeli Knesset, shown in Figure 5.6, during a period from October 1999 to November 2000 from which I collected a sample of votes. First, the far greater fragmentation of the Israeli party system and governing coalition structure is evident. Israeli parties also show somewhat more variance in voting unity across the different indicators, and their overall levels demonstrate less unity and some vote losses, even among parties in the governing coalition, because of disunity.

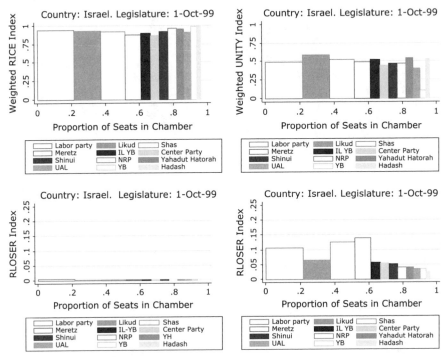

Figure 5.6 WRICE, WUNITY, RLOSER, and ULOSER indices for Israel, 1999–2000.

A similar complexity and fragmentation are also evident in Brazil's party system during the first administration of President Fernando Henrique Cardoso, 1995–99, shown in Figure 5.7. Here, the president's party is shown, toward the right of each panel, in black, with other parties in the governing coalition (i.e., holding cabinet portfolios) in white, and the various others in gray hues. As scholarship on that country frequently notes, Brazil exhibits relatively low voting unity overall, by any index, and high levels of vote losses because of disunity. But there is also substantial variance across parties. The Workers' Party (PT) and the Communist Party of Brazil (PC do B), both in opposition, for example, show high levels of unity and mobilization, and virtually no losses owing to disunity. The governing parties, by and large, are less unified.

Finally, consider the United States House of Representatives during the 104th Congress, 1995–97, in Figure 5.8. The two-party hegemony of the Republicans and Democrats stands in sharp contrast to the fragmented

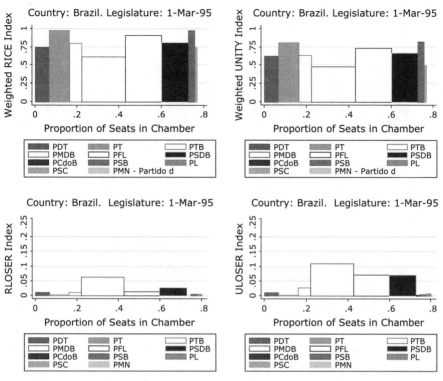

Figure 5.7 WRICE, WUNITY, RLOSER, and ULOSER indices for Brazil, 1995–1998.

Israeli and Brazilian systems. The relatively low $WRICE_i$ indices illustrate a substantial amount of cross-voting with which even casual observers of the U.S. Congress are familiar, but the near parity between $WRICE_i$ and $WUNITY_i$ also shows that U.S. legislators are diligent about getting to the floor to vote. Most of the disunity in the U.S. Congress comes in the form of cross-voting, rather than nonvoting. As a result, while both the loss-based indices are high for the United States, RLOSER is nearly as high as ULOSER, especially for the Republicans, the majority party during this Congress.

Because the voting unity indices developed in this chapter summarize vast amounts of legislative activity in relatively simple statistics, it possible to compare distinct legislatures, or the same legislature in different periods, or both, according to common metrics. This is useful for describing and visualizing legislative party systems, but the goal of developing these tools

111

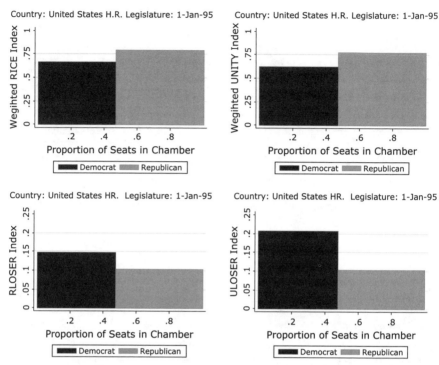

Figure 5.8 WRICE, WUNITY, RLOSER, and ULOSER indices for the United States, 1995–97.

is to explain the conditions that generate high and low levels of voting unity, mobilization, and ultimately partisan and government success or failure on the floor. The next chapter focuses on that task.

Chapter 5 Appendix 1: Illustrations of RICE and UNITY Indices

Appendix Table 5.1 shows examples of RICE and UNITY scores, and their relative sensitivity to both cross-voting and nonvoting, in a hypothetical 300-member legislature with three parties of 100 members each. The first column shows the overall tally for each vote in the format (aye, nay, non-vote). The next column shows values for a measure of how closely contested each vote is. The next columns show the tally for each party on each of six votes, followed by the parties' $UNITY_{ij}$ and $RICE_{ij}$ scores.

On the first vote, all three parties mobilize only half their members, but within each party all members who cast decisive votes vote the same way; thus $UNITY_{ij}$ scores in each case are relatively low at .50, whereas $RICE_{ij}$

scores are "perfect" at 1.00. Voting participation increases across the six votes in every party – that is, the number of nonvotes declines. Now consider the pattern of Party A, which experiences increasing cross-voting as more of its members cast decisive votes; thus, its $RICE_{Aj}$ scores plummet faster than its $UNITY_{Aj}$ scores, converging at zero on the last vote. Party B experiences substantial cross-voting on early votes but pulls together subsequently such that both $RICE_{Bj}$ and $UNITY_{Bj}$ rise and converge as more legislators mobilize on later votes. Party C experiences no cross-voting on any votes, so $UNITY_{Cj}$ rises to converge with $RICE_{Cj}$ as mobilization increases.

Chapter 5 Appendix 2: Weighting by CLOSEness

When votes are consensual in the legislature as a whole, voting unity scores for any subset of legislators will necessarily be high, at least as measured by $RICE_{ij}$. Counting all votes equally, including lopsided ones, therefore, inflates unity indices. This presents a particular problem for cross-national comparisons where there is variance across cases in the average closeness of votes owing to characteristics of legislatures entirely unrelated to party unity. For example, if rules in Legislature A require recording votes on every motion, the vast majority of which are perfunctory and consensual, whereas in Legislature B only votes on substantive (and potentially divisive) motions are recorded, then unweighted indices from the two legislatures would show higher unity in A, even in the absence of any real effect on legislative decision making.

The conventional response in studies of recorded votes is to establish some criterion for throwing out votes that are "too consensual" to be considered relevant to party unity. Established criteria in studies of the two-party U.S. Congress often focus on whether the majorities or the leaderships of the two main parties oppose each other on a given vote (Brady, Cooper, and Hurley 1977; Cox and McCubbins 1993). In the multiparty environment of most other democracies, however, such criteria are of little use. Which votes meet the selection criterion would vary according to which parties' majorities or leaderships are considered. Another approach is to include all votes on which some minimum proportion of legislators votes on the losing side (Mainwaring and Pérez-Liñán 1997; Figueiredo and Limongi 2000). But such thresholds are necessarily arbitrary, and they count all votes, no matter how far above threshold, equally, contradicting the basic intuition behind selection criteria in general – that the sternest test of unity is whether members of a party or coalition vote

Appendix Table 5.1. *Examples of RICE and UNITY Scores, and Weighted and Unweighted Indices, in a Hypothetical Legislature*

Tally	CLOSE$_j$	Party A			Party B			Party C		
		Tally$_A$	UNITY$_{Aj}$	RICE$_{Aj}$	Tally$_B$	UNITY$_{Bj}$	RICE$_{Bj}$	Tally$_C$	UNITY$_{Cj}$	RICE$_{Cj}$
[150,0,150]	0.00	[50,0,50]	.50	1.0	[50,0,50]	.50	1.00	[50,0,50]	.5	1.00
[162,18,120]	.20	[54,6,40]	.48	.80	[48,12,40]	.36	.60	[60,0,40]	.6	1.00
[168,42,90]	.40	[56,14,30]	.42	.60	[42,28,30]	.14	.20	[70,0,30]	.7	1.00
[168,72,60]	.60	[56,24,20]	.32	.40	[32,48,20]	.16	.20	[80,0,20]	.8	1.00
[162,108,30]	.80	[54,36,10]	.18	.20	[18,72,10]	.54	.60	[90,0,10]	.9	1.00
[150,150,0]	1.00	[50,50,0]	0.00	0.00	[0,100,0]	1.00	1.00	[100,0,0]	1.0	1.00
Unweighted indices			.32	.50		.45	.60		.75	1.00
Weighted indices			.20	.27		.55	.60		.87	1.00

together when doing so matters to legislative outcomes, and therefore that the more hotly contested a vote is, the more relevant it is to a measure of unity.

This suggests $RICE_i$ and $UNITY_i$ indices calculated as follows:

$$WRICE_i = \sum RICE_{ij} * CLOSE_j / \sum CLOSE_j$$

$$WUNITY_i = \sum UNITY_{ij} * CLOSE_j / \sum CLOSE_j,$$

where

$$CLOSE_j = 1 - (1/THRESHOLD * |THRESHOLD - \%AYE|)^6$$

for legislature as a whole on vote j.

These indices are summary statistics for voting unity in party i, weighting votes by how closely they were contested, according to the basic intuition that, for a party seeking to influence outcomes, unity is more critical the more likely it is that defection (or defection *and* nonvoting, in the case of $UNITY_i$) of any member(s) will be pivotal.

In Appendix Table 5.1, the bottom two rows illustrate this weighting system for the hypothetical legislature. The second column of the table shows how closely contested each vote was ($CLOSE_j$ is described in the appendix). On each successive vote in this example, the legislature as a whole is more closely divided, and these more closely contested votes count more heavily under the weighting scheme than if the index were a simple, unweighted mean of scores.

Because Party A displays increasing cross-voting on the more contentious votes, and because cross-voting drives down $UNITY_{Aj}$ and $RICE_{Aj}$ alike, Party A's weighted indices are both well below its corresponding unweighted indices. Next, consider Party B. The first vote is consensual, so all parties are, by definition, perfectly unified as measured by RICE scores (although their UNITY scores lag because of nonvoting). Beyond this vote, Party B exhibits greater cross-voting on the relatively lopsided votes and pulls together on the more closely contested and heavily weighted ones. Because more closely contested votes count more under

---

[6] When the threshold for passing a measure is a simple majority of those voting, the formula can be written as: $CLOSE = 1 - (2 * |50\% - \%AYE|)$. However, when passage requires an extraordinary majority, the more general formula still applies. This form of the general equation was suggested to me by Jeanne Giraldo.

the weighting system, WUNITY$_B$ is higher than UUNITY$_B$, and WRICE$_B$ pulls even with URICE$_B$. Party C exhibits a similar pattern, with no cross-voting and so perfect RICE scores but increasing mobilization on closer votes. The trajectories of UNITY and RICE scores for each party as closeness varies rise across the six votes described in Appendix Table 5.1, as are illustrated in Appendix Figure 5.1. By and large, if a voting unity index rises with closeness, then its weighted measure > unweighted, whereas if it is inversely related to closeness, the opposite is true.

Chapter 5 Appendix 3: Legislative Success Index

To determine whether a party "won" on a given measure, it is necessary to infer each party's preference. I rely on the votes themselves, attributing to each party the preference supported by the majority of its voting members. For every party, *i*, on every vote, *j*:

PREF$_{ij}$ = Approve if AYE$_{ij}$ > NAY$_{ij}$, Reject if NAY$_{ij}$ < AYE$_{ij}$, No Preference AYE$_{ij}$ = NAY$_{ij}$

Thus if most of a party's decisive votes were aye and the measure is approved, it counts as a win; if most of its votes were aye and the measure is rejected, it counts as a loss, and so on.[7]

Chapter 5 Appendix 4: RLOSER and ULOSER

RLOSER$_{ij}$ = 1 if:

- PREF$_{ij}$ = Approve, AND Outcome$_j$ = Reject, AND TotalAYE$_j$ + NAY$_{ij}$ > Threshold$_j$,

or if

- PREF$_{ij}$ = Reject, AND Outcome$_j$ = Approve, AND TotalAYE$_j$ − AYE$_{ij}$ < Threshold$_j$

ULOSER$_{ij}$ = 1 if:

- PREF$_{ij}$ = Approve, AND Outcome$_j$ = Reject, AND TotalAYE$_j$ + NAY$_{ij}$ + NONVOTES$_{ij}$ > Threshold$_j$,

[7] In a handful of legislatures, such as Brazil's Chamber of Deputies and the U.S. Congress on some votes, parties' formal positions on specific measures are reported as part of the assembly's published record. This practice, however, is sufficiently rare as not to be viable for broad cross-national analysis.

116

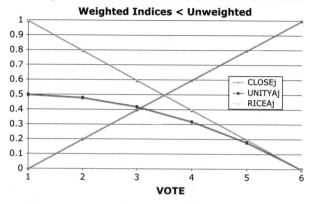

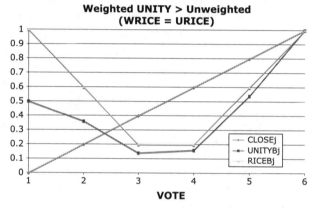

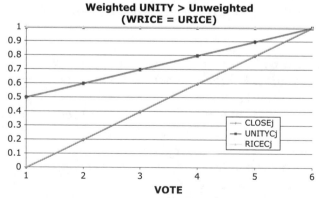

Appendix Figure 5.1 Patterns of UNITY and RICE scores, and effects on weighted versus unweighted indices, as CLOSEness varies.

or if

- $PREF_{ij} = Reject$, AND $Outcome_j = Approve$, AND $TotalAYE_j - AYE_{ij} - NONVOTES_{ij} < Threshold_j$

where, for every vote, j:

- $Threshold_j = $ number of votes necessary to approve the measure
- $Outcome_j = [Approve, Reject]$

$RLOSER_{ij}$ and $ULOSER_{ij}$ identify votes on which, *given how all other parties voted*, a party lost despite the fact that it could have prevailed had it been fully unified or mobilized. Appendix Table 5.2 illustrates some scenarios in a hypothetical legislature with 100 members and two parties, A and B, with 60 and 40 seats, respectively.

A party "loses" a vote whenever the outcome runs contrary to that supported by a majority of its voting members. When the parties vote together, neither loses, as in Votes 1 and 2. When both parties vote along party lines (high $RICE_{ij}$ scores for both), as in Votes 3 and 4, Party B loses *provided* that $UNITY_{ij}$ scores are closely correlated – that is, provided that both parties mobilize around the same proportion of their members to vote. Note, however, that on Vote 4, Party B could have prevailed, given how Party A voted, had it mobilized its full complement of legislators to vote nay. Thus, on Vote 4, Party B is a ULOSER.

Votes 5 through 8 represent losses by Party A because of disunity of various sorts. Vote 5 shows a straightforward breakdown within Party A, with some members voting against the party majority, swinging the outcome in favor of the united and mobilized Party B. The results of Vote 6 are similar, where Party A suffers a combination of defections among voting and nonvoting members while confronting a unified and mobilized opposition. In Votes 7 and 8, Party A is both divided and fails to mobilize, while Party B lags on either one or the other count but prevails on the vote outcome. In each of these cases, Party A's disunity allows B to win (i.e., costs A the vote). On Votes 5, 6, and 7, Party A could have won (i.e., passed the measure) if all of its voting members had voted aye, and obviously had it fully mobilized. In these cases, therefore, Party A is both the RLOSER and ULOSER. On Vote 8, Party A could have won had it fully mobilized, but not merely had all its voting members voted aye, so it is a ULOSER but not an RLOSER.

As long as $UNITY_{ij}$ is strongly correlated across the parties on a given vote, the outcome will reflect the distribution of seats across parties.

Appendix Table 5.2. *Illustrations of RLOSER and ULOSER in a Hypothetical 100-Member Legislature (tallies are [aye–nay–nonvote])*

Vote	TALLY$_{Aj}$	TALLY$_{Bj}$	Losing Party	RICE$_{Aj}$	RICE$_{Bj}$	RLOSER	UNITY$_{Aj}$	UNITY$_{Bj}$	ULOSER
1	[60–0–0]	[40–0–0]	None	1.00	1.00	None	1.00	1.00	None
2	[30–0–30]	[20–0–20]	None	1.00	1.00	None	.50	.50	None
3	[60–0–0]	[0–40–0]	B	1.00	1.00	None	1.00	1.00	None
4	[30–0–30]	[0–20–20]	**B**	1.00	1.00	None	.50	.50	Party B
5	[45–15–0]	[0–40–0]	A	.50	1.00	Party A	.50	1.00	Party A
6	[40–10–10]	[0–40–0]	A	.60	1.00	Party A	.50	1.00	Party A
7	[20–10–30]	[0–20–20]	A	.33	1.00	Party A	.17	.50	Party A
8	[15–5–40]	[10–30–0]	A	.50	.50	None	.17	.50	Party A

119

Outcomes unreflective of the seat distribution become possible when UN-ITY$_{ij}$ scores come uncoupled. In the example of Appendix Table 5.2, where there is a majority party, for Party A to be defeated, its UNITY$_{Aj}$ must drop more than that of its opponents. The same does not necessarily apply for RICE$_{ij}$ scores, as Vote 8 shows.

Given that RLOSER$_{ij}$ and ULOSER$_{ij}$ are calculated with respect to the outcome of each vote, I do not weight them in creating summary indices, RLOSER$_i$ and ULOSER$_i$, for each party, but simply report proportions – for example, on how many votes, out of all votes analyzed, was a party an RLOSER.

Chapter 5 Appendix 5: Nonvotes and Relative versus Absolute-Vote Thresholds

Consider first the mechanics of the rules for approving measures that are put to a legislative vote. Although some votes may require extraordinary majority support (60%, 67%, or 75%) for approval, most votes in most legislatures require simple majority support (> 50%). But a majority of whom? In most cases, chamber rules stipulate the proportion of members that constitutes a quorum, and approval of standard measures requires support from a majority of those voting aye or nay when a quorum is present. Thus, the precise number for approving a measure is set in relative terms – relative to the number voting.

Under a relative threshold, if I disagree with my party's position, either I might withhold my support from the party by not voting (whether through abstention, or not showing up, or simply not pressing a button on my electronic voting device), or I could *not only* withhold my support *but also* give my vote to the other side. The latter is a more visible breach of unity than the former and does correspondingly more damage to the party's collective brand name; and if the vote is close, the latter is twice as damaging to my party's prospects of winning than the former. This difference is at the heart of the distinction between the traditional RICE$_{ij}$ score and the UNITY$_{ij}$ score developed previously.

In some legislatures, however, thresholds are set in absolute terms, as a percentage of the full membership of the assembly. Among the cases analyzed in this book, the Russian Duma and Nicaraguan and Guatemalan assemblies require absolute thresholds to pass any measure. Under such rules, nonvotes, whatever their intent, are equivalent to nays in their effect on outcomes. For the purposes of calculating voting unity indices, my point of departure is to

Appendix 5

Non-votes = Nay

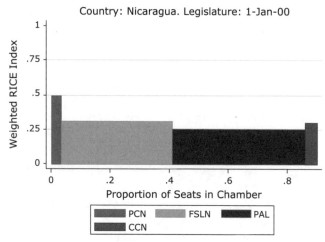

Non-votes ignored.

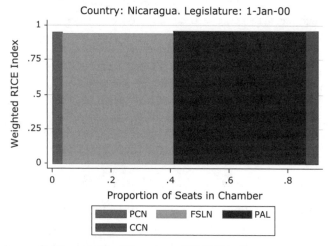

Appendix Figure 5.2   Nicaraguan WRICE indices.

treat them as such – that is, to count nonvotes as nays when their effects on outcomes are equivalent to nay votes.

This approach warrants careful consideration, however, because count-ing nonvotes as nays renders $RICE_{ij}$ scores, in particular, and the indices built from them, highly sensitive to nonvoting. For example, Appendix Figure 5.2 compares $WRICE_i$ indices for parties in the Nicaraguan

Assembly, first calculated with nonvotes as nays, then discounting nonvotes altogether. In the figure, weighted $RICE_i$ indices are represented by the height of each bar on the y axis. Each party's share of assembly seats is represented by the width of its column along the x axis.[8]

The second panel, with near-perfect $WRICE_i$ indices across the board, illustrates that cross-voting was nearly absent from this Nicaraguan Assembly. Yet ignoring nonvotes, as in this panel, overestimates party voting unity as it affects vote outcomes, because any legislator who does not like a measure her party supports can oppose it as effectively by not voting as by overtly crossing the aisle to vote nay. As the $WRICE_i$ indices in the first panel show, Nicaraguan deputies did not reliably deliver their votes to support their parties' positions.

How, then, ought one treat nonvoting under absolute-threshold voting rules? Cautiously, and with explicit consideration of what one is looking for. With respect to outcomes, nonvotes are equivalent to nays under absolute thresholds, so if one is interested in effects of votes on outcomes, nonvotes = nays is appropriate. With respect to the communicative element of voting – the extent to which legislative votes are expressions of a party's policy positions – the situation is murkier. Nonvoting is, effectively, passive opposition to a measure. If passive opposition is markedly less visible to copartisans and to citizens than explicit opposition, then not voting when one's party supports a measure represents something less than a full-scale breach of party unity, but ignoring nonvotes altogether probably fails to capture the dissent they imply. Moreover, when one's party opposes a measure, ignoring nonvotes fails to capture the party unity they entail.

Chapter 5 Appendix 6: Measuring Voting Unity in Small Parties

The various measures of voting unity confront three types of limitations associated with small parties. First, the $RICE_{ij}$ score is not relevant for a party with only one member because cross-voting is, by definition, impossible. Thus, $RICE_{ij}$ scores are not calculated for parties with only one legislator, or for votes on which only one member of a party participates.

Second, $RLOSER_{ij}$ is calculated only for parties where $N > 2$. $RLOSER_{ij}$ is derived from simulated vote outcomes under alternative, "more unified" permutations of a party's votes, given the party's inferred

---

[8] The columns do not necessarily reach the 100 percent mark, as indices are not calculated for independents who remained unaffiliated with any party bloc or for single-member parties.

preference on the vote. Where $N \leq 2$, the party either has no inferred preference (i.e., splits [1–1]) or is perfectly unified, in which case no alternative, more unified permutation is possible. $ULOSER_{ij}$ can be calculated for parties with two members or more because, for example, a [1–0–1] tally indicates a partisan preference for aye, on which the party could have mobilized more effectively with [2–0–0].

The third consideration is that both $RICE_i$ and $UNITY_i$ are subject to upward bias as a combined function of a group's size and the underlying proclivity of its members to vote together (Desposato 2005). The bias is more severe the smaller the group and the less inclined its members are to vote alike. The problem is that the probability of observing instances of high party unity (e.g., all voting aye, or all nay) is higher the fatter are the tails of the binomial distribution of the proportion of "alike" votes. Observations in these tails reflect higher $RICE_i$ and $UNITY_i$ values than the underlying probability of voting alike would suggest, biasing the measures upward. The tails of the distribution are fatter when N is smaller, and the resulting bias is more pronounced when the underlying probability of voting together is smaller. (Think of the likelihood of observing all "heads" – that is, "perfect unity" – when tossing a pair of coins, as opposed to when tossing ten coins.) The magnitude of small-group bias declines rapidly as party size and underlying cohesiveness increase.

Desposatos's (2005) analysis suggests that the potential bias in cohesiveness scores can be corrected by estimating deviance factors for RICE and UNITY scores, which are functions of group size and the underlying proclivity of members to vote together, then subtracting that factor from the score. The process I use is as follows. For any party i on vote j, one can calculate the proportions of legislators who vote together (T) with most of the group, or who vote in dissent (D):

- $T_{ij} =$ maximum [AYE, NAY], as a percentage of those voting
- $D_{ij} =$ minimum [AYE, NAY], as a percentage of those voting

One can also calculate analogous proportions of legislators mobilized (M), those opposed (O), and those not voting (NV) based on the size of the group, rather than just those who vote:

- $M_{ij} =$ maximum [aye, nay] as a share of all legislators
- $O_{ij} =$ minimum [aye, nay] as a share of all legislators
- $NV_{ij} = 1 - M_{ij} - O_{ij}$

The $RICE_{ij}$ score is just $T_{ij} - D_{ij}$, and the $UNITY_{ij}$ score is $M_{ij} - O_{ij}$.

The corresponding $RICE_i$ and $UNITY_i$ indices are summations of $T_i - D_i$, and $M_i - O_i$ across all votes. The indices, then, reflect estimates of the underlying probabilities of voting "against" the group, or withholding one's vote from the group.

For each party group, i, I calculate the expected upward bias due to small party size as:

- $RICEdeviance_i = D_i / N_i$
- $UNITYdeviance_i = O_i / N_i$

where N_i is the number of members in the cohort. I then calculate the "empirically corrected" indices for each cohort by subtracting its deviance factor from its "raw" index. The indices are "empirically corrected" because the estimates of underlying probabilities of D_i and O_i are based on the observations of behavior across all votes. The deviance factors grow as the probability of cross-voting grows, and shrink as N_i grows. For expositional simplicity, I do not include the word "corrected" each time I refer to the corrected indices, but all indices presented in this book are corrected for potential bias.

6

Explaining Voting Unity

6.1. Legislative Parties and Institutional Context

The institutional environment in which parties operate is widely held to affect their voting unity. Parties in parliamentary systems are generally characterized as highly unified, and those in presidential systems as more fractious and less disciplined, with resulting difficulty for presidents in the legislative arena (Diermeier and Feddersen 1998; Hix, Noury, and Roland 2006; Persson and Tabellini 2003; Shugart 1998). Federalism, by encouraging the organization of parties at the subnational level, is posited to foster divisions within parties at the national level (Mainwaring 1999; Weyland 1996). Electoral systems that provide for competition among legislative candidates within the same party for personal votes are portrayed as encouraging disunity relative to closed-lists election rules (Ames 1995; Golden and Chang 2001; Hix 2004). The leadership of parties that are older and better established may be more autonomous and less vulnerable to pressure from presidents (Stokes 2001).

These assertions are not uniformly accepted. On the basis of a broad cross-national study, Cheibub, Przeworski, and Saiegh (2004) argue that presidents are on par with parliamentary executives in forming legislative coalitions to pass legislation. After completing a case study of Brazil, a presidential federal system with intraparty electoral competition – all the characteristics listed as undermining party unity – Figueiredo and Limongi (2000) argue that various provisions centralizing control over the legislative agenda provide leverage to control wayward parliamentarians and govern as efficiently as governments that confront none of these institutional obstacles ostensibly do.

It is difficult to know whether institutions matter to party unity, which institutions, and how much, without cross-national studies with sufficient breadth to allow for variance in the institutional factors of interest. Morgenstern (2003) makes an ambitious contribution along these lines, but his empirical analysis includes five countries, all presidential, which limits his ability to test for the effects of constitutional structure, and its interaction with party-level factors, on voting unity. Sieberer's (2006) study is similarly constrained by including only European parliaments. Drawing on the data and measures of unity described in Chapter 5, this chapter tests for how the institutional environment affects legislative party unity.

I begin by reviewing three distinct potential mechanisms that might produce party unity in legislative voting – cohesiveness, discipline, and agenda control – and argue that the logic of competing principals operates through the first and second of these. Then I use cross-national voting data to shed some light on the relationship between cohesiveness and discipline across the parties included in this analysis. Drawing on the logic of competing principals, I spell out a number of explicit hypotheses regarding factors that should affect legislative voting unity. After presenting the models used to test the hypotheses against the cross-national data and the results, I extend the analysis of voting unity from individual parties to governing and opposition coalitions.

6.2. Competing Principals and Existing Accounts of Party Unity

There are three potential sources of legislative party unity: cohesiveness, discipline, and agenda control. Cohesiveness implies that elections produce legislative parties whose members have similar preferences and therefore vote in harmony. Discipline refers to the combination of responses, generally administered by party leaders, used to reward voting loyalty and deter or punish breaches in solidarity. Strong discipline should raise party voting unity, other things being equal. Agenda control implies that those who control the flow of legislative traffic steer it so as to determine whether proposals that would divide a given party or coalition come to a vote. Where control of a legislative chamber's agenda is monopolized by the leaders of a given party or coalition – an agenda cartel – we should expect them to minimize agenda access for measures that would divide the party, and so we might expect that levels of voting unity should vary according to which parties control the agenda (Cox and McCubbins 2005).

The competing principals theory advanced in this book derives hypotheses based on electoral sources of party cohesiveness and the institutional resources that drive discipline within parties. For example, electoral rules that centralize control over nominations allow party leaders to screen potential candidates for ideological compatibility with national party priorities, and so to foster cohesiveness among those ultimately elected. The same centralization over nominations – or of list positions in closed-list systems – also provides leaders with formidable sanctions should legislators breach party voting unity against the leadership's wishes. Mavericks can be denied renomination or moved down lists to marginal or unwinnable positions.

It is easy to posit how other institutional factors might also affect party cohesiveness or discipline. For example, parties in federal systems are more apt to have autonomous subnational organizations than those in unitary systems. If the same party's reputation and priorities vary according to diverse interests across subnational electorates, then national legislative party groups should be less cohesive in federal than in unitary systems. As another example, presidentialism creates a potential rival to legislative party leaders, endowed with considerable resources to command responsiveness among legislators to an alternative set of demands, possibly undermining the effect of legislative party discipline.

The competing principals explanation, therefore, bears directly on both cohesiveness-based and discipline-based stories for why party unity may be high or low. A competing principals theory of party unity, by itself, is less directly relevant to the agenda cartel account of party unity, for a number of reasons. Agenda cartel theory focuses on the direction of policy changes under specific governing coalitions, whereas the competing principals model does not make claims about legislative outcomes in a theoretical policy space (Cox and McCubbins 2005). The implications of agenda control theory regarding voting unity focus on the specific subset of legislative votes – on key procedural matters or those that ratify final passage of new policies, for example. Unfortunately, the data available across the range of legislatures included in this analysis often do not make it possible to identify and separate out such votes. In part this is due to the quality of the data, but in part it has to do with the diversity of legislative procedures cross-nationally. The mechanics of final passage itself are context-specific. The voting process whereby various alternative proposals are sifted until a surviving contender is pitted against the status quo is characteristic of the specific amendment procedure used in the U.S. Congress, but not in many other legislatures (Rasch 2000; Weldon 1997). More broadly still, the set of rules governing who can bring motions to the assembly floor for a vote varies across countries and legislative chambers, with control vested in chamber directorates in some cases, monopolized by executives drawn from the chamber in others, and shared with independently elected executives in others.

In short, the data and theory presented here provide substantial leverage in testing for party unity driven by cohesiveness and discipline across the full spectrum of legislative votes, but more limited leverage in testing for unity driven by the specific mechanism and conditions posited by agenda cartel theory. The results here shed light on cohesiveness of preferences among copartisans and the relative monopoly on discipline imposed by legislative party leaders.

6.3. Cohesiveness and Discipline: Weighted and Unweighted Indices

The terms "cohesiveness" and "discipline" are both frequently used in reference to the voting unity within legislative parties, but it is important to keep in mind the conceptual distinction between the terms. The former refers to the degree to which the members of a group share similar preferences; the latter, to the degree to which group leaders are able to elicit unified voting on the part of the group, regardless of member preferences. Unless there is reason to believe that a particular pattern of voting behavior is caused by either cohesiveness or discipline, I use the more generic term "unity" to describe the proclivity of copartisan legislators to vote together.

The difficulty of distinguishing party cohesiveness from discipline is familiar to students of American politics, and debate over the relative contribution of each to party unity in U.S. congressional voting constitutes a substantial literature in its own right (Krehbiel 2000; Snyder and Groseclose 2000; Cox and Poole 2004). As the previous chapter described, I rely on a weighted index of $RICE_{ij}$ scores ($WRICE_i$) as one of my summary indicators of party unity, but comparing the unweighted mean ($URICE_i$) of a party's $RICE_{ij}$ scores with $WRICE_i$ can provide leverage on whether it is cohesiveness among copartisans or discipline that accounts for the levels of unity we observe.

Consider first the "discipline-free" scenario. On votes that are consensual across an entire legislature, $RICE_{ij}$ scores will necessarily be high for all parties. As votes diverge from consensus, low party unity scores become possible. Disunity within parties is still not inevitable, because lack of consensus at the level of the legislature could be the product of conflict between or among highly unified parties, but the presence of dissenting votes at the assembly level allows for the prospect of internal party disunity whereas consensus at the assembly level does not. The more hotly votes are contested in the legislature overall, the more "room" there is, arithmetically, for disunity within parties. Thus, in the discipline-free scenario, $RICE_{ij}$ scores decline as $CLOSE_j$ rises, and $WRICE_i$ is lower than $URICE_i$.

Now consider the scenario with party discipline – that is, where party leaders are able to compel their legislators to vote together. $RICE_{ij}$ scores must still be high on consensual votes, by definition. Where votes are moderately contested, there is the potential for disunity within parties. But as votes approach toss-ups (i.e., as $CLOSE_j$ approaches 1.0), such that prevote head counts suggest a handful of switched votes one way or the other could turn the outcome, party leaders should be increasingly inclined to impose discipline (King and Zeckhauser 2003). Thus, the more that discipline, as opposed to cohesiveness, accounts for levels of unity, the more we should observe elevated $RICE_{ij}$ scores as $CLOSE_j$ approaches 1.0 – that is, on the votes that enter most heavily in my weighting scheme. It follows that the more that discipline, as opposed to cohesiveness, drives voting unity, the higher the ratio of $WRICE_i$ to $URICE_i$.[1]

In Table 6.1 and Figure 6.1, Party A illustrates the discipline-free scenario, and Party B the disciplined scenario, for RICE scores and indices across six votes in a hypothetical 300-member legislature. In Party A, $RICE_{Aj}$ declines as successive votes are contested more closely at the level of the legislature as a whole; thus, the weighted index is substantially lower than the unweighted. Party B experiences divisions on some moderately contested votes but pulls together on the closest votes, with the effect that its weighted index is higher than its unweighted. Party C experiences only one instance of dissent, on a close vote, such that its weighted index, like A's, is lower than its unweighted (although not by as much).

A relevant statistic, then, is the ratio between $WRICE_i$ and $URICE_i$.[2] A lower ratio indicates a tendency for intraparty splits, when they do occur, to

---

[1] Snyder and Groseclose (2000) use a variation on this insight to gain leverage on the cohesiveness-versus-discipline debate on roll call voting in the U.S. Congress. They suggest that, whatever levels of dissent are evident, lopsided votes should nevertheless contain information about legislators' unconstrained policy preferences (and so, about cohesiveness), on the grounds that party leaders should have no interest in imposing discipline on votes that are not expected to be close.

[2] Note that the information in the analogous relationship between $WUNITY_i$ and $UUNITY_i$ is, again, more ambiguous. $UNITY_{ij}$ can be low if many members abstain or do not vote, even on consensual votes (i.e., low $CLOSE_j$). As a result, the relationship between weighted and unweighted $RICE_i$ indices provides better purchase than that between weighted and unweighted $UNITY_i$ indices on cohesiveness versus discipline.

Table 6.1. *Cohesiveness, Discipline, and Weighted and Unweighted RICE Indices in a Hypothetical Legislature*

		Party A		Party B		Party C	
Tally	CLOSE$_j$	Tally	RICE$_{ij}$	Tally	RICE$_{ij}$	Tally	RICE$_{ij}$
[300,0]	0 = 1–2*|.5–1|	[100,0]	1.00	[100,0]	1.00	[100,0]	1.00
[270,30]	.2 = 1–2*|.5–.9|	[95,5]	.9	[75,25]	.50	[100,0]	1.00
[240,60]	.4 = 1–2*|.5–.8|	[90,10]	.8	[50,50]	0.00	[100,0]	1.00
[210,90]	.6 = 1–2*|.5–.7|	[85,15]	.7	[25,75]	.50	[100,0]	1.00
[180,120]	.8 = 1–2*|.5–.6|	[80,20]	.6	[0,100]	1.00	[100,0]	1.00
[150,150]	1.0 = 1–2*|.5–.5|	[75,25]	.50	[0,100]	1.00	[75,25]	.50
WRICE$_i$		.63		.73		.83	
URICE$_i$		.75		.67		.92	
Weighted:Unweighted		.84		1.09		.90	

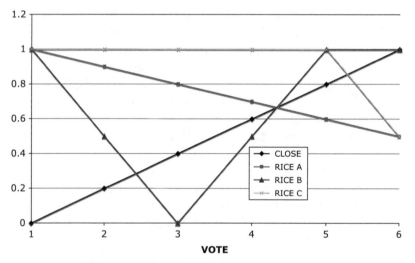

Figure 6.1   RICE scores for three parties: Cohesiveness versus discipline.

happen on closely contested votes. Higher ratios indicate parties that may experience splits on lopsided votes but pull together on closer ones. Across the cases examined here, it turns out that weighted indices tend to be slightly lower than unweighted, but there is substantial variance. The mean WRICE:URICE ratio = .95, but the standard deviation = .12. So in the typical party, unity does not deteriorate "when it matters most" as chronically as for Party A, but neither does the average party rally when the chips are down as reliably as Party B.

If we assume that party leaders value unity more, and are less tolerant of cross-voting, on close votes than lopsided ones, then the ratio is an indicator of the leader's ability to impose discipline (Snyder and Groseclose 2000; King and Zeckhauser 2003). The ratio, therefore, provides a rough proxy for the relative contribution of discipline to a party's overall voting unity.

It is worth noting that ratios do not necessarily correspond to overall levels of party unity. The following combinations are all possible:

- *low unity, low ratio*, indicating a party that is neither cohesive nor disciplined;
- *low unity, high ratio*, indicating a pervasive lack of cohesiveness, but the party pulls together more on close votes than on lopsided ones, suggesting some measure of discipline;
- *high unity, low ratio*, indicating a party that is generally cohesive, but what breaches occur come on close votes, suggesting a lack of discipline; or
- *high unity, high ratio*, indicating a party that is consistently unified, and airtight on close votes.

Comparing a party's ratio with its level of voting unity can inform us about the relative contributions of cohesiveness and discipline to overall unity. In making this comparison, it is preferable to use $URICE_i$ rather than $WRICE_i$, the formula for which emphasizes close votes and so already encompasses more of the information reflected in the ratio itself. Consider Figure 6.2.[3]

There are cases of discipline without unity (i.e., low unity, high ratio) in the lower right section, but the unity-without-discipline upper left corner of the graph is sparsely populated. The ratio and $URICE_i$ are correlated at .34, and the general pattern is that parties with higher ratios are more unified.[4]

---

[3] The Philippines case is dropped because it is an extreme outlier in its near absence of even moderately contested floor votes, leaving ratios that are hypersensitive to a handful of close votes (see Table 5.1).

[4] Plotting $WRICE_i$ against the weighted:unweighted ratio yields a tighter scatter, with no low-ratio parties extremely low on $WRICE_i$ and a stronger positive correlation (.63), although the lower right quadrant (high discipline, low unity) remains well populated. This stronger relationship is to be expected, given that both $WRICE_i$ and the ratio are drawing on the same proclivity of copartisans to vote together on close votes. Nevertheless, the pattern confirms that among highly unified parties, the proclivity to vote with one's copartisans is more pronounced on close votes, precisely when party leaders should be watching.

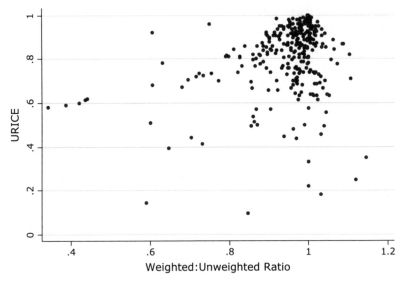

Figure 6.2 Scatterplots of URICE$_i$ against the ratio of WRICE$_i$:URICE$_i$.

The relationship is far from ironclad, and there are cases of all the combinations of cohesiveness and unity outlined previously, but the overall pattern is consistent with the idea that some measure of discipline on close votes, in addition to innate cohesiveness, accounts for party unity in legislative voting.

6.4. Hypotheses: Legislative Parties and Competing Principals

6.4.1. First Principals

Building on the logic of competing principals outlined in Chapter 1, I begin with the premise that party leaders are important actors to whose demands legislators might respond. In all democratic systems, national legislatures are organized by parties, and almost all legislators are members of party groups within their assemblies. To varying degrees, the leaders of these groups control resources – appointment to key committees, control over the legislative agenda, office space, staff, and perks – valued by rank-and-file members. Legislative party leaders may also share command of national party organizations, which often control resources critical to legislators' political career prospects, such as nominations for reelection to the legislature or for other offices, appointed posts, and access to campaign finance.

Thus, virtually all legislators are subject to influence by at least one principal – their legislative party leadership.

Whether they are subject to pressure from other, competing principals depends on the institutional context in which they operate. The hypotheses that follow posit the impact of various factors that affect the relative commitment of legislators to the national party's collective reputation and those that could pull legislators in other directions.

6.4.2. Competing Principals Hypotheses

First consider the extent to which legislators' electoral connection to voters might pull them in directions contrary to the demands of legislative party leaders. Where party leaders exercise strong influence over a legislator's election, the demands to which the legislator must respond in order to pursue reelection and the demands from those who control the distribution of resources within the assembly are consistent. The principal to whom the legislator must respond on both counts is the party leadership. Where voters exercise relatively more control over legislators' electoral prospects and party leaders less, legislators may face demands from their electoral principals that compete with those of party leaders.

The rules by which legislators are elected affect their relative responsiveness to party leaders and to alternative interests in the electorate (Shugart, Valdini, and Suominen 2005; Hix 2004). Where party leaders draw up lists of candidates that are presented in general elections and cannot be altered by voters, or can be altered only under extraordinary circumstances, electoral responsiveness to a competing principal is minimized. By contrast, where candidates compete against copartisans for voter support and that competition determines which candidates from a party win seats, then legislators have reason to cultivate reputations distinct from their copartisans'.[5]

---

[5] The degree to which electoral rules encourage personal vote seeking among candidates can be parsed more precisely than the dichotomy on which I rely here. Even in Carey and Shugart's (1995) full rank ordering of electoral systems, however, the key distinction – which determines whether increases in district magnitude will push toward more or less personalism – is whether or not voters are afforded the opportunity to cast votes among competing copartisans that determine which candidates within the party win seats. Given the amount of empirical variation on electoral rules represented in my data, the best option is to rely on this yes-no dichotomy on intraparty competition to characterize institutional forces operating on the connection between legislators and their principals.

H1: Party unity should be lower where legislative candidates compete against members of their own parties for personal votes than where nominations are controlled by party leaders and electoral lists are closed.

Next, consider the effects of unitary versus federal systems of government. Under the former, the strongest level of party organization is generally national, the level at which the leaders who control the party group in the national legislature operate. Under federal systems, by contrast, the primary level of party organization, where politicians build careers and win or lose renomination for office, is often a subnational political unit (e.g., state or province). Heterogeneity across these units may be reflected within parties at the national level, subjecting legislators to competing pulls from principals at the national versus subnational levels and undermining voting unity in the national legislature.

H2: Party unity should be lower in federal systems than in unitary ones.

The next hypotheses focus on the effects of constitutional regime type – specifically, presidentialism versus parliamentarism – and how regime type interacts with a party's status in government or in opposition to affect party voting unity. It is widely held that presidentialism undermines party unity whereas parliamentarism fosters it (APSA 1950; Diermeier and Feddersen 1998; Gerring, Thacker, and Moreno 2005). Yet there are various ways this might work. In this section I articulate a competing principals account of presidential disunity, and in the next I consider an alternative account of parliamentary unity based on the confidence vote. The key point for now is that the implications of the accounts differ in some of the hypotheses they suggest.

The core of the competing principals account of presidential disunity is that popularly elected presidents, whether in pure presidential or hybrid regimes, are potentially powerful competitors with party leaders for legislators' attention and responsiveness. Presidential elections allow the possibility that politicians whose political careers and fortunes are built outside the legislative party system occupy the chief executive office, and they may use their influence and authority toward ends at odds with legislative voting discipline (Linz 1994). Most presidents have substantial constitutional powers over lawmaking, many have extensive controls over the legislative agenda, and many also control substantial fiscal resources that legislators covet (Shugart and Carey 1992; Carey and Shugart 1998; Baldez and Carey

1999; Figueiredo and Limongi 2000; Aleman and Tsebelis 2005). Presidents also command the attention of national media, and Calvo (2007) demonstrates that strong public approval enhances presidents' ability to sway legislators toward their proposals.

Given their considerable resources, where presidents' demands contradict those of legislative party leaders, their influence should undermine voting unity in systems with popularly elected presidents relative to pure parliamentary systems. To the extent that presidents might use their resources to pull votes from any and all legislators, the effect should be present across all parties.

> H3: Party unity should be lower in systems with popularly elected presidents than in pure parliamentary system.

Next consider the difference between regimes with presidents and those without with respect to how a party's status, in government or in opposition, ought to affect party unity. The resources of the executive branch reinforce the influence of legislative party leaders in the absence of a president, but they can undermine this influence if vested in an independent president. Consider first the no-president scenario. In parliamentary systems, the party leadership is the principal most influential over any given legislator, and in the case of government parties, the legislative party leaders and the executive are one and the same. Where legislative leadership and executive leadership are fused, parties in government have more resources to impose discipline than do those in opposition (Laver and Shepsle 1996). This suggests:

> H3a: Party unity should be higher in governing parties than opposition parties under parliamentarism.

Under presidentialism, and in hybrid regimes with elected presidents, the situation is more complex. The general story from Hypothesis 3, that presidents compete with party leaders for legislator loyalties, applies, but presidential attention and influence fall more heavily on the presidents' copartisans and coalition partners than on legislators from outside the presidents' coalition. During interviews in various presidential countries, I asked, "On what are voting coalitions based – common ideology, party, electoral interests, control of the legislative agenda, support for the executive, etc.?" Party was the most commonly cited foundation for legislative voting, consistent with the premise that legislators are beholden to legislative party leaders. Next most frequent, however, were responses that pointed toward the executive. Oscar Hernández (interview) suggested that legislative party strength in Costa Rica hinges on a party's relationship to the presidency:

When a party wins, that party group generally forms a stronger connection to the executive. The strongest relationship is legislative group-to-executive – president of the Republic, ministers and all the apparatus of public administration. The losing party group does not maintain much of a strong connection with its party organization. Parties in this country are not strong ideological structures, such as would elicit discipline from each deputy. Parties at the national level have been converted into electoral platforms more than the classical concept of an ideological bloc.

The interviews illustrated the mechanisms by which presidential resources – budgetary and regulatory resources and often the ability to influence the legislative agenda directly – are employed to pressure copartisans and to build legislative majorities. For example, according to Nicaraguan deputy Luis Urbina (interview), of President Arnaldo Aleman's Liberal Party,

The executive normally works better when it has an assembly majority. The majority party tries to support projects from the executive, of which it is part. . . . So when the executive wants to submit a law, it calls on the majority party, explains the benefits of approving the law, and generally we vote in line with the directives we are given. This doesn't mean we are obliged to, but normally that's what happens.

Urbina's account relies on an inherent compatibility between the executive's interests and those of his legislative copartisans, or at least on some inherent loyalty to the executive. More frequently, legislators pointed to concrete resources by which executives elicit support. Critics of Urbina's Liberal Party in Nicaragua, for example, invariably pointed to patronage as the source of support for the executive (Baltodano and Hurtado interviews). As Jorge Samper (interview) of the Sandinista Renewal Movement put it,

The Liberal group has been very obedient, through presidential discipline more than party discipline. They take almost no decisions autonomously from the president, and when they have done so, they have had to backtrack when it produces a presidential veto. One or another deputy has voted against the president's wishes, and then along comes some bit of patronage that makes him change his vote, and we vote again the way the president orders. [*Interviewer*: What are examples of patronage?] Public jobs, for deputies and relatives. The deputy might be made ambassador to some country, and maybe they send his family or relatives. . . . The rest of the deputies, that are not from the Sandinista or Liberal groups, many of them have formed alliances with the government . . . [but] these aren't real political alliances, but rather alliances based on patronage.

136

Samper's account of presidential influence is consistent with Nicaragua's reputation, and that of the Aleman administration in particular, for corruption. Accounts of presidential influence elsewhere do not always hinge on exchanges that reek so much of impropriety, but they share a focus on the resources executives control that appeal to legislators' ambitions. Ricardo Combellas (interview) cites President Chavez's control over party nominations to all electoral posts as the main source of his influence within the Movimiento Quinta República (Chavez's party in the early years of the 2000 decade) in Venezuela. Carlos Vargas Pagán (interview) cites the Costa Rican president's ability to expedite, or hold up, disbursement of funds budgeted for projects in deputies' districts as a source of influence.

There is a consensus in the interview responses that presidents control resources that can be employed to influence legislative votes. The interviews raise some questions, however, about exactly how presidential influence should manifest itself in party unity. First, the accounts of presidential influence offered in the interviews rely on executive-legislative exchanges that – even if not overtly corrupt – might attract criticism if exposed to public scrutiny. This suggests that presidential influence might be mitigated by visible voting. The obstacle to testing this proposition empirically is that where votes are not recorded, party unity cannot be measured, so it remains conjecture. Second is the matter of whether presidential influence ought to raise or diminish party voting unity. The Hernández and Urbina interviews suggest that party unity is boosted when a party holds the presidency relative to some baseline level. This outcome may be true in the cases of the parties and presidents Hernández and Urbina had in mind, but whether it is the effect of alliance with presidents more generally is not obvious. Presidential influence ought to depend on whether the legislative party leadership consistently agrees with the president's wishes or, if it does not, on the relative influence of each of these actors over the legislative rank and file.[6]

More specifically, when the two principals of governing-party legislators (party leaders and the president) concur on a given measure before the

---

[6] For example, Weldon (1997) demonstrates that the source of unity in the archetypal case of airtight party discipline under presidentialism – Mexico's Partido Revolucionario Institucional during its long hegemony – was the elaborate institutional structure that afforded presidents not only their constitutional authorities but also control over all the partisan and procedural resources that, in other political systems, normally fall in the domain of legislative party leaders. The secret of PRI unity throughout much of the twentieth century was that legislators had only one meaningful principal.

Table 6.2. *Legislators' Principals under Presidentialism, Parliamentarism, Government, and Opposition*

	Opposition Parties	Government Parties
Parliamentarism	Legislative party leadership	Legislative party leadership fused with executive authority and resources
		H3a: Reinforces party unity relative to opposition parties
Presidentialism	1. Legislative party leadership	1. Legislative party leadership
	2. Some independent pressure from president	2. Heightened independent influence from president
	H3: Undermines party unity relative to all parties in pure parliamentary systems	*H3b: Undermines party unity relative to governing parties under parliamentarism*

assembly, the effect should be similar to that under parliamentarism – providing a boost to unity owing to the additional resources with which the president can pressure legislators. On the other hand, when the president and legislative party leadership disagree and pull in opposite directions, party unity should suffer in governing parties. Whether the net effect of competing principals is to diminish voting unity among governing parties under presidentialism depends on how frequently the principals pull in opposite directions and on their relative influence over legislators. To the extent the principals compete *at all*, however, voting unity in government parties should suffer under presidential systems relative to parliamentary systems.

All of this suggests the following effect of alliance with the president on party voting unity:

H3b: Party unity in governing parties should be lower under presidentialism than under parliamentarism.

The logic of H3, H3a, and H3b is summarized in Table 6.2.

6.4.3. Further Hypotheses on Party Unity

Beyond those generated specifically by the logic of competing principals, a few more hypotheses merit consideration – one that focuses on the

138

parliamentary-presidential distinction, and two that focus on the venerability of regimes and parties and its potential effect on unity.

Among the most prominent propositions regarding the effects of formal institutions on party unity is that the authority of the executive in parliamentary systems to offer legislative proposals as matters of confidence accounts for more unified parties in parliamentary than in presidential systems. The intuition is that the confidence provision raises the stakes for all parties because rejecting such a measure triggers the collapse of the government and perhaps early elections. If a party splits, and loses as a result, on a vote subject to a confidence provision, the costs are greater than just forgoing the new policy for the status quo, or vice versa (Bagehot 1867; Cox 1987; Diermeier and Feddersen 1998; Huber 1996). This implies the following hypothesis.

> H4: Party unity should be higher in systems with confidence vote provisions than those without.

The confidence vote story is compelling but not without proviso. First, even where confidence vote provisions exist, they are not formally summoned on most votes, so technically there is room for party voting disunity that does not threaten government survival. More important, note that the confidence vote is not restricted to pure parliamentary systems but is a characteristic of hybrid regimes as well (Valenzuela 1994; Shugart and Carey 1992). The best-known case combining a confidence vote provision for the cabinet with a more-than-ceremonial elected presidency is the French Fifth Republic (1958–present), but such hybrid arrangements are common among newer regimes (Frye 1997). In short, the distinction between regimes with and without confidence vote provisions does not map perfectly onto the distinction between those with and without elected presidents. In principle, this ought to allow leverage to distinguish between H3 and H4, to determine whether differences in voting unity between pure presidential and pure parliamentary regimes are the product of competing principals, confidence votes, or some combination of the two. In practice, scarcity of data from hybrid regimes hampers my ability to test for that distinction, for now. I return to this matter in the discussion of the statistical model and results.

Next, consider the age of the regime. Scholarship on comparative party systems posits that parties in new democracies are weaker than those in better-established systems (Mainwaring and Scully 1995; Coppedge 1998; Carroll, Cox, and Pachon 2006). It follows that legislators' expectations about which parties will thrive are less solid and that their commitment to any particular party's collective reputation should be lower in new rather than established political systems. There should be diminishing returns to the effect of time on expectations, such that the difference between a regime that is one year old and one that is eleven years old should be greater than that between one that is eleven and one that is twenty-one, and so on. This suggests:

> H5: Party unity should increase with the age (logged) of the political regime.

Although new political regimes frequently give birth to new parties and party systems, such that the age of parties is strongly correlated with the age of the regimes in which they operate ($p = .66$), the two remain distinct. New parties are occasionally born and take root in established regimes, such as the U.S. Republicans in the 1850s or Israel's Shas in the 1980s. By the same token, established parties frequently survive through authoritarian interludes and thrive after the reestablishment of a democratic regime, such as Argentina's Radicals (UCR) and Peronists (PJ) in the 1980s or the Christian Democrats in Chile and in the Czech Republic in the 1990s. By the same logic as in H5, legislators' expectations about the future value of a party's label ought to be strengthened the better established that label is and the more durable it has proved to be over time (Roberts and Wibbels 1999; Stokes 2001).

> H6: Party unity should increase with the age (logged) of the party.

Finally, formal models of party competition represent the inherent level of agreement among copartisans, described here as cohesiveness, as proximity in an N-dimensional policy space (Shepsle 1991). If legislative party groups comprise ideological neighbors, then for a policy space of a given size and dimensionality, greater party fragmentation would imply more cohesive party groups (Cox 1990). Given that cohesiveness is a key source of voting unity, it follows that party voting unity may be higher in more fragmented party systems.

> H7: Party unity should increase with fragmentation of the legislative party system.

Among the factors posited here to affect legislative voting unity, some (e.g., existence of a presidency or confidence vote, the electoral system, federalism, regime age, or the fragmentation of the party system) are fixed across all parties in any given assembly, whereas others (e.g., government or opposition status, party age) vary across parties within the same assembly. Table 6.3 presents descriptive statistics for the system-level variables for the

Table 6.3. *System-Level Variables for Lower Legislative Chambers, by Country*

Country	Intraparty Competition	Federal	President	Confidence Vote	Regime Age (log)	Effective Number of Parties
Argentina	No	Yes	Yes	No	0.69–2.56	2.21–3.59
Australia	No	Yes	No	Yes	4.56	2.61
Brazil	Yes	Yes	Yes	No	1.61–3.00	4.48–9.30
Canada	No	Yes	No	Yes	4.86	2.26
Chile	No	No	Yes	No	1.95–2.20	4.85–5.12
Czech Republic	No	No	No	Yes	0.69–1.61	3.80–5.90
Ecuador	No	No	Yes	No	2.94	5.05
France IV Republic	No	No	No	Yes	0–2.40	4.30–6.76
Guatemala	No	No	Yes	No	2.30–2.71	2.16–3.46
Israel	No	No	No	Yes	3.91	8.50
Mexico	No	Yes	Yes	No	4.28	2.86
New Zealand	No	No	No	Yes	5.02–5.04	1.81–2.87
Nicaragua	No	No	Yes	No	2.77	2.86
Peru	Yes	No	Yes	No	1.79–2.08	2.66–4.01
Philippines	Yes	No	Yes	No	3.71	2.15
Poland	Yes	No	Yes	Yes	2.20	3.17
Russia	No	Yes	Yes	No	1.39	5.66
United States	Yes	Yes	Yes	No	5.31–5.34	1.90–2.00
Uruguay	Yes	No	Yes	No	0.69–1.95	2.87–3.34

assemblies included in the quantitative analysis in this chapter. In cases of assemblies where data were available for more than one period, Table 6.3 shows mean values across periods for the effective number of parties (Laakso and Taagepera 1979) and for regime age (log) during the first year in each legislature.

6.5. Picturing Party Unity across Systems

The indices developed in Chapter 5 can illustrate cross-national patterns of voting unity. In the literature on comparative legislatures, the most prevalent explanations for levels of unity refer to electoral rules (Wallack, Gaviria, Panizza, and Stein 2003; Shugart, Valdini, and Suominen 2005) and to the confidence vote procedure (Bagehot 1867; Cox 1987; Huber 1996; Diermeier and Feddersen 1998; Gerring, Thacker, and Moreno

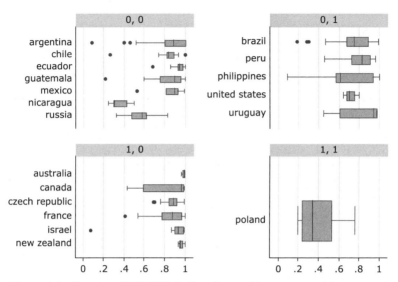

Figure 6.3 Boxplot of WRICE$_i$ indices by confidence vote and intraparty competition.

2005).[7] Figure 6.3 presents WRICE$_i$ indices for the parties in each country for which I have data according to whether the constitution includes a confidence vote provision and whether assembly elections provide for competition among candidates from the same party. In the bottom left panel are systems with the confidence vote and without intraparty competition. By and large, voting unity as measured by WRICE$_i$ is high, with the average more than .90. Parties in France's Fourth Republic are widely regarded to have been chronically factionalized, but even its mean WRICE$_i$ is .85. Canada and Israel each have a derelict outlier, but in each case these are two-member parties in which a 1–1 split vote would drive the RICE$_{ij}$ score to zero. Overwhelmingly, the legislators in these parliamentary systems voted together with their copartisans.

The bottom right panel shows the one case of a confidence vote system with intraparty competition, Poland. Note that, in addition to the confidence

[7] Federalism is frequently mentioned as a source of party disunity at the national level, but in the most careful analysis of the issue to date, Desposato (2004b) finds evidence for only a remarkably small drag on voting unity in Brazil, where low party unity had often been attributed to a federalism effect (Weyland 1996; Mainwaring 1999). Jones and Hwang (2005) similarly are unable to detect an effect of provincial forces on voting in the Argentine Congress, although they confront substantial challenges in identifying what effect alliance with governors ought to have on allied deputies.

vote provision, Poland also has a popularly elected presidency. It is the one hybrid regime from which I was able to collect recorded voting data.[8] $WRICE_i$ is extraordinarily low. Poland's open-list proportional representation may contribute to individualism among members of the Sejm. The Polish presidency may also contribute to disunity among some parties. It is worth noting that, of eight parties in the Sejm, President Kwasniewski's Social Democrats (SLD) had the lowest $WRICE_i$ index, consistent with the competing principals logic outlined in H3b. We should be cautious about drawing inferences based on this case, however. The Polish vote data are from a twenty-month period following the adoption of a new constitution and the inauguration of a new government facing an opposition president. The rules of the game, and the party system itself, were relatively young, and voting in subsequent periods may show increased unity. Nevertheless, the Polish data at hand are consistent with the propositions that intraparty competition and the presence of an elected president, as well as alliance with the president, generate drags on party unity.

The top left panel of Figure 6.3 shows the nonconfidence vote (i.e., pure presidential) systems without intraparty competition. Nicaragua and Russia are very low, of course, but $WRICE_i$ indices there must be eyed warily in light of their absolute-majority threshold voting rules. Elsewhere, levels of $WRICE_i$ are higher – a bit lower than under confidence vote systems without intraparty competition but generally in the .8 to .9 neighborhood. Finally, the top right panel shows systems without confidence votes and with intraparty competition, and the indices suggest more modest levels of voting unity overall, averaging in the .7 to .8 neighborhood, and with considerable spreads.

Figure 6.4 presents the same set of boxplots for the $RLOSER_i$ index, and here the pattern is similar, although Poland is less extreme. Among the pure parliamentary cases without intraparty competition, parties almost never lose votes that they could, but for party cross-voting, have won. In Poland, the median party lost about 2 percent of all votes because of such divisions. (It should be noted that this party, the Peasant Party [PSL], was on the winning side of 92 percent of all votes, so its losses due to disunity accounted for a quarter of all its losses.) At any rate, caution is again in

---

[8] Attentive readers might note that both the Peruvian (Art. 134) and Russian (Art. 111) constitutions provide for removal of the cabinet by vote of a parliamentary majority. However, both constitutions also allow the president to dissolve the legislature in this instance, raising the costs to legislators enormously of wielding the no-confidence vote over presidential resistance. Given these provisions, I do not code Peru or Russia as no-confidence vote systems.

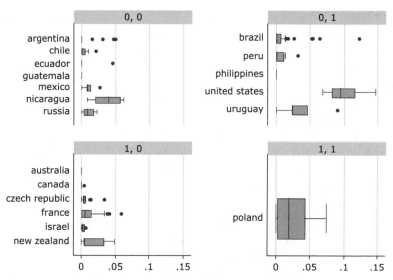

Figure 6.4 Boxplot of RLOSER$_i$ indices by confidence vote and intraparty competition.

order in drawing inferences about this particular combination of institutional variables from the Polish data alone. The top left panel shows pure separation-of-powers systems with no intraparty competition, again showing a larger spread of values and slightly greater disunity overall than in the analogous pure parliamentary cases. Finally, the top right shows the pure separation-of-powers systems with intraparty competition and, as expected, exhibits the greatest incidence of lost votes because of disunity. The United States is the outlier, with a median value of around 9 percent of all votes lost because of disunity, but values in the 2 to 5 percent range are not unusual in Peru and Uruguay, and indices run still higher in Brazil.

Analogous boxplot graphs for WUNITY$_i$ and ULOSER$_i$ are much less striking, showing larger spreads across the board but no clear patterns. The next two figures contrast WRICE$_i$ with WUNITY$_i$ (Figure 6.5) and RLOSERi with ULOSER$_i$ (Figure 6.6), pooling observations from countries according to whether they have directly elected presidents and intraparty electoral competition.

In Figure 6.5, the darker boxes represent WRICE$_i$, and the lighter WUNITY$_i$. There is a clear overall pattern by which WRICE$_i$ indices trend higher in parliamentary systems than in those with elected presidents, and among presidential systems, lower with intraparty competition than

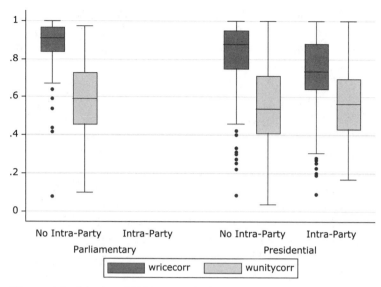

Figure 6.5 Boxplot of WRICE$_i$ and of WUNITY$_i$ indices by intraparty competition and presidentialism, pooled across countries.

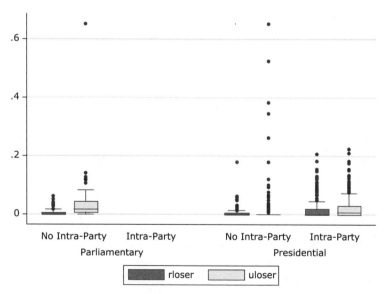

Figure 6.6 Boxplot of RLOSER$_i$ and of ULOSER$_i$ indices by intraparty competition and presidentialism, pooled across countries.

without. (There are no recorded vote data from parliamentary systems with intraparty competition.) There is no analogous pattern among $WUNITY_i$ indices, which exhibit wider spreads and no apparent responsiveness to regime type or electoral rules. Figure 6.6, with the darker boxes representing $RLOSER_i$ and the lighter $ULOSER_i$, shows a similar contrast, with larger increasing $RLOSER_i$ values from parliamentary to presidential systems, and from no intraparty competition to intraparty competition within presidential systems, but no corresponding pattern for $ULOSER_i$. On the whole, the mobilization-based indices, $WUNITY_i$ and $ULOSER_i$, appear to be more susceptible than the cross-voting-based indices, $WRICE_i$ and $RLOSER_i$, to distortion via nonvoting equilibria, as discussed in Chapter 5, which limits their usefulness for cross-national comparisons.

On the whole, the graphical patterns of $WRICE_i$ and $RLOSER_i$ suggest that party unity is lower in presidential regimes and in the presence of intraparty electoral competition. The statistical analysis below adds variables, operating at both the level of political system and the level of individual parties, to gain additional purchase on sources of party voting unity, and disunity.

6.6. Models

6.6.1. Challenges Presented by the Data

The structure of the data presents some challenges in testing the hypotheses developed here. Each observation represents the characteristics of a party group in a given assembly. Multilevel modeling is appropriate for the multivariate analysis because each party group is clustered within a higher-level unit, a legislative assembly. Factors like party age or government-opposition status that vary across parties within each assembly are posited to affect voting unity, but the hypotheses also refer to system-level factors, like presidentialism or electoral rules, that are constant across parties within a given assembly but vary across assemblies (Singer 1998; Steenbergen and Jones 2002).

Another data issue is covariance between two of the system-level variables. The data include only one hybrid constitution, combining a popularly elected and powerful president with a confidence vote provision for the cabinet – that of Poland. Otherwise, presidentialism and the existence of a confidence vote procedure are perfect complements of each other, making it difficult to distinguish their effects statistically. Ideally, vote data from more hybrid systems will become available, so these factors can vary independently to a greater degree. In the meantime, multicollinearity means it is not feasible to include both a Confidence Vote variable and a Presidentialism variable in the same regression estimating voting unity. The results presented here include the Presidentialism variable for two reasons. First, testing H3b requires including a cross-level interactive variable, Government Party * Presidentialism, and there are compelling statistical reasons to include the component variables when using an interactive variable (Brambor, Clark, and Golder 2006).[9] Second, in some specifications, Presidentialism shows a statistically significant impact on voting unity, whereas the Confidence Vote variable never does. I report this latter (non)result in the text but show the statistical results of the models including the Presidentialism variable.

6.6.2. The Multilevel Model

The basic statistical model is to estimate voting unity as a function of both party-level and system-level explanatory variables, as follows:

$$\text{UNITY}_{ij} = \pi_0 j + \pi_1 P_1 + \ldots + \pi_4 P_4 + e_{ij}$$

$$\pi_{0j} = \beta_{00} + \beta_{01} S_1 + \ldots + \beta_5 S_5 + r_{0j}$$

P1–P4 and S1–S5 refer to party-level and system-level variables. The party-level coefficients (π_{1}–π_{4}) are estimated as fixed across countries. The party-level intercept (π_{0j}) is a function of both party-level and system-level effects. To estimate the cross-level interaction, government party status by presidentialism (per H3b), a party-level coefficient is modeled as a function of system-level variables.

The dependent variables are the two cross-voting-base measures of voting unity developed in Chapter 5, WRICE_i and RLOSER_i, as well as the parties' overall averages ($\%\text{WON}_i$) on recorded votes.[10]

Note that all three voting unity indices under examination are constrained to values between zero and one, with WRICE_i fairly normally

---

[9] I thank an anonymous Cambridge University Press reviewer for pointing me toward the Brambor, Clark, and Golder (2006) article, which illustrates the importance of including all component variables along with any interactive term. An earlier version of this study (Carey 2007), not fully appreciating this imperative, presents models including Confidence Vote, rather than Presidential, alongside the Government Party * Presidential interactive term.

[10] Analyses on the mobilization-based indices, WUNITY_i and ULOSER_i, are not included in the analyses presented in this chapter because the sensitivity of those indices to nonvoting makes them less reliable measures of unity, at least until effective means of identifying and accounting for nonvoting equilibria can be established.

distributed around a mean of .79; %WON$_i$ fairly uniformly distributed with mean .59; and RLOSER$_i$, clustered around zero, with mean $= .014$ and standard deviation $= .032$. The assumptions of the linear model are under the most serious strain for the analyses of RLOSER$_i$, given its clustering to the left of the scale. To verify the results from the linear model, I replicated the analyses using multilevel ordered logit, grouping ranges of values on the dependent variables into bins where necessary. All significant results from the linear models are confirmed in the ordered logits, and in some instances, the logit coefficients are significant where the linear models' estimates fall just short. I report on the linear multilevel models for simplicity of exposition and interpretation of coefficients, noting on occasion where the ordered logits confirm hypotheses that are ambiguous in the linear models.

System-level explanatory variables include the following:

Intraparty Competition is coded 1 if the electoral system requires that candidates for the assembly compete against their own copartisans for preference votes; 0 otherwise.

Presidential is coded 1 if the country has a popularly elected presidency endowed with substantial constitutional powers; 0 otherwise.

Federal is coded 1 if the country has a federal constitution and subnational units are meaningful arenas of political competition and the distribution of political resources; 0 otherwise.

Regime Age (log) is the log of the number of years since the founding of the current democratic regime.

Effective Number of Parties is the Laakso and Taagepera (1979) index of party system fragmentation for a given chamber.[11]

Party-level variables are as follows:

Party Age (log) is the log of the number of years since a given party's founding.

---

[11] Note that both the Effective Number of Parties and the previous system-level variable, Regime Age, can vary across assemblies within a given legislature. From Table 5.1, for example, note that the data include votes from three different Brazilian assemblies, two from Chile, but one from Australia. Potentially, then, there are three levels of data – party within an assembly, the specific iteration of the assembly, and the constitutional system in which the iterations of that assembly exist. In the interest of simplicity, however, I combine these last two levels, assigning mean values for the Effective Number of Parties and Regime Age across observations from a given legislature. In practice, there is little variance on either variable across assemblies within each system for the data included.

Seat Share is the proportion of seats held by the party in a given assembly.
Government Party is coded 1 if the party holds at least one cabinet port-
folio in the current cabinet; 0 otherwise.
*Government Party * Presidential* is the interaction of Government Party
with Presidential.

The logic of the independent variables and expectations about their
effects are mostly straightforward from the hypotheses section, but a few
comments are in order. The default status implied by the models is for an
opposition party in a parliamentary system. The variable Presidential estimates the effect on the dependent variable of being in a presidential regime.
The coefficient on Government Party represents the effect of being in
government, as opposed to out, in parliamentary systems. The coefficient
on Government Party * Presidential picks up the marginal difference between government parties in systems with directly elected presidents and
those in parliamentary systems. The comparison between government
and opposition parties within presidential systems is also of interest, so
below the list of coefficients from each model the tables show the linear
combination of Government Party + Government Party * Presidential –
Presidential.

Seat Share is included as a control variable, but its logic depends on
the dependent variable. When the dependent variable is $\%WON_i$, expectations regarding Seat Share are clear-cut – a greater share of seats should
lead to more wins. When the dependent variable is $WRICE_i$, expectations
are less firm. Parties that comprise larger shares of their chambers may
encompass more-diverse viewpoints and thus be subject to disunity. On the
other hand, increasing seat shares generally provides increasing access to the
legislative resources that party leaders employ to elicit compliance and to
mobilize their rank and file (Hurtado interview). Finally, when the dependent variable is the $RLOSER_i$ index of vote losses due to disunity, the effect
of Seat Share should be positive, notwithstanding the fact that bigger parties win more, because a split within a larger party should be more likely to
reverse a vote outcome than the same split in a smaller one.[12]

---

[12] I also ran the models on vote loss due to disunity controlling for WIN%, on the grounds
that only parties that win votes stand to lose some through breakdowns in unity. That is, if
a party's winning percentage is zero or close to it, we might reasonably expect that it is
merely in perpetual and futile opposition, rather than that it *might* have won, say, 3 percent
of those lost votes but for internal splits. This turns out not to be the case, however; the
coefficient on WIN% was never close to significant.

6.7. Results

Models 1a–c, in Table 6.4, regress $WRICE_i$ on sets of both system-level and party-level explanatory variables. Model 1a includes the full set of variables implied by the preceding hypotheses, plus a control for each party's share of assembly seats. It is, perhaps, most straightforward to note at the outset the hypotheses for which there is no support in any model. Contrary to H2, there is no evidence that federalism undermines party voting unity, as measured either by WRICE or by one of the vote-outcome (%WON or RLOSER) indices. Nor is there evidence that the existence of a confidence vote provision (H4), regime age (H5), or party system fragmentation (H7) matters under any model specifications. With regard to the confidence vote, statistical results are not shown in Table 6.4 because Confidence Vote cannot be included in the same model with Presidential, but alternative specifications dropping Presidential (and Government Party * Presidential) show no measurable effect of Confidence Vote on any of the dependent variables.

6.7.1. Party Age Fosters Unity

In Model 1a, the coefficients on all system-level variables fall short of conventional significance levels (although that on Presidential just barely, with p < .12). The only party-level variable with any leverage is Party Age (log). The effect of party longevity is modest but consistent. An increase in one natural log unit (say, from a 1-year-old party to a 3-year-old party, or from 3 to 8 years, 8 to 20, 20 to 55, or 55 to 150) is expected to increase $WRICE_i$ by .02. Moving from the youngest parties in the data (newborns populate many assemblies) to the oldest (e.g., the major parties in Uruguay or the United States) is expected to push $WRICE_i$ up by .10, or half a standard deviation, other things being equal. To the extent that legislative voting unity reflects a party's brand name, such reputations gradually grow clearer and more informative over time. None of the other party-level variables provides any traction in explaining WRICE. Neither a party's share of seats nor its status in government or out has any measurable effect.

6.7.2. Intraparty Competition and Presidents Disrupt Unity

The effects of two system-level variables of interest, however, warrant further exploration. With usable data from only nineteen assemblies, there are substantial degrees of freedom constraints at the system level.

Table 6.4. *Multilevel Analysis of Legislative Voting Unity within Parties*

	Dependent Variables						
	WRICE$_i$			%WON$_i$	RLOSER$_i$		
Independent Variables	1a	1b	1c	2	3a	3b	3c
System level							
Intraparty Competition	−.04 (.10)	−.05 (.10)	−.16** (.07)	.09 (.07)	.017* (.010)	.018* (.009)	.021** (.010)
Presidential	−.17 (.11)	−.19* (.10)	−.06 (.07)	.14* (.08)	.004 (.010)	.002 (.010)	−.003 (.011)
Federal	.02 (.09)			−.12** (.06)	.004 (.009)		
Regime Age (log)	.02 (.04)			−.02 (.03)	.003 (.004)		
Effective Number Parties	.01 (.03)			.01 (.02)	−.000 (.003)		
Party level							
Party Age (log)	.02*** (.01)	.02** (.01)	.02** (.01)	.38*** (.11)	.035*** (.008)	.036*** (.008)	.036*** (.008)
Seat Share	.05 (.08)	.05 (.08)	−.01 (.07)	.25*** (.05)	.001 (.003)	.001 (.003)	.001 (.003)
Government Party	−.05 (.04)	−.05 (.04)	−.05 (.03)	−.18** (.06)	.010** (.004)	.010** (.004)	.012** (.004)
GovPty * Presidential	.01 (.05)	.01 (.05)	−.00 (.04)	.51*** (.15)	−.010 (.020)	−.001 (.007)	−.001 (.007)
Constant	.77*** (.21)	.89*** (.08)	.90*** (.05)	−.07 (.09)	.007 (.011)	.009 (.010)	.015 (.011)
H0: Government Party + GovPty * Presidential − Presidential = 0	.13 (.11)	.15 (.11)	.01 (.08)				
Proportion of variance explained							
System level	.31	.28	.60	.39	.47	.45	.52
Party level	.05	.05	.06	.19	.22	.22	.24
N (parties)	206	206	184	309	254	254	229
N (assemblies)	19	19	16	19	19	19	16

Note: Models 1c and 3c exclude observations from Russia, Nicaragua, and Guatemala, where nonvotes are counted as nay votes. * Significant at > .10 level. ** Significant at > .05 level. *** Significant at > .01 level. All models include only parties with two or more legislators.

151

Therefore, Models 1b and 1c (as well as 3b and 3c) drop those system-level variables for which there is no hint of a measurable effect on party unity, retaining those for which the graphical representation of data, as well as bivariate analyses, suggests some impact. Model 1b replicates 1a, but without the Federal, Regime Age, and Effective Number of Parties variables. The estimated impact of presidentialism on voting unity increases slightly, and the standard error shrinks, such that the coefficient is now significant at .06. The shift from a parliamentary regime to one with an elected president drops $WRICE_i$ by .18 – nearly a full standard deviation. This suggests confirmation of H3, yet sorting out the relative impact of presidentialism and intraparty electoral competition remains thorny.

Note that among these data, all cases of intraparty competition are in regimes with elected presidents. Recall further, from Chapter 5 (Section 5.3.2 and Appendix 5), that applying the $WRICE_i$ index to assemblies where all nonvotes are counted as nays is particularly awkward and may yield unduly low values. All three such assemblies in the data, those of Nicaragua, Guatemala, and Russia, are in presidential systems without intraparty competition (see Figure 6.3). Model 1c drops these observations, with a resulting shift in the relative scope, and the statistical significance, of the Presidential and Intraparty Competition variables. With the nonvote = nay-vote observations excluded, Intraparty Competition is associated with a .16 drop in $WRICE_i$, significant at .02. The estimated effect of presidentialism remains negative but falls short of significance (analogous to Intraparty Competition when the nonvote = nay-vote assemblies are included). In short, presidentialism and intraparty electoral competition both appear to diminish $WRICE_i$, but although the cross-national breadth of these data is unprecedented, statistical leverage at the system level is limited, so uncertainty as to the relative impact of these factors remains.

6.7.3. Overall Averages: Governing Parties Win, but Presidents Get in the Way

Model 2, estimating %WON, begins to shed light on the differences between governing parties in parliamentary and presidential systems. Note that all nonconsensual votes pit some winners against some losers, and the hypotheses derived previously do not suggest that the proclivity of parties to be on the winning side should differ according to system-level factors. Nevertheless, to generate as clear a picture as possible of what characteristics of parties contribute to winning and losing votes, Model 2 regresses $\%WON_i$ across all recorded votes on both system-level and party-level explanatory variables.[13] The system-level coefficients indicate that legislative bandwagons are more prevalent in presidential than parliamentary systems and less pronounced in federal than unitary systems, suggesting a greater proclivity among parties in parliamentary and federal regimes to take a stand – even a losing one.

Moving to party-level factors, the coefficient on the Seat Share control variable is positive and significant. For every additional percentage of chamber seats a party holds, its expected winning rate rises by nearly four-tenths of a percent. It is, of course, not surprising that bigger parties tend to win more. Turning to the variables of greater interest, the coefficient on Government Party shows that, in parliamentary systems, government parties win at a much greater rate than do opposition parties – 25 percent more, over and above the effects of Seat Share. The coefficient on Government Party * President shows that this advantage is largely wiped out for governing parties under presidentialism – and the difference across systems in the effect of governing party status is strongly significant. Just as striking is the linear combination of regime-type governing status, and their interaction, shown in the next section. Accounting for seat share, the legislative averages of governing parties in presidential systems are statistically indistinguishable from – and in the event slightly *lower* than – those of opposition parties.

6.7.4. Disunity Losses: Intraparty Competition and Presidents (Again)

Why are government parties in presidential systems not more effective at winning votes? Model 3 indicates that a substantial share of losses is attributable to breakdowns in unity. Beginning, as previously, with the system-level variables, neither federalism, presidentialism, regime age, party system fragmentation, nor the existence of a confidence vote provision (not shown) has any measurable effect on RLOSER$_i$'s failing to confirm Hypotheses 2, 3, 4, or 5. The estimated coefficient on Intraparty Competition is positive and significant at .07 or better across all three models. RLOSER$_i$ jumps by around 2 percent (standard deviation is 3 percent) with Intraparty Competition, in

---

[13] In analyses of %WON and RLOSER, the Party Age variable is never significant. Its inclusion or exclusion does not affect the direction or significance of any other variables, but because I was unable to determine Party Age for almost a third of all parties included in the data, including the variable in any analysis "costs" a lot of observations. Therefore, Party Age is dropped from Models 2 and 3. The system-level variables are included as controls in Model 2, although they are not of substantive interest. The effects of party-level variables are the same whether the system-level variables are included or not.

further support of Hypothesis 1. When copartisans compete for electoral support, their inclination to distinguish themselves from each other evidently outweighs party loyalty in some instances that are pivotal to vote outcomes.

Moving to party-level effects, the Seat Share variable is a strong and significant contributor to RLOSER$_i$ rates, confirming that splits in large parties are more consequential to vote outcomes than analogous splits in small parties. There is also further support in Model 3 for Hypothesis 3b. First, note that governing parties in parliamentary systems lose votes because of breakdowns in unity at effectively the same rate as opposition parties, which, in practice, is to say only very rarely. The estimated effect of being in government in systems with presidents, by contrast, is substantial. Governing parties in systems with presidents lose because of disunity a full percent more than do governing parties in parliamentary systems. They even lose votes they could have won, but for cross-voting, at higher rates than opposition parties in presidential systems.[14]

An additional 1 percent more losses – whether owing to intraparty competition or governing status in a presidential regime, may appear to be only a moderate disadvantage, but consider that the mean RLOSER rate across *all* parties is 1.4 percent. Governing parties under presidentialism lose far more than their fair share of votes because of disunity. Furthermore, governing parties, even under presidentialism, win 82 percent of all votes (as against 84 percent for governing parties in parliamentary systems), so membership in government can be expected to boost a party's overall rate of floor losses by around 5 percent through its effect on RLOSER alone, accounting for half the overall difference in the governing parties' averages between presidential and parliamentary systems.

6.7.5. Illustrative Cases

Returning to the "snapshots" of party systems in specific assemblies illustrates the overall results. Figure 6.7 shows unity indices based on votes from the Canadian House of Commons in 1994–97. In this federal system with no intraparty competition, a confidence vote provision, and no elected president, WRICE$_i$ is uniformly near perfect. WUNITY$_i$ is lower but strongly correlated across parties, suggesting nonvoting equilibria, and RLOSER$_i$ and ULOSER$_i$ levels are near zero.

[14] The coefficient on the linear combination of regime type and governing status falls short of significance in the models shown in Table 6.4, but is positive and significant at .01 in the ordered logit version of Model 3c.

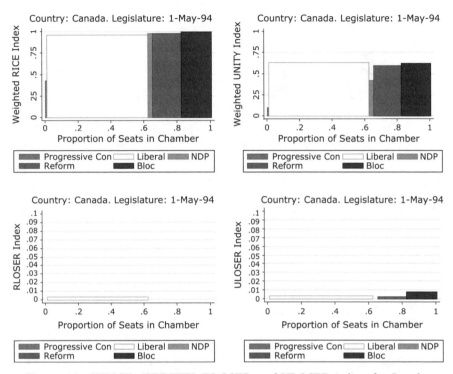

Figure 6.7 WRICE_i, WUNITY_i, RLOSER_i, and ULOSER_i indices for Canada, 1994–97.

The case of Brazil during the second administration of Fernando Henrique Cardoso, 1999–2003, is shown in Figure 6.8.[15] The president's Social Democratic Party (PSDB) is shown in black, second from the left, while other parties in the government coalition are in white, with the opposition in various gray hues. Voting unity is lower by all indices among the governing parties, which also experience markedly higher loss rates because of to cross-voting and undermobilization.

Those familiar with Brazilian politics will note that among the more highly unified opposition parties is the Worker's Party (PT) led by Luiz Ignacio (Lula) da Silva, which has long been noted for its strong discipline even within Brazil's famously fractious and fluid party system. Lula won the presidential election following Cardoso's second term, bringing the PT to

---

[15] Indices from Cardoso's first administration were shown in Figure 5.8, and the picture is strikingly similar.

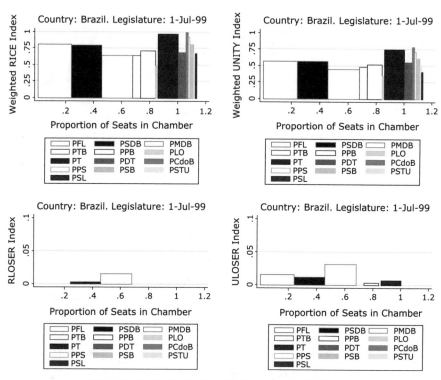

Figure 6.8 WRICE$_i$, WUNITY$_i$, RLOSER$_i$, and ULOSER$_i$ indices for Brazil, 1999–2003.

power in coalition with a left-leaning bloc of parties. Given their prior reputations, one might expect these parties to be more unified than their predecessors in government, and Figure 6.9 shows this to be correct for votes during Lula's first two years, 2003–5. Note, however, that the PT's WRICE$_i$ during the previous two periods was .98, but it fell to .91 even during Lula's honeymoon, and qualitative accounts suggest that divisions within the PT, between legislators loyal to Lula's and those who objected to the president's centrist governing strategy, drove PT unity levels down further still as Lula's presidency wore on (Fleischer 2004).

6.7.6. Summing up the Results on Party Unity

Table 6.5 summarizes the empirical evidence regarding the seven hypotheses on voting. Most, but not all, of the competing principals hypotheses

Results

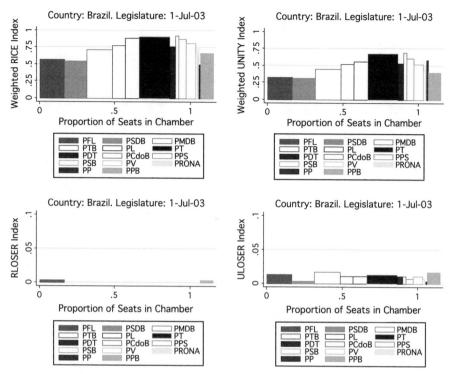

Figure 6.9 WRICE$_i$, WUNITY$_i$, RLOSER$_i$, and ULOSER$_i$ indices for Brazil, 2003–5.

find some support. H1 is supported insofar as intraparty electoral competition is associated with lower values of WRICE$_i$ (the effect is statistically significant when assemblies where nonvotes = nay votes are excluded), and higher values of RLOSER$_i$. Where electoral rules provide for intraparty competition, thus strengthening the influence of personal vote constituencies relative to party leaders, there is more cross-voting, leading to increased vote loss rates. H2 fares less well, with no support from the statistical analyses for the proposition that federalism affects party unity. The graphical comparisons of voting unity indices across regimes with and without elected presidents suggest that presidentialism disrupts party unity, consistent with H3, and there is some statistical support for this proposition, although the effect is significant only when assemblies where nonvoting = nay are included in the analysis.

Both H3a and H3b, regarding the relative impact of being in government in systems with and without elected presidents, find some support in

Table 6.5. *Summary of Hypothesis Tests*

Hypothesized Effect	WRICE$_i$	%WON$_i$	RLOSER$_i$
Competing principals hypotheses			
H1: Intraparty electoral competition reduces unity	(✔)		✔
H2: Federalism reduces unity			
H3: Presidentialism reduces party unity	(✔)		
H3a: Parliamentarism strengthens governing parties		✔	
H3b: Governing parties weaker under			
presidentialism than parliamentarism		✔	✔
Other hypotheses			
H4: Confidence vote increases unity			
H5: Parties more unified in longer-established regimes			
H6: Older parties more unified than newer ones	✔		
H7: Parties more unified in fragmented party systems			

the results on vote outcomes. In parliamentary systems, governing parties win more than their share of votes (%WON). Governing parties in presidential systems, by contrast, win at lower rates, and when they lose, they do so more frequently due to cross-voting. Presidentialist governing parties, in fact, appear to be at no legislative advantage even relative to their own opposition. Controlling for Seat Share, they win at no higher rate and suffer disunity losses more often.

Table 6.5 summarizes the evidence for each hypothesis against WRICE$_i$, %WON$_i$, and RLOSER$_i$. Check marks indicate that the hypothesis finds support in the multilevel analysis. The competing principals hypotheses are listed at the top. All except H2, regarding federalism, find some support.

The hypotheses based on other, noncompeting principals rationales find little support. There is no evidence that existence of a confidence vote affects voting unity, although it is important to acknowledge that the data here make it difficult to estimate separately the potential effects of the confidence vote from the effects of independently elected presidents at the system level. As more legislative voting data become available from hybrid systems, it will be possible to disentangle these stories. Nor is there support for the idea that parties are more unified in longer-established regimes, nor in regimes with greater levels of party system fragmentation. Older parties exhibit lower levels of cross-voting (WRICE$_i$), making H6 the only noncompeting principals hypothesis supported by the multilevel analysis.

6.8. Extending the Analysis

6.8.1. Governing and Opposition Coalitions

Most party systems do not regularly produce single-party legislative majorities. Multiparty coalitions are generally necessary to form and sustain a government under regimes that include the confidence vote provision, and scholarship on presidential democracies increasingly recognizes the key role played by multiparty coalitions in organizing executives and building legislative majorities (Amorim Neto 2002, 2006; Carey 2002; Powell 2000; Siavelis 2000). The central role of coalitions in legislative politics suggests that it is worthwhile to take advantage of the flexibility of the voting unity indices developed here to apply them to governing and opposition coalitions as wholes, in order to run another analysis complementary to that on parties themselves.

For the purpose of calculating government and opposition voting unity indices, I coded all legislators in an assembly from parties that held cabinet portfolios for more than half of the period from which votes were collected as being inside the government coalition. All others are lumped into a single opposition coalition. This means that the opposition "coalition" is frequently not a coalition in any formal sense but rather a residual category that may well include legislators with widely disparate preferences and ideological tendencies. There may be organized and internally coherent opposition blocs in many legislatures – for example, parties that had formed preelectoral coalitions before the previous election – but because I did not have information on such blocs across all the assemblies and time periods, I relied on the crude method of lumping all nongovernment legislators together. This means the baseline level of unity to be expected within opposition coalitions is modest.

6.8.2. Adapting the Statistical Model

Having calculated the familiar voting unity indices for government and opposition coalitions in each assembly, I rely on the familiar multilevel statistical model, as in the preceding analysis of parties. The independent variables describing political institutions and regime age are the same. I do not include a measure of party system fragmentation, given that the analysis includes only a single government and opposition coalition within each assembly. I do, however, include a coalition-level variable, Multiparty Coalition, indicating whether a coalition consisted of legislators from more than one party. The Seat Share variable is the percentage of assembly seats held by all the parties in a given coalition.

As in the b and c models from Table 6.4, I am parsimonious about including system-level variables in the models on WRICE$_i$ and RLOSER$_i$ to preserve degrees of freedom at that level. I include Intra-party Competition, which is associated with lower WRICE$_i$ indices, and Presidential, given the prominence of the cross-level interactive variable, Government Coalition * Presidential (Brambor, Clarke, and Golder 2006).

6.8.3. Results: Government Bonus under Parliamentarism but Not Presidentialism

Table 6.6 presents the results of the regressions. As with parties, intraparty electoral competition diminishes voting unity in coalitions. This may be a manifestation of the diminution of voting unity fostered by such competition within the parties that make up broader coalitions, but it may also reflect a greater level of legislative individualism within such assemblies generally. The effect is large, negative, and significant at .01 on coalition WRICEi indices, and positive (as expected) but not significant for RLOSER$_i$. By contrast, presidentialism has no measurable impact on either of the coalition voting unity measures. All system-level variables, including Federal and Regime Age, are included as controls in Model 5.

Moving to the coalition-level variables, bigger coalitions experience a bit more cross-voting (lower WRICE$_i$, per Model 4) than smaller ones, although the estimated effect falls short of statistical significance. Bigger coalitions win more frequently (Model 5), as expected, and they lose because of vote defections more often (Model 6). Multiparty coalitions experience more cross-voting than single-party groups, win less frequently, and lose because of defections more, although the latter two effects are not significant.

Of primary interest in the coalition analysis, however, are the conditional effects of being in or out of government. Governing coalitions in parliamentary systems are more unified than opposition coalitions, with nearly a full standard deviation boost in WRICE$_i$ (.15), a 38-point boost in percentage of

Table 6.6. *Multilevel Analysis of Legislative Voting Unity within Governing and Opposition Coalitions*

Independent Variables	Dependent Variables		
	WRICE$_i$ Model 4	%WON$_i$ Model 5	RLOSER$_i$ Model 6
System level			
Intraparty Competition	−.17*** (.07)	.10* (.06)	.008 (.030)
Presidential	.03 (.08)	.16* (.09)	.002 (.035)
Federal		−.16*** (.06)	
Regime Age (log)		−.02 (.02)	
Party level			
Seat Share	−.22 (.14)	.63*** (.17)	.010* (.060)
Multiparty Coalition	−.14** (.06)	−.09 (.07)	.020 (.025)
Government Coalition	.15** (.07)	.38*** (.08)	−.051* (.030)
Government Coalition* Presidential	−.08 (.08)	−.23*** (10)	.009 (.035)
Constant	.91*** (.10)	.37** (.15)	.012 (.045)
H0: Government Coalition + GovCoal* Presidential − Presidential = 0	.04 (.10)	−.02 (.12)	−.044 (.046)
Proportion of variance explained			
System level	.53	.60	.04
Party level	.31	.55	.21
N (coalitions)	68	68	68
N (assemblies)	14	14	14

Note: Observations from Philippines (no information on governing coalition), Russia (nonpartisan president), Nicaragua and Guatemala (nonvotes = nays), and Uruguay (records only from votes in joint sessions on constitutional amendments) excluded.
* Significant at > .10 level. ** Significant at > .05 level. *** Significant at > .01 level.

votes won, and a 5.1 percent reduction in the rate of losses due to cross-voting – the mean rate of which across all observations is 6.9 percent.

Whereas governing coalitions in parliamentary systems are more unified, win more votes, and lose less frequently because of disunity than opposition coalitions, the coefficients on Governing Coalition * Presidential indicate that this unity boost is diminished in presidential regimes (more cross-voting, more losses, and more defection losses), although the marginal effect reaches statistical significance only with regard to winning percentage. The linear combination of Government Coalition + GovCoal * Presidential – Presidential (at the bottom of Table 6.6) indicates that governing coalitions in regimes with presidents are statistically indistinguishable from opposition coalitions in presidential systems on either of the unity indices or on overall average. Recall, however, that in each assembly, unity indices for opposition coalitions lump all nongovernment parties together, so the bar for a governing coalition to surpass is quite low. This makes the result on overall legislative win rates, in particular, all the more striking. As with parties, these results suggest that presidents are no legislative asset at all to the coalitions through which they endeavor to govern. In pure parliamentary systems, government coalitions are more unified and more successful (even controlling for Seat Share) in winning votes, but the government unity boost vanishes altogether in the presence of presidents.

6.9. Conclusion: Competing Principals Disrupt Voting Unity

The evidence in this chapter supports the competing principals approach to legislative representation, the basic idea of which is that almost all legislators are subordinate to party leaders within their assembly, and the extent to which party groups are unified or cohesive depends on whether other principals, with competing demands, also control resources to pressure legislators. To the extent that such competing principals elicit responsiveness from legislators, they drive wedges into party groups, which we observe in vote patterns and vote outcomes. This chapter looked for sources of competition among principals in the constitutional and electoral rules that govern legislative politics, and in how these institutions interact with the status of parties inside and outside government.

6.9.1. Electoral Rules Matter

The evidence here supports some arguments, but fails to support others, about the effects of institutions on legislative party unity that have either been derived theoretically, or advanced on the basis of evidence from a smaller number of cases, or both. These results are based on a broader cross-national dataset than any previous study, which affords greater leverage in estimating system-level effects and for disentangling these from party-level effects. For example, a number of scholars have attributed disunity within parties to intraparty preference voting (Cain, Ferejohn, and Fiorina 1987; Mainwaring and Pérez-Liñán 1997; Garman, Haggard, and Willis 2001), whereas others rightly cautioned that, in the absence of evidence from legislative voting itself, inferring levels of party cohesiveness from voting rules alone was premature (Figueiredo and Limongi 2000). The results here should dispel uncertainty on this count.

6.9.2. *No Evidence of a Federalism Effect*

Federalism has been identified as weakening national-level parties in case studies of India and Brazil (Chhibber and Kollman 1998; Mainwaring 1999), although the most sophisticated studies to date of legislative voting patterns estimate the effect on party voting unity to be relatively small or undetectable (Desposato 2004b; Jones and Hwang 2005). The results here, with considerably extended empirical reach, find no evidence that federalism per se affects levels of legislative voting unity. It may be that the blunt measure of constitutional federalism employed here is insufficiently sensitive to capture varying levels to which power within national parties is decentralized, or to which there is regional heterogeneity within parties, or both.

6.9.3. *Governments Differ in Parliamentary and Presidential Systems*

The most important new results are found in the differences between parliamentary and presidential systems on governing party unity. The differences reported here do not rely on the presence or absence of the confidence vote provision, which is at the center of many discussions of party discipline. Rather, they are based on how the existence and influence of a popularly elected president can disrupt party voting unity generally, and an account of how being in government differs in presidential and parliamentary regimes. Take two parties, or two coalitions, of the same size. Put one in government under parliamentarism, and the additional resources should boost its legislative effectiveness. By contrast, hand that party or coalition the presidency, and you should expect no such advantage.

Studies of the presidency in specific countries frequently conclude that the office is unusually strong, even dominant over the legislature. In the literature, presidents appear to be an unusually potent breed. The results here suggest reassessing this verdict, at least with regard to legislative influence. Parties allied with presidents do not do any better on the floor of the legislature than others. Presidents may dominate their local political theaters in various ways but not by directing the actions of unified battalions of legislators.

For all their stature and the resources they command, presidents are disruptive to party unity because they present a potentially competing source of directives against those of party leaders within the legislature. Legislative leaders in parties outside government need not contend with such a formidable competitor in coordinating the actions of their troops. The incentives for presidents to stake out positions "above" politics and to carry themselves as suprapartisan actors, even when they have won election on the basis of party support, buttress this effect. And the resources – political and material – that presidents command in most systems provide them ample currency with which to curry legislative favor. By this account, it is not presidential weakness per se that is the source of party disunity but presidential power. Power can be understood as a source of party disunity, however, only if one is attentive to the institutional environment in which legislative parties operate. The aim of the competing principals theory is to focus attention on the elements of that environment that shape the strength of party leaders and the various actors with whom they compete for legislators' loyalties.

7

The Individual-Collective Balance

7.1. Transparency, Party Unity, Votes, and Accountability

This book asks, Who are the political actors in a position to place demands on lawmakers and, given the mix of pressures, what kind of legislative accountability can we expect? The focus throughout is on legislators' votes. Whatever other important representative and policymaking activities transpire in assemblies, votes remain the core blocks on which legislative decisions are built. I concentrate on whether votes can be easily monitored by those outside the legislature – their visibility – and, in those legislatures where votes are recorded and available for analysis, on patterns of voting among parties.

These two elements of legislative voting, transparency and party unity, are key components of two distinct types of legislative accountability: individual and collective. When the votes of individual legislators are not visible, it is difficult for those outside the legislature to know whether a representative has acted in accordance with their preferences. Some measure of voting unity within groups is necessary for collective accountability as well, because, if its members do not vote together regularly, a group cannot be regarded as shaping legislative outcomes.

Transparency and voting unity are matters of degree, not absolutes, and much of the book is an effort to document and then to explain how much of each we see across various legislatures. The first task is primarily one of mapping – of visiting legislatures, personally and virtually, in order to discover what information about votes is available. Where voting records can be had, we can expand and improve the map by turning the quantity of ayes, nays, and nonvotes into statistical descriptors of voting unity. The explanatory work in the book relies on a combination of "soaking and poking" (Fenno 1978) to determine which political actors favor transparency and which do not, and developing a model of the forces that play on legislators, and so affect their proclivities toward party voting unity. I refer to the actors that apply these pressures as legislators' principals, and I argue that party unity is a product of the extent to which these principals pull in different directions.

The explanations of transparency and party unity are related because principals that apply competing pressures force a measure of individualism upon legislators. Deciding how to vote when one's legislative party pulls one way and the president another, for example, is an act of self-definition. If the vote is visible to citizens, then the same act that diminishes party unity, and so might erode collective accountability, can also provide a building block for individual accountability.

7.2. Reviewing the Major Points

- The ideal of legislative accountability is afflicted by a fundamental tension between individualism and collectivism.

Individual accountability implies that legislators answer to the specific demands of citizens in their behavior, including voting. Collective accountability implies that teams of legislators – mainly parties and coalitions, in most legislatures – act collectively to promote a policy agenda and are evaluated by citizens as a group according to their effectiveness in advancing it. Where constituents – even supporters of the same party or coalition – put diverse demands on legislators, the demands of individual accountability can contradict the collective action on which collective accountability is based.

- Academic work on legislative accountability displays a normative proclivity for the collective variety, but there are signs of a push toward individual accountability in legislatures themselves.

There is a venerable tradition of scholarship on legislative accountability that extols strong-party government, mainly on the grounds that strong parties facilitate clear options for voters over policy platforms. Nevertheless, political reforms in many Latin American countries have aimed at boosting individual accountability, even at the expense of strong parties. Politicians' survey responses demonstrate a pronounced bent toward greater individualism. Survey responses may be cheap talk, perhaps reflecting only what the politicians think citizens want to hear. Even if so, though, this would indicate that politicians believe that citizens want more individualistic and less party-centered representation from their legislators. What limited evidence is available from public opinion surveys suggests that this is, indeed, what citizens want. At any rate, there appears to be a disjuncture between what much of the academic literature on legislative representation prescribes and what politicians and reformers aim to deliver.

- Visible votes are an essential component of individual accountability. They are in scarce supply in many legislatures, but time and technology push toward more visible voting.

The mechanics of voting in legislative assemblies can produce a fundamental asymmetry in the ability of legislative insiders (most prominently, legislative party leaders) and outsiders (everyone else, including citizens, organized interest groups, the media, and academics) to monitor legislators' behavior. The historical and institutional contexts differed considerably, but the adoption and expansion of recorded voting in the United States and in some countries in Latin America have pushed accountability in similar directions. On the whole, visible voting has been favored by opposition legislators and has been used to force unpopular measures advanced by majority parties and coalitions onto the public record. Interviews support the idea that recording and publishing legislative votes facilitate external monitoring, foster fair play in legislative procedures, discourage legislators from obfuscating their records, allow voters to reward or punish legislators for votes in elections, and may affect legislative decisions in anticipation of such effects.

The supply of recorded votes is limited in most Latin American legislatures, largely because of reluctance about visible voting on the part of party leaders who strive to maintain a tight grip on the rules of legislative procedure. Nevertheless, the increasing availability of secure and efficient electronic voting systems has driven down dramatically the procedural costs of recording votes and making them visible. Moreover, once some set of conditions – a presidential initiative, for example, or a successful minority-led reform – allows for the establishment of visible voting as standard operating procedure, the practice appears difficult to revoke, perhaps owing to the widespread belief among politicians that citizens want more transparency in legislative institutions, even at the cost of strong party control.

167

- Electoral rules matter to what sort of accountability legislators deliver. The familiar SMD-versus-PR distinction is not what drives the individualism-versus-collectivism trade-off, but it does affect incentives for candidates to deliver information that facilitates individual accountability.

The distinction between single-member districts and proportional representation is central to so much scholarship on electoral systems that academic attention frequently gravitates there unreflectively. Yet one finds highly individualist, and highly collectivist, legislative representation on both sides of the SMD-PR divide. Electoral rules can encourage, or discourage, individualism, but they do so by shaping the range of principals to whom legislators respond. The more a centralized national party leadership monopolizes access to the electoral resources legislators value, the more dominant the party is as its legislators' common principal, and representation is more collective. When electoral resources are more decentralized, legislators of the same party diversify their appeals, responding to a more heterogeneous group of principals, placing a greater premium on individualistic representation. The trade-off here has little to do with single-member districts versus proportional representation and much to do with the number and nature of principals to which legislators respond.

Although either SMD or PR electoral systems can foster individualistic (or collective) representation, the number of candidates competing for votes in a given district affects the electoral advantage to be had by publicizing the record of one's electoral opponents. Specifically, the fewer other candidates competing, the greater the expected gain to any given candidate from critically exposing an incumbent legislator's record. The number of candidates tends to rise with district magnitude. Therefore, this particular transmission belt for information about incumbent legislators' voting records – negative campaigning by other candidates – should be more effective in elections with low district magnitudes than where magnitudes are higher.

- Recording votes, in addition to making individual-level visibility possible, also makes it possible to measure voting unity across parties, coalitions, or any group of interest within an assembly.

The indices developed here can be used to generate statistics that describe the voting unity of any group. Because parties are the universal unit of collective representation in modern democratic legislatures, and because party unity is widely regarded as a key condition for collective accountability, party voting unity is of natural interest. I generate statistics to describe parties' levels of mobilization, cross-voting, their overall success in winning recorded votes, and their incidence of losses attributable to undermobilization and cross-voting. These statistics allow for cross-national and cross-temporal comparisons of party unity, for example, either statistically or graphically.

- Other things being equal, the more the institutional context establishes alternative principals with control over resources legislators value, the lower is party unity.

The institutional context affects the relative value to legislators of collective party labels versus individualism in voting. For example, longer-established political parties tend to mobilize their legislators at higher levels, and levels of cross-voting are lower, suggesting that the communicative value of party labels increases with time. For some institutional factors, I find no evidence of effects on voting unity. The voting indices do not support hypotheses that federalism undermines party unity, or that the availability of a confidence vote mechanism boosts it. There is support, however, for other hypotheses regarding the effects of competing principals on unity. When candidates must compete with their own copartisans for individual support among voters, their responsiveness to personalized constituencies diminishes party voting unity. Presidents represent another potential principal to compete with party leaders for legislators' loyalties, and cross-voting is more common across the board in systems with elected presidents. Moreover, although governing parties in parliamentary systems are highly unified and successful at winning votes, governing parties in presidential systems have no advantage in voting unity. They are no more unified or successful on the floor, other things being equal, than opposition parties. The same distinction applies to governing coalitions in parliamentary versus presidential systems. Whereas the resources associated with membership in government may be an asset to voting unity under parliamentarism, the potential for presidents to compete with legislative party and coalition leaders appears to render them a liability to voting unity.

7.3. The Optimal Mix?

7.3.1. The Cases For, and Against, Various Institutional Arrangements

The crux of the competing principals account of party unity advanced here is that when more than one actor (principal) influences who gets elected under a party label and controls resources legislators care about, divergence in the demands of these principals will reduce legislative party unity. The case for collective accountability regards party voting unity as a necessary condition. I have suggested that institutional arrangements that increase legislators' responsiveness to principals other than national party leaders can push in the direction of individual accountability. The tension between individual and collective accountability raises the inevitable question of whether there is some optimal mix of the two, and whether the design of political institutions can affect whether legislative representation hits that target.

Academic research on accountability up to now does not provide a conclusive answer. Some of the most creative recent theoretical work on accountability focuses on governments or representatives as monolithic selectors of policy (Manin, Przeworski, and Stokes 1999; Fearon 1999; Ferejohn 1999), or else on the accountability of presidents alone (Stokes 2001). Among research that discusses legislators and parties explicitly, the enduring argument for strong-party government holds unity as an unqualified collective good, both in providing coherent options to voters in elections and in delivering decisive government (American Political Science Association 1950).

The theme remains central in contemporary scholarship. Powell and Whitten (1993) include party cohesion as one of the four factors that determine whether voters can assign responsibility to their elected representatives for policy outcomes, and so hold them accountable. Johnson and Crisp (2003) demonstrate that the ideological predisposition of legislative majorities can account for economic policies where president-centered explanations cannot, but that the connection between legislative party platforms and the policies implemented is stronger when electoral rules discourage individualism. The implication is that collective representation strengthens the connection between what voters ask for and what they get. Gerring, Thacker, and Moreno (2005) make a more sweeping claim, that political institutions that centralize government authority in strong national parties produce superior policy outcomes on dimensions ranging from bureaucratic efficiency to investment security to public health and education. The clear prescription is that representation works best when legislators answer directly and unequivocally to their parties as principals.

The related theme that institutions that encourage party disunity produce political pathologies is also prominent. Golden and Chang (2001) attribute corruption scandals in campaign finance to the degree of intraparty competition among Christian Democratic legislators in Italy. Hallerberg and Mairer (2004) contend that personal vote seeking generates common-pool resource problems whereby legislators under-value fiscal discipline.

Yet there are competing claims in the scholarship on accountability, with respect both to centralization of authority and to the idea that legislative individualism is an unmitigated liability. On centralization, the Madisonian theme that the division of legislative from executive authority enhances accountability of representatives retains some support. Persson, Roland, and Tabellini (1997) argue that competition between the branches, institutionalized under presidentialism, increases the amount of information politicians supply to citizens about other politicians' misdeeds, such that the cumulative effect of increased individual accountability is improved government accountability in the aggregate. Hellwig and Samuels (2007) show that electoral support for presidents' parties more closely tracks economic growth rates than does that of prime ministers' parties in pure parliamentary systems. It may be that the separation of powers allows for a more specialized brand of accountability whereby voters can evaluate presidents and legislators according to their responsiveness to separate sets of demands (Samuels and Shugart 2003), or that presidentialism's fixed terms prevent midterm replacements of the chief executive so common under parliamentarism, which in turn weaken accountability by sheltering those responsible for policy failures from voters' wrath (Cheibub and Przeworski 1999).

Finally, intraparty competition in legislative elections has its own defenders. Kunicová and Rose-Ackerman (2005) argue that open-list competition discourages collusion among would-be rent seekers, and their data from across ninety-four countries suggest such elections reduce corruption. Farrell and McAllister (2004) argue that voters regard the fairness of elections to be higher and are more satisfied with democracy overall, where elections allow for personal preference votes among individual legislative candidates than in closed-list systems.

Current scholarship on democratic institutions provides evidence to support both the normative goal of collective accountability and the idea that individual accountability is a democratic asset. Yet the two types of accountability make contradictory demands on legislators, and we know relatively little about how the trade-off between these ideals operates. Discussions of individualism versus collectivism in legislative representation tend to proceed as though the trade-off were a straightforward matter of swapping a unit of one sort of accountability for a unit of the other, but

171

accountability is notoriously difficult to measure. And even if we could measure both individual and collective accountability among legislators, there is no reason to assume that the substitution of one for the other is always zero sum.

7.3.2. Individualism versus Individual Accountability

The subtle but critical distinction here is between legislative individualism and individual accountability. Consider, for example, the model of legislative individualism proposed by Carey and Shugart (1995), and refined and applied in various studies since (Wallack, Gaviria, Panizza, and Stein 2003; Hallerberg and Mairer 2004). The model posits that, in elections with intra-party competition, incentives for individualism rise monotonically, and those for collectivism drop correspondingly, as the number of copartisans against which a given candidate must compete rises. There is empirical evidence to support this proposition about individualism (Crisp and Ingall 2002; Carey and Reinhardt 2004; Shugart, Valdini, and Suominen 2005). Yet it does not follow that maximizing individualism per se also maximizes individual accountability. Accountability rests on the coordination of behavior, information, and sanctioning mechanisms among representatives and their constituents. Intraparty competition in large multimember districts might maximize individualism, but larger districts also decrease the quality of information delivered to voters about specific candidates and increase coordination problems among voters in sanctioning incumbents (Desposato 2004a; Cox 1997). Recall, for example, the elections in Afghanistan under the single nontransferable vote (SNTV) rule, described in Chapter 1.

It follows that the conditions to enhance individual accountability are not necessarily those which maximize individualism and minimize collective representation. Specifically, individual accountability thrives when citizens are provided sufficient information about the actions of individual legislators and are able to use that information to reward or punish at the polls. When the number of candidates grows too high, the supply and quality of information about each legislator's record decline, and the cognitive challenge voters face in processing candidate-specific information rises (Desposato 2004a; Reynolds 2006). The distinction between legislative individualism and individual accountability suggests that the tension between individual and collective accountability might be better represented as a maximization problem than as an even swap. I defer to future research the formidable task of measuring the contours of this trade-off empirically, but the case of Chilean democracy since the reestablishment of civilian government in 1990 offers an instructive example.

7.3.3. Chile's Blend of Individualism and Party Unity

In 1989, on the eve of Chile's transition from military authoritarianism back to civilian democracy, the outgoing government imposed a unique system for legislative elections. It called for all elected legislators to be chosen in open-list competition, but with every district electing two representatives (i.e., magnitude = 2).[1] Votes for both candidates from each electoral alliance, or list, are first pooled in order to determine the distribution of seats across lists in the district, then candidates from winning lists are awarded seats in order of their personal preference votes. Thus, the collective performance of the list affects candidates' prospects, but candidates from the same list also compete with each other for preference votes.[2]

Chile's open-list elections in low-magnitude districts have contributed to the formation and maintenance of stable multiparty coalitions among both governing and opposition parties (Siavelis 2000; Londregan 2001). The coalitions have proved relatively unified in the legislature, to a greater degree than the ideological proximity of their component parties alone would predict, and have developed collective reputations that convey substantial information to voters (Carey 1998). At the same time, Chile's combination of presidentialism and personal vote seeking in elections moderates the tendency toward collectivism in legislative representation. Figure 7.1 shows $WRICE_i$ and $RLOSER_i$ indices for parties in the Chilean Chamber of Deputies, based on recorded votes for a nine-month period at the end of the second post-transition congress.[3] The president's Christian

---

[1] The outgoing regime's motives for choosing this system were not benign. It sought to cushion the anticipated defeat of its civilian politician allies in the ensuing elections. The unusual conditions by which Chile's electoral rule was imposed over the objections of its incipient governing majority mitigate the problem of endogeneity of institutions that is intractable in much of comparative politics (Przeworski 2007). As a result, Chile presents an unusually favorable environment for testing the effects of institutions on political behavior.

[2] Note that I refer here to electoral alliances as running lists, rather than parties. This is because Chilean electoral law allows parties to coalesce to run lists, and indeed almost all seats in Chilean elections under this system have been won by candidates from coalition lists. As a result, Chilean elections have been characterized by intracoalition competition but not by intraparty competition.

[3] A figure based on votes from the third congress is virtually identical. The mobilization-based indices, $WUNITY_i$ and $ULOSER$, are suspect in the Chilean case, because the uniform drop-off across parties from $WRICE_i$ to $WUNITY_i$ suggests nonvoting equilibria.

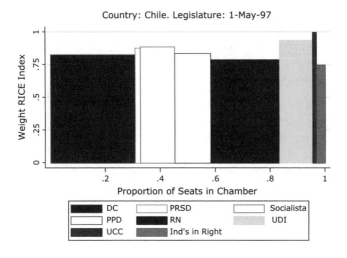

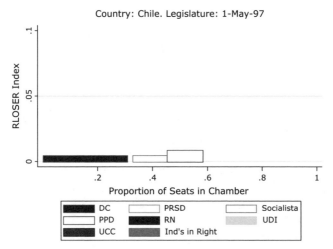

Figure 7.1 WRICE$_i$ and RLOSER$_i$ in the Chilean Chamber of Deputies, 1997–98.

Democratic (DC) party is shown at the left of each panel in black with the other parties in the governing coalition in white, and opposition parties in varying gray hues toward the right of each panel.

The parties in Chile's governing coalition experienced more cross-voting (mean WRICE$_i$ = .86) than do governing parties in pure parliamentary systems (mean WRICE$_i$ = .93), but less than governing parties in other presidential systems (mean WRICE$_i$ = .76). Chile's opposition parties were, on average, just slightly more unified (mean $WRICE_i = .87$) than their government counterparts. Opposition parties experienced no floor losses due to cross-voting in this period and governing parties were RLOSERs on 0.6 percent of votes – the same rate as governing parties in parliamentary regimes, and below the 3 percent average among governing parties elsewhere under presidentialism. These figures suggest sufficient party unity so that collective representation is viable in Chile, even while individual legislators seek personal votes and voters maintain the ability to retain or reject specific representatives. In the election following the period on which Figure 7.1 is based, 85 of 120 Chamber incumbents were nominated for reelection, and of these, 72 – that is, 85 percent of those on the ballot, 60 percent of all incumbents – won a successive term.

Chilean political institutions are not beyond criticism, and the electoral system, in particular, is subject to regular proposals for reform (Altman 2005; Huneeus 2006).[4] Yet Chilean democracy since 1990 has delivered a respectable combination of collective and individual legislative accountability (Cox 2006b). Elections have produced governing coalitions that are easily identifiable by voters and that, once in office, have generally advanced the policies and platforms on which they campaigned. Governments have met with regular, although not uniform, success on the floor of Congress. Chilean presidents throughout this period have occasionally been publicly at odds with the leaders of their allied parties and coalition, but the more common scenario has been mutual cooperation. As a result, government-sponsored legislative proposals have mostly been successful, although sometimes only after prolonged periods of legislative deliberation (Siavelis 2000; Londregan 2001). The conventional economic indicators by which governments are judged have been consistently strong in Chile during this period, and voters have rewarded the governing coalition with reelection to the presidency three times and returned majorities from that coalition to the legislature in four consecutive elections. These same

---

[4] The most persistent criticisms stem from the lack of proportionality and the high barriers to entry inherent in the two-member district system. Increasing district magnitude could remedy this, as opportunities for minority-party representation increase rapidly with increments in magnitude in this range. In order to improve proportionality while maintaining the conditions for effective individual accountability and avoiding rampant individualism, reformers might retain candidate preference voting but embrace only modest increases in magnitude. At magnitudes above 5 or 6, the informational demands on Chilean voters imposed by open-list competition would threaten individual accountability, and the incentives for individualism could undermine party unity sufficiently to threaten collective accountability.

voters can select individual legislators from among fields of candidates small enough that campaigns are not mere cacophonies of individualistic appeals. They have taken the opportunity to exercise that discretion, rewarding some, but not all, incumbents with reelection.

7.3.4. What's Next?

The search for the optimal balance between collective and individual accountability among legislators may turn out to be dissatisfying in the same way as Goldilocks's method for identifying good porridge. Critics tend to think they know too much collectivism when they see it, and widespread complaints about "partyarchy" and boss rule suggest they see it a lot. Other critics see too little collectivism and are prone to complain about particularism and rudderless parties. There is no mix of individual and collective accountability widely recognized to be "just right."

This book might represent a step toward identifying that balance, but its primary goals are descriptive and explanatory, not normative. It describes two types of accountability and explains how legislative votes can be the medium through which each is delivered. It documents the levels of transparency and party unity of legislative voting across a wide array of legislatures. It offers explanations for why voting transparency has increased in some instances, and for how and why it can be expected to increase in others. It explains levels of voting unity according to how the institutional environment in which legislative parties operate shapes the diversity of demands placed on lawmakers.

The empirical contribution here is largely one of mapping more of the legislative world in terms of transparency and party unity. The field of legislative studies is highly developed in the United States, largely because the long record of voting transparency in the U.S. Congress has fueled a vibrant field of study on recorded votes. Transparency is in its relative infancy in many other legislatures, but has made big strides recently, and we should expect further advances. This will facilitate mapping the world of legislative voting more completely and precisely, as well as the development of analytical tools that may provide better leverage in evaluating accountability, and the conditions that enhance and subvert it in its distinct forms.

Appendix: Interview Subjects by Country

Name	Office	Party[a]
Bolivia (La Paz, May 14–16, 2001)		
Bedregal, Guillermo	Deputy	MNR
Brockmann, Ericka	Senator; party leader	MIR
Cárdenas, Víctor Hugo	Ex-deputy, ex-vice president of the Republic	MRTA
Carvajal Donoso, Hugo	Cabinet minister; ex-president of Chamber of Deputies	MIR
Ferrufino, Alfonso	Ex-deputy	MBL
Sánchez de Lozada, Gonzalo	Party leader, ex-president of the Republic	MNR
Sánchez Bezraín, Carlos	Deputy	MNR
Colombia (Bogota, May 1–4, 2001)		
Acosta, Amilkar	Senator	PL
Andrade, Hernán	Representative	PC
Blum de Barberi, Claudia	Senador	Movimiento '98
Devia, Javier	Representative	PC
García Valencia, Jesús Ignacio	Representative	PL
Gómez Gallo, Luis Humberto	Senator	PC
Guerra, Antonio	Senator	PL
Gutiérrez, Nancy Patricia	Representative	PL
Holguín Sardi, Carlos	Senator	PC
Navarro, Antonio	Senator	MVA
Orduz, Rafael	Senator	ASI/MCA
Rivera Salazar, Rodrigo	Senator	PL

(continued)

Name	Office	Party[a]
Costa Rica (San Jose, May 22–26, 2000)		
Castillo, Fernando	Auditor general of the Republic	
De La Cruz, Vladimir	Deputy; party leader	PFDN
Gonzalez, Eladio	Assembly staff	
Guevara, Otto	Deputy	ML
Guido, Célimo	Deputy; party leader	PFDN
Hernández, Oscar	Assembly staff	
Morales, Humberto	Assembly staff	
Sibaja, Alex	Deputy; party leader	PLN
Vargas, Eliséo	Deputy; party leader	PUSC
Vargas Pagán, Carlos	Deputy; ex-president of the Assembly	PUSC
Ecuador (Quito, May 18–22, 2001)		
Albornoz, Vicente	Deputy	PS
González, Carlos	Deputy	ID
Landazuri, Guillermo	Deputy	ID
Lucero, Wilfredo	Deputy; party leader	ID
Neira, Xavier	Deputy; party leader	PSC
Pons, Juan José	Deputy	DP
Vajello Arcos, Andrés	Ex-deputy; ex-president of Congress	ID
Vajello López, Carlos	Deputy; ex-president of Congress	
Vela, Alexandra	Deputy	DP
El Salvador (San Salvador, August 16–18, 2000)		
Alvarenga, Aristides	Deputy	PDC
Alvarenga, Rolando	Deputy; party leader	ARENA
Duch, Juan	Deputy; ex-president of Assembly	ARENA
Pineda, Armando	Assembly staff	
Zamora, Rubén	Ex-deputy; party leader	CD
Nicaragua (Managua, August 21–22, 2000)		
Baltodano, Mónica	Deputy	FSLN
Bolaños, María Lourdes	Deputy	FSLN
Hurtado, Carlos	Deputy; party leader	AC
Samper, Jorge	Deputy	MRS
Urbina Noguera, Luis	Deputy	PLC

Appendix

Name	Office	Party[a]
Peru (Lima, May 7–9, 2001)		
Blanco Oropeza, Carlos	Deputy; ex-president of Congress	C90-NM
Cevasco Piedra, José	Assembly staff	
De Althaus, Jaime	Political talk show host (*La Hora N*)	
Masías, Manuel	Deputy	Independent
Ortiz de Zevallos, Gabriel	Pollster (Instituto de Apoyo)	
Pease, Henry	Deputy; party leader	UPP
Venezuela (March 2–10, 2000)		
Combellas, Ricardo	Deputy (Constituent Assembly)	Independent
Fernández, Julio César	Deputy (Interim Assembly)	Independent
Murillo, Alexis	Assembly staff	
Tarek Saab, William	Deputy	MVR

[a] AC: Accion Conservador; ARENA: Alianza para la Renovacion Nacional; ASI/MCA: Alianza Social Indigena/MCA; C90-NM: Cambio 90 – Nueva Mayoria; CD: Convergencia Democratica; DP: Democracia y Progreso; FSLN: Frente Sandinista para la Liberacion Nacional; ID: Izquierda Democratica; MBL: Movimiento Bolivia Libre; MIR: Movimiento Izquierdista Revolucionario; ML: Movimiento Libertario; MNR: Movimiento Nacional Revolucionario; MRS: Movimiento Renovacion Sandinismo; MRTA: Movimiento Revolucionario Tupac Amaru; MVA: Movimiento Via Alterna; MVR: Movimiento Quinta Republica; PC: Partido Conservador; PDC: Partido Democrata Cristiana; PFDN: Partido Frente Democratico Nacional; PL: Partido Liberal; PLC: Partido Liberal Constitucionalista; PLN: Patido Liberacion Nacional; PS: Partido Socialista; PSC: Partido Social Cristiano; PUSC: Partido Union Social Cristiano; UPP: Union por el Peru.

References

Adserá Alicia, Carles Boix, and Mark Payne. 2003. "Are You Being Served? Political Accountability and Quality of Government." *Journal of Law, Economics, and Organization* 19(2): 445–90.

Alcántara, Manuel. 1994–2000. *Proyecto Elites Latinoamericanos (PELA)*. Salamanca, Spain: Instituto Interuniversitario de Iberoamérica (Universidad de Salamanca).

Aldrich, John H. 1995. *Why Parties? The Origin and Transformation of Political Parties in America*. Chicago: University of Chicago Press.

Aleman, Eduardo, and George Tsebelis. 2005. "Presidential Conditional Agenda Setting in Latin America." *World Politics* 57(3): 396–420.

Altman, David. 2005. *"De un sistema paralelo a un compensatorio (proporcional personalizado)."* Santiago, Chile: Instituto de Ciencia Politica, Pontificia Universidad Catolica de Chile.

American Political Science Association. 1950. *Toward a More Responsible Two-Party System*. New York: Rinehart.

Ames, Barry. 1995. "Electoral Strategy under Open List Proportional Representation." *American Journal of Political Science* 39(2): 406–33.

———. 2002. "Party Discipline in the Chamber of Deputies." In *Legislative Politics in Latin America*, ed. Scott Morgenstern and Benito Nacif, 185–221. Cambridge: Cambridge University Press.

Amorim Neto, Octavio. 2002. "Presidential Cabinets, Electoral Cycles, and Coalition Discipline in Brazil." In *Legislative Politics in Latin America*, ed. Scott Morgenstern and Benito Nacif, 48–78. Cambridge: Cambridge University Press.

———. 2006. *Presidencialismo e governabilidade nas Americas*. Rio de Janeiro: Editora Fundacion Getulio Vargas.

Amorim Neto, Octavio, Gary W. Cox, and Mathew D. McCubbins. 2003. "Agenda Power in Brazil's Camara dos Deputados, 1989–98." *World Politics* 55(4): 550–78.

Asamblea Nacional de Panamá. 2005. http://www.asamblea.gob.pa/.

Associación de Derechos Civiles. 2004. "Ley de Reforma Laboral: Falencias de su votación." Buenos Aires, Argentina.

Austen-Smith, David. 1994. "Strategic Transmission of Costly Information." *Econometrica* 62: 955–64.

Bagehot, Walter. 1867. *The English Constitution*. Reprint, Ithaca, NY: Cornell University Press, 1963.

Baldez, Lisa A., and John M. Carey. 1999. "Presidential Agenda Control and Spending Policy: Lessons from General Pinochet's Constitution." *American Journal of Political Science* 43(1): 29–55.

Barczak, Monica. 2001. "Representation by Consultation? The Rise of Direct Democracy in Latin America." *Latin American Politics and Society* 43(3): 37–60.

Bianco, William T., David B. Spence, and John D. Wilkerson. 1996. "The Electoral Connection in the Early Congress: The Case of the Compensation Act of 1816." *American Journal of Political Science* 40(1): 145–71.

Bowler, Shaun, David M. Farrell, and Richard S. Katz. 1999. "Party Cohesion, Party Discipline, and Parliaments." In *Party Discipline and Parliamentary Government*, ed. Shaun Bowler, David M. Farrell, and Richard S. Katz, 3–22. Columbus: Ohio State University Press.

Brady, David W., Joseph Cooper, and Patricia A. Hurley. 1977. "The Electoral Basis of Party Voting: Patterns and Trends in the U.S. House of Representatives." In *The Impact of the Electoral Process*, ed. Louis Misel and Joseph Cooper, 133–65. Beverly Hills: Sage.

Brambor, Thomas, William R. Clark, and Matthew Golder. 2006. "Understanding Interaction Models: Improving Empirical Analysis." *Political Analysis* 14: 63–82.

Brennan, Geoffrey, and Philip Pettit. 1990. "Unveiling the Vote." *British Journal of Political Science* 20(3): 311–33.

Burke, Edmund. 1774. *The Works of the Right Honourable Edmund Burke*. London: Henry G. Bohn.

Burns, John F., and Nat Ives. 2005. "Shiites Win Most Votes in Iraq, Election Results Show." *New York Times*, February 13, International sec., 1–22.

Cain, Bruce, John Ferejohn, and Morris Fiorina. 1987. *The Personal Vote: Constituency Service and Electoral Independence*. Cambridge, MA: Harvard University Press.

Calvo, Ernesto. 2007. "The Responsive Legislature: Public Opinion and Discipline in a Highly Disciplined Legislature." *British Journal of Political Science* 37: 263–80.

Canes-Wrone, Brandice, David W. Brady, and John F. Cogan. 2002. "Out of Step, Out of Office: Electoral Accountability and House Members' Voting." *American Political Science Review* 96(1): 127–40.

Carey, John M. 2002. "Parties and Coalitions in Chile in the 1990s." In *Legislative Politics in Latin America*, ed. Scott Morgenstern and Benito Nacif, 222–53. Cambridge: Cambridge University Press.

———. 2003. "Discipline, Accountability, and Legislative Voting in Latin America." *Comparative Politics* 35(2): 191–211.

———. 2007. "Competing Principals, Political Institutions, and Party Unity in Legislative Voting." *American Journal of Political Science* 51(1): 92–107.

References

Carey, John M., and Gina Yanitell Reinhardt. 2004. "State-Level Institutional Effects on Legislative Coalition Unity in Brazil." *Legislative Studies Quarterly* 29(1): 23–47.

Carey, John M., and Matthew Soberg Shugart. 1995. "Incentives to Cultivate a Personal Vote: A Rank Ordering of Electoral Formulas." *Electoral Studies* 14(4): 417–39.

   1998. "Calling Out the Tanks, or Filling Out the Forms?" In *Executive Decree Authority*, ed. John M. Carey and Matthew Soberg Shugart, 1–32. Cambridge: Cambridge University Press.

Carroll, Royce, Gary W. Cox, and Monica Pachon. 2006. "How Political Parties Create Democracy, Chapter 2." *Legislative Studies Quarterly* 31(2): 153–74.

Centro de Estudios Públicos. 2007. *Estudio nacional de opinion pública*. Santiago, Chile: Centro de Estudios Públicos.

Cevasco Piedra, José. 2000. *El Congreso del Perú: Un modelo de modernización*. Lima: Ediciones del Congreso del Perú.

Cheibub, Jose Antonio, and Adam Przeworski. 1999. "Democracy, Elections, and Accountability for Economic Outcomes." In *Democracy, Accountability, and Representation*, ed. Bernard Manin, Adam Przeworski, and Susan C. Stokes, 222–50. Cambridge: Cambridge University Press.

Cheibub, José Antonio, Adam Przeworski, and Sebastian M. Saiegh. 2004. "Government Coalitions and Legislative Effectiveness under Presidentialism and Parliamentarism." *British Journal of Political Science* 34: 565–87.

Chhibber, Pradeep, and Ken Kollman. 1998. "Party Aggregation and the Number of Parties in India and the United States." *American Political Science Review* 92(2): 329–42.

Clarín. 2004a. "La justicia resolvera si debe quedar registrado como vota cada diputado porteno." Buenos Aires, Argentina. February 17. www.clarin.com.

   2004b. "Otra forma de votar las leyes." Buenos Aires, Argentina. February 18. www.clarin.com.

Cleary, Matthew R., and Susan C. Stokes. 2006. *Democracy and the Culture of Skepticism: Political Trust in Argentina and Mexico*. New York: Russell Sage Foundation.

Colomer, Josep M. 2001. *Political Institutions: Democracy and Social Choice*. New York: Oxford University Press.

Condorcet, Marquis de. 1785. *Essay on the Application of Analysis to the Probability of Majority Decisions* (Essai sur l'application de l'analyse à la probabilté des decisions rendues a la pluralité des voix). Paris: De l'Imprimerie royale.

Congreso del Perú. 1998. Diario de los debates. Primera Legislatura Ordinaria de 1998, 11ª Sesión, 24 de setiembre.

Coppedge, Michael J. 1994. *Strong Parties and Lame Ducks: Presidentialism, Partyarchy, and Factionalism in Venezuela*. Stanford: Stanford University Press.

   1998. "The Dynamic Diversity of Latin American Party Systems." *Party Politics* 4(4): 547–68.

Corrado, Anthony. 2002. "A History of Federal Campaign Finance Law." In *The New Campaign Finance Sourcebook*, ed. Anthony Corrado, Thomas Mann,

Daniel Ortiz, and Trevor Potter. Washington, DC: Brookings Institution. http://www.brook.edu/dybdocroot/gs/cf/sourcebk01/HistoryChap.pdf.

Cox, Gary W. 1987. *The Efficient Secret*. Cambridge: Cambridge University Press.

1990. "Centripetal and Centrifugal Incentives in Electoral Systems." *American Journal of Political Science* 34(4): 903–35.

1997. *Making Votes Count: Strategic Coordination in the World's Electoral Systems*. Cambridge: Cambridge University Press.

2006a. "The Organization of Democratic Legislatures." In *Oxford Handbook of Political Economy*, ed. Barry Weingast and Donald Wittman, 141–61. New York: Oxford University Press.

2006b. "Evaluating Electoral Systems." *Revista de Ciencia Política* 26(1): 212–15.

Cox, Gary W., and Mathew D. McCubbins. 1993. *Legislative Leviathan: Party Government in the House*. Berkeley: University of California Press.

2005. *Setting the Agenda: Responsible Party Government in the U.S. House of Representatives*. Cambridge: Cambridge University Press.

Cox, Gary W., Mikitaka Masuyama, and Mathew D. McCubbins. 2000. "Agenda Power in the Japanese House of Representatives." *Japanese Journal of Political Science* 1(1): 1–12.

Cox, Gary W., and Keith T. Poole. 2004. "On Measuring Partisanship in Roll-Call Voting: The US House of Representatives, 1877–1999." *American Journal of Political Science* 46(3): 477–89.

Cox, Gary W., and Matthew S. Shugart. 1995. "In the Absence of Vote Pooling: Nomination and Vote Allocation Errors in Colombia." *Electoral Studies* 14(4): 441–60.

Cox, Gary W., and Michael F. Thies. 1998. "The Cost of Intraparty Competition: The Single, Nontransferable Vote and Money Politics in Japan." *Comparative Political Studies* 31(3): 267–91.

Crisp, Brian F., and Rachel E. Ingall. 2002. "Institutional Engineering and the Nature of Representation: Mapping the Effects of Electoral Reform in Colombia." *American Journal of Political Science* 46(4): 733–48.

Crisp, Brian, and Juan Carlos Rey. 2001. "The Causes of Electoral Reform in Venezuela." In *Mixed-Member Electoral Systems: The Best of Both Worlds*, ed. Matthew S. Shugart and Martin P. Wattenberg, 173–93. New York: Oxford University Press.

Culver, William W., and Alfonso Ferrufino. 2000. "Diputados uninominales: La participacion politica en Bolivia." *Contribuciones* 1: 1–28.

Dallas Morning News. 2003a."Editorial: Let the Sun Shine – Legislature Needs to Get Online with Records." *Dallas Morning News Online*, April 1. http://www.dallasnews.com/.

2003b."Editorial: Let the Sun Shine – Excuses for Not Recording Votes Are Flimsy." *Dallas Morning News Online*, March 31. http://www.dallasnews.com/.

Dawisha, Adeed, and Larry Diamond. 2006. "Iraq's Year of Voting Dangerously." *Journal of Democracy* 17(2): 89–103.

Desposato, Scott. 2004a. "Going Negative in Comparative Perspective: The Impact of Electoral Rules on Campaign Strategy." Paper presented at the annual meeting of the American Political Science Association, Boston, August 30–September 3.

2004b. "The Impact of Federalism on National Party Cohesion in Brazil." *Legislative Studies Quarterly* 29(2): 259–85.

2005. "Correcting for Small-Group Cohesion in Roll Call Cohesion Scores." *British Journal of Political Science* 35(4): 731–44.

2006a. "Parties for Rent? Ambition, Ideology, and Party-Switching in Brazil's Chamber of Deputies." *American Journal of Political Science* 50(1): 62–80.

2006b. "Brazilian Political Reform: What Needs Fixing and How to Fix It." Paper presented at the Center for Brazilian Studies, Oxford University, June 5.

Diermeier, Daniel, and Timothy J. Feddersen. 1998. "Cohesion in Legislatures and the Vote of Confidence Procedure." *American Political Science Review* 92(3): 611–22.

Diez Canseco, Javier. 2001. "Impondra el Congreso mano blanda y lucro cesante?" *La Republica*, May 6, p. 24.

Duverger, Maurice. 1954. *Political Parties, Their Organization and Activity in the Modern State*. New York: Wiley.

El Tiempo. 2002. "Alvaro Uribe Velez radico proyecto de referendo en su primer acto de gobierno." August 7. http://www.eltiempo.com/.

Erickson, Robert S. 1971. "The Electoral Impact of Congressional Roll Call Voting." *American Political Science Review* 65: 1018–32.

Farrell, David M., and Ian McAllister. 2004. "Voter Satisfaction and Electoral Systems: Does Preferential Voting in Candidate-Centered Systems Make a Difference?" Paper presented at the University of California, Irvine. Posted in eScholarship Repository: http://repositories.cdlib.org/csd/04-04.

Fearon, James D. 1999. "Electoral Accountability and the Control of Politicians: Selecting Good Types versus Sanctioning Poor Performance." In *Democracy, Accountability, and Representation*, ed. Bernard Manin, Adam Przeworski, and Susan C. Stokes, 55–97. Cambridge: Cambridge University Press.

Fenno, Richard F., Jr. 1978. *Home Style: House Members in Their Districts*. Boston: Little, Brown.

Ferejohn, John. 1999. "Accountability and Authority: Toward a Theory of Political Accountability." In *Democracy, Accountability, and Representation*, ed. Bernard Manin, Adam Przeworski, and Susan C. Stokes, 131–53. Cambridge: Cambridge University Press.

Figueiredo, Argelina Cheibub, and Fernando Limongi. 2000. "Presidential Power, Legislative Organization, and Party Behavior in Brazil." *Comparative Politics* 32(2): 151–70.

Fleischer, David. 2004. "The Politics of the Lula PT-led Coalition." Paper prepared for the conference of the Latin American Studies Association, Las Vegas, NV, November 4–6.

Frye, Timothy. 1997. "A Politics of Institutional Choice: Post-Communist Presidencies." *Comparative Political Studies* 30(5): 523–52.

Gallagher, Michael. 1991. "Proportionality, Disproportionality and Electoral Systems." *Electoral Studies* 10: 33–51.

Garman, Christopher, Stephan Haggard, and Eliza Willis. 2001. "Fiscal Decentralization: A Political Theory with Latin American Cases." *World Politics* 53(2): 205–36.

Gerring, John, and Strom C. Thacker. 2008. *A Centripetal Theory of Democratic Governance*. Cambridge: Cambridge University Press.

Gerring, John, Strom C. Thacker, and C. Moreno. 2005. "Centripetal Democratic Governance: A Theory and Global Inquiry." *American Political Science Review* 99(4): 567–81.

Golden, Miriam A., and Eric C.C. Chang. 2001. "Competitive Corruption: Factional Conflict and Political Malfeasance in Postwar Italian Christian Democracy." *World Politics* 53(4): 588–622. http://muse.jhu.edu/journals/world_politics/ v053/53.4golden.pdf.

Gonzalez Bertomeu, Juan F. 2004. *Cada voto con su nombre: Votaciones nominales en el Poder Legislativo*. Buenos Aires: Asociación por los Derechos Civiles.

Gunson, Phil. 2006. "Chavez's Venezuela." *Current History* 105(688): 58–63.

Hallerberg, Mark, and Patrik Mairer. 2004. "Executive Authority, the Personal Vote, and Budget Discipline in Latin American and Caribbean Countries." *American Journal of Political Science* 48(3): 571–87.

Haspel, Moshe, Thomas Remington, and Steven S. Smith. 1998. "Electoral Institutions and Party Cohesion in the Russian Duma." *Journal of Politics* 60(2): 417–39.

Hellwig, Timothy, and David Samuels. 2007. "Electoral Accountability and the Variety of Democratic Regimes." *British Journal of Political Science* 38: 65–90.

Hix, Simon. 2002. "Parliamentary Behavior with Two Principals: Preferences, Parties, and Voting in the European Parliament." *American Journal of Political Science* 46(3): 688–98.

2004. "Electoral Institutions and Legislative Behavior – Explaining Voting Defection in the European Parliament." *World Politics* 56(2): 194–223.

Hix, Simon, Abdul Noury, and Gerard Roland. 2006. "Dimensions of Politics in the European Parliament." *American Journal of Political Science* 50(2): 494–511.

Huber, John D. 1996. "The Vote of Confidence in Parliamentary Democracies." *American Political Science Review* 90(2): 269–82.

Huber, John D., and G. Bingham Powell. 1994. "Congruence between Citizens and Policymakers in Two Visions of Liberal Democracy." *World Politics* 46: 291–326.

Huneeus, Carlos. "Binominalismo y calidad democratica." *La Tercera, Santiago, Chile*, August 8, 2006, Opinion sec.

International Institute for Democracy and Electoral Assistance. 1997. *Handbook of Electoral Systems*. Stockholm, Sweden: IDEA.

Jenkins, Jeffrey A. 1999. "Examining the Bonding Effects of Party: A Comparative Analysis of Roll-Call Voting in the US and Confederate Houses." *American Journal of Political Science* 43(4): 1144–65.

2000. "Examining the Robustness of Ideological Voting: Evidence from the Confederate House of Representatives." *American Journal of Political Science* 44(4): 811–22.

References

Jenkins, Jeffrey A., and Charles Stewart III. 2003. "Out in the Open: The Emergence of Viva Voce Voting in House Speakership Elections." *Legislative Studies Quarterly* 28(4): 481–508.

Johnson, Chris, William Maley, Alexander Thier, and Ali Wardak. 2003. *Afghanistan's Political and Constitutional Development*. London: Overseas Development Institute and U.K. Department for International Development.

Johnson, Gregg, and Brian F. Crisp. 2003. "Mandates, Powers, and Policies." *American Journal of Political Science* 47(1): 127–41.

Jones, Mark P., and W. Hwang. 2005. "Party Government in Presidential Democracies: Extending Cartel Theory beyond the US Congress." *American Journal of Political Science* 49(2): 267–82.

Katz, Richard S. 1994. "The 1993 Parliamentary Electoral Reform." In *Italian Politics*, ed. Carol Mershon and Gianfranco Pasquino, 93–112. 9th ed. Boulder, CO: Westview Press.

Kile, Orville M. 1948. *The Farm Bureau through Three Decades*. Baltimore: Waverly Press.

King, David C., and Richard J. Zeckhauser. 2003. "Congressional Vote Options." *Legislative Studies Quarterly* 28(3): 387–411.

Krehbiel, Keith. 1998. *Pivotal Politics: A Theory of U.S. Lawmaking*. Chicago: University of Chicago Press.

2000. "Party Discipline and Measures of Partisanship." *American Journal of Political Science* 44(2): 212–27.

Kulischeck, Michael, and Brian F. Crisp. 2001. "The Consequences of Electoral Reform in Venezuela." In *Mixed-Member Electoral Systems: The Best of Both Worlds?*, ed. Matthew S. Shugart and Martin P. Wattenberg, 404–31. New York: Oxford University Press.

Kunicová, Jana, and Susan Rose-Ackerman. 2005. "Electoral Rules and Constitutional Structures as Constraints on Corruption." *British Journal of Political Science* 35(4): 573–606.

La Gaceta. 2001. "Congresistas que votaron y en contra de la revocatoria." *La Gaceta*, 6 May, sec. 2.

La Raja, Raymond J. 2003. "Why Soft Money Has Strengthened Parties." In *Inside the Campaign Finance Battle: Court Testimony on the New Reforms*, ed. Anthony Corrado, Thomas E. Mann, and Trevor Potter, 69–98. Washington, DC: Brookings Institution Press.

Laakso, Markku, and Rein Taagepera. 1979. "Effective Number of Parties: A Measure with Application to West Europe." *Comparative Political Studies* 12: 3–27.

Lanfranchi, Prisca, and Ruth Luthi. 1999. "Cohesion of Party Groups and Interparty Conflict in the Swiss Parliament: Roll Call Voting in the National Council." In *Party Discipline and Parliamentary Government*, ed. Shaun Bowler, David M. Farrell, and Richard S. Katz, 99–120. Columbus: Ohio State University Press.

Latin America Data Base. 2001. "Nicaragua: Governing Party and Sandinistas Nominate Presidential Candidates." *NotiCen: Central American & Caribbean Political & Economic Affairs* 6(3).

Latinobarómetro. 2003 *Summary Report: Democracy and Economy*. www .latinobarometro.org.

Laver, Michael, and Kenneth Shepsle. 1996. *Making and Breaking Governments: Cabinets and Legislatures in Parliamentary Democracies*. Cambridge: Cambridge University Press.

Lijphart, Arend. 1994. *Electoral Systems and Party Systems: A Study of 27 Democracies, 1945–1990*. New York: Oxford University Press.

——— 1999. *Patterns of Democracy: Government Forms and Performance in Thirty-Six Countries*. New Haven: Yale University Press.

Linz, Juan J. 1994. "Presidentialism or Parliamentarism: Does It Make a Difference?" In *The Failure of Presidential Democracy*, ed. Juan J. Linz and Arturo Valenzuela, 3–90. Baltimore: Johns Hopkins University Press.

Londregan, John. 2001. *Legislative Institutions and Ideology in Chile*. Cambridge: Cambridge University Press.

Lowry, W. R., and C. R. Shipan. 2002. "Party Differentiation in Congress." *Legislative Studies Quarterly* 27(1): 33–60.

Luna, Juan P., and Elizabeth J. Zechmeister. 2005. "Political Representation in Latin America: A Study of Elite-Mass Congruence in Nine Countries." *Comparative Political Studies* 38(4): 388–416.

Lupia, Arthur, and Mathew D. McCubbins. 1998. *The Democratic Dilemma: Can Citizens Learn What They Need to Know?* Cambridge: Cambridge University Press.

Mainwaring, Scott P. 1999. *Rethinking Party Systems in the Third Wave of Democratization: The Case of Brazil*. Stanford: Stanford University Press.

Mainwaring, Scott P., and Aníbal Pérez-Liñán. 1997. "Party Discipline in the Brazilian Constitutional Congress." *Legislative Studies Quarterly* 22(4): 453–83.

Mainwaring, Scott P., and Timothy R. Scully. 1995. "Party Systems in Latin America." In *Building Democratic Institutions: Party Systems in Latin America*, ed. Scott Mainwaring and Timothy R. Scully, 1–36. Stanford: Stanford University Press.

Manin, Bernard, Adam Przeworski, and Susan C. Stokes. 1999. "Elections and Representation." In *Elections, Accountability, and Representation*, ed. Bernard Manin, Adam Przeworski, and Susan C. Stokes, 29–54. Cambridge: Cambridge University Press.

Mann, Thomas E. 2003. "Linking Knowledge and Action: Political Science and Campaign Finance Reform." *Perspective on Politics* 17(1): 69–83.

Marlowe, Ann. 2007. "Life of the Parties." *Wall Street Journal*, January 29, A17.

Mayhew, David. 1974. *Congress: The Electoral Connection*. New Haven: Yale University Press.

Mayorga, Rene. 2001. "Electoral Reform in Bolivia: Origins of the Mixed-Member Proportional System." In *Mixed-Member Electoral Systems: The Best of Both Worlds?*, ed. Matthew S. Shugart and Martin P. Wattenberg, 194–208. New York: Oxford University Press.

McCoy, J. L. 1999. "Chavez and the End of 'Partyarchy' in Venezuela." *Journal of Democracy* 105(3): 64–77.

References

McCubbins, Mathew D., and Frances McCall Rosenbluth. 1995. "Party Provision for Personal Politics: Dividing the Vote in Japan." In *Structure and Policy in Japan and the United States*, ed. Peter F. Cowhey and Mathew D. McCubbins, 35–55. Cambridge: Cambridge University Press.

McKelvey, Richard. 1976. "Intransitivities in Multidimensional Voting Models: Some Implications for Agenda Control." *Journal of Economic Theory* 12: 472–82.

Moe, Terry M., and Michael Caldwell. 1994. "The Institutional Foundations of Democratic Government: A Comparison of Presidential and Parliamentary Systems." *Journal of Institutional Theoretical Economics* 150(1): 171–95.

Molinar Horcacitas, Juan, and Jeffrey Weldon. 2001. "Reforming Electoral Systems in Mexico." In *Mixed-Member Electoral Systems: The Best of Both Worlds?*, ed. Matthew Soberg Shugart and Martin P. Wattenberg, 209–30. Oxford: Oxford University Press.

Morgan, Jana, Rosario Espinal, and Mitchell A. Seligson. 2006. *The Political Culture of the Dominican Republic in 2006*. Nashville, TN: Latin American Public Opinion Project.

Morgenstern, Scott. 2003. *Patterns of Legislative Politics: Roll Call Voting in Latin America and the United States*. Cambridge: Cambridge University Press.

Morone, James A. 1990. *The Democratic Wish: Popular Participation and the Limits of American Government*. New York: Basic Books.

Nicolau, Jairo Marconi. 2007. "O Sistema Eleitoral De Lista Aberta no Brasil." In *Instituições representativas no Brasil: Balanço e reforma*, ed. Jairo Marconi Nicolau and Timothy J. Power, 97–122. Rio de Janeiro: IUPERJ.

Odegard, Peter H. 1928. *Pressure Politics: The Story of the Anti-Saloon League*. New York: Columbia University Press.

Pérez-Liñán, Aníbal. 2007. *Presidential Impeachment and the New Political Instability in Latin America*. Cambridge: Cambridge University Press.

Persson, Torsten, Gerard Roland, and Guido Tabellini. 1997. "Separation of Powers and Political Accountability." *Quarterly Journal of Economics* 112: 1163–1202.

Persson, Torsten, and Guido Tabellini. 2003. *The Economic Effects of Constitutions*. Cambridge, MA: MIT Press.

Persson, Torsten, Guido Tabellini, and F. Trebbi. 2003. "Electoral Rules and Corruption." *Journal of the European Economic Association* 1: 958–89.

Pharr, Susan J., Robert D. Putnam, and Russell J. Dalton. 2000. "A Quarter-Century of Declining Confidence." *Journal of Democracy* 11(2): 500–25.

Poole, Keith T. 1998. "Recovering a Basic Space from a Set of Issue Scales." *American Journal of Political Science* 42(3): 954–93.

Poole, Keith T., and Howard Rosenthal. 1985. "A Spatial Model for Legislative Roll Call Analysis." *American Journal of Political Science* 29(2): 357–84.

1997. *Congress: A Political-Economic History of Roll Call Voting*. New York: Oxford University Press.

2001. "D-Nominate after 10 Years: A Comparative Update to Congress; A Political-Economic History of Roll-Call Voting." *Legislative Studies Quarterly* 26(1): 5–30.

Powell, G. Bingham. 2000. *Elections as Instruments of Democracy: Majoritarian and Proportional Visions*. New Haven: Yale University Press.

Powell, G. Bingham, and Georg Vanberg. 2000. "Election Laws, Disproportionality and Median Correspondence: Implications for Two Visions of Democracy." *British Journal of Political Science* 30(3): 383–411. http://www.journals.cup.org/bin/bladerunner?REQUNIQ=1028572637&;;REQSESS=75269&117000REQEVENT=&REQINT1=1202&REQAUTH=0.

Powell, G. Bingham, and Guy D. Whitten. 1993. "A Cross-National Analysis of Economic Voting: Taking Account of the Political Context." *American Journal of Political Science* 37(2): 391–414.

Proyecto Élites Parlamentarias Latinoamericanas. 2006. *Boletín n°6: Disciplina de voto y lealtad partidista*. Salamanca, Spain: Instituto Interuniversitario de Iberoamérica (Universidad de Salamanca).

Przeworski, Adam. 2007. "Is the Science of Comparative Politics Possible?" In *Oxford Handbook of Comparative Politics*, ed. Carles Boix and Susan C. Stokes, 117–39. New York: Oxford University Press.

Quinn, Kevin M., Burt L. Monroe, Michael Colaresi, Michael H. Crespin, and Dragomir R. Radev. 2006. "An Automated Method of Topic-Coding Legislative Speech over Time with Application to the 105th–108th U.S. Senate." Paper presented at the annual meetings of the American Political Science Association, Philadelphia, September 2.

Rachadell, Manuel. 1991. "El sistema electoral y la reforma de los partidos." In *Venezuela, democracia y futuro: Los partidos politicos en la decada de los 90. Reflexiones para un cambio neceario*, ed. Carlos Blanco and Edgar Paredes Pisani, 203–10. Caracas: Comision Presidencial para la Reforma del Estado.

Rasch, Bjorn E. 2000. "Parliamentary Floor Voting Procedures and Agenda Setting in Europe." *Legislative Studies Quarterly* 25(1): 3–23.

Reynolds, Andrew. 2006. "The Curious Case of Afghanistan." *Journal of Democracy* 17(2): 104–17.

Rice, Stuart A. 1925. "The Behavior of Legislative Groups." *Political Science Quarterly* 40: 60–72.

Riker, William H. 1982. *Liberalism against Populism*. Prospect Heights, IL: Waveland Press.

Roberts, Kenneth, and Erik Wibbels. 1999. "Party Systems and Electoral Volatility in Latin America: A Test of Economic, Institutional, and Structural Explanations." *American Political Science Review* 93(3): 575–90.

Rosas, Guillermo. 2005. "The Ideological Organization of Latin American Legislative Parties: An Empirical Analysis of Elite Policy Preferences." *Comparative Political Studies* 7(824): 849.

Rose-Ackerman, Susan. 1999. *Corruption and Government: Causes, Consequences, and Reform*. Cambridge: Cambridge University Press.

Rosenthal, Howard, and Erik Voeten. 2004. "Analyzing Roll Calls with Perfect Spatial Voting: France 1946–1958." *American Journal of Political Science* 48(3): 620–32.

References

Rousseau, Jean Jacques. 1763. "Voting." In *On the Social Contract*, book IV, ch. XX. New York: St. Martin's Press, 1978.

Rubin, Barnett R. "The Wrong Voting System." *International Herald Tribune*, March 16, International section.

Samuels, David. 2000. "Ambition and Competition: Explaining Legislative Turnover in Brazil." *Legislative Studies Quarterly* 25(3): 481–97.

2004. "Presidentialism and Accountability for the Economy in Comparative Perspective." *American Political Science Review* 98(3): 425–36.

Samuels, David, and Matthew S. Shugart. 2003. "Presidentialism, Elections, and Representation." *Journal of Theoretical Politics* 15(1): 33–60.

Sartori, Giovanni. 1976. *Parties and Party Systems: A Framework for Analysis*. Cambridge: Cambridge University Press.

Scarrow, Susan E. 2001a. "Direct Democracy and Institutional Change: A Comparative Investigation." *Comparative Political Studies* 34(688): 651–65.

2001b. "Germany: The Mixed-Member System as a Political Compromise." In *Mixed-Member Electoral Systems: The Best of Both Worlds?*, ed. Matthew S. Shugart and Martin P. Wattenberg, 55–69. New York: Oxford University Press.

Seligson, Mitchell A., Abby B. Cordova, Juan Carlos Donoso, Daniel Moreno Morales, Diana Orces, and Vivian Schwarz Blum. 2007. *Democracy Audit: Bolivia 2006 Report*. Nashville, TN: Latin American Public Opinion Project.

Shepsle, Kenneth. 1991. *Models of Multiparty Electoral Competition*. New York: Harwood Academic.

Shugart, Matthew S. 1998. "The Inverse Relationship between Party Strength and Executive Strength: A Theory of Politicians' Constitutional Choices." *British Journal of Political Science* 28(1): 1–29.

Shugart, Matthew S., and John M. Carey. 1992. *Presidents and Assemblies: Constitutional Design and Electoral Dynamics*. Cambridge: Cambridge University Press.

Shugart, Matthew S., Erika Moreno, and Luis E. Fajardo. 2006. "Deepening Democracy by Renovating Political Practices: The Struggle for Electoral Reform in Colombia." In *Peace, Democracy, and Human Rights in Colombia*, ed. Christopher Welna and Gustavo Gallon, 202–66. Notre Dame, IN: Notre Dame University Press.

Shugart, Matthew S., Melody E. Valdini, and K. Suominen. 2005. "Looking for Locals: Voter Information Demands and Personal Vote-Earning Attributes of Legislators under Proportional Representation." *American Journal of Political Science* 49(2): 437–49.

Shugart, Matthew S., and Martin P. Wattenberg, eds. 2001. *Mixed-Member Electoral Systems: The Best of Both Worlds?* New York: Oxford University Press.

Siavelis, Peter. 2000. *The President and Congress in Postauthoritarian Chile: Institutional Constraints to Democratic Consolidation*. University Park: Pennsylvania State University Press.

Sieberer, Ulrich. 2006. "Party Unity in Parliamentary Democracies: A Comparative Analysis." *Journal of Legislative Studies* 12(2): 150–78.

Singer, Judith D. 1998. "Using SAS PROC MIXED to Fit Multilevel Models, Hierarchical Models, and Individual Growth Models." *Journal of Educational and Behavioral Statistics* 24(4): 323–55.

Skeen, C. Edward. 1986. "Vox Populi, Vox Dei: The Compensation Act of 1816 and the Rise of Popular Politics." *Journal of the Early Republic* 6(253): 274.

Smith, Steven S. 1989. *Call to Order: Floor Politics in the House and Senate.* Washington, DC: Brookings Institution Press.

Snyder, James M., and Tim Groseclose. 2000. "Estimating Party Influence in Congressional Roll-Call Voting." *American Journal of Political Science* 44(2): 193–211.

Snyder, James M., and Michael M. Ting. 2005. "Why Roll Calls? A Model of Position Taking in Legislative Voting and Elections." *Journal of Law, Economics, and Organization* 21(1): 153–78.

Steenbergen, Marco R., and Bradford S. Jones. 2002. "Modeling Multilevel Data Structures." *American Journal of Political Science* 46(1): 218–237.

Stokes, Susan C. 2001. *Mandates and Democracy: Neoliberalism by Surprise in Latin America.* Cambridge: Cambridge University Press.

Sundquist, James L. 1981. *The Decline and Resurgence of Congress.* Washington, DC: Brookings Institution Press.

Taagepera, Rein, and Matthew Sobert Shugart. 1989. *Seats and Votes: The Effects and Determinants of Electoral Systems.* New Haven: Yale University Press.

Tapia G., Sady. 2004. "Legisladores 'huyen' del voto electrónico." *La Prensa,* March 25. La Prensa Web, http://www.prensa.com/.

Texas State Legislature. 2005. "Texas Legislature Online." http://www.capitol.state.tx.us/tlo/legislation/voteinfo.htm.

Thames, Francis C. 2007. "Searching for the Electoral Connection: Parliamentary Party Switching in the Ukrainian Rada, 1998–2002." *Legislative Studies Quarterly* 32(2): 223–56.

Tsebelis, George. 1999. "Veto Players and Law Production in Parliamentary Democracies: An Empirical Analysis." *American Political Science Review* 93(3): 591–608.

Ungar Bleier, Elisabeth. 2002. "Consideraciones sobre la reforma politica." *Testimony before the Comisión Primera Constitucional del Senado de la República.* Bogotá.

United States Supreme Court. 1958. Majority Decision in NAACP v. Alabama Ex Rel. *Patterson, Attorney General. No. 91 Supreme Court of the United States 357 U.S.* 449; 78 S. Ct. 1163.

Valenzuela, Arturo. 1994. "Party Politics and the Crisis of Presidentialism in Chile: A Proposal for a Parliamentary Form of Government." In *The Failure of Presidential Democracy: The Case of Latin America,* vol. 2, ed. Juan J. Linz and Arturo Valenzuela, 91–150. Baltimore: Johns Hopkins University Press.

VoteWorld. 2008. *VoteWorld: The International Legislative Roll-Call Voting Website.* http://ucdata.berkeley.edu:7101/new_web/VoteWorld/voteworld/.

Wallack, Jessica S., A. Gaviria, Ugo Panizza, and Eduardo Stein. 2003. "Particularism around the World." *World Bank Economic Review* 17(1): 133–43.

References

Weldon, Jeffrey. 1997. "Political Sources of *Presidencialismo* in Mexico." In *Presidentialism and Democracy in Latin America*, ed. Matthew S. Shugart and Scott P. Mainwaring, 225–58. Cambridge: Cambridge University Press.

——— 2001. "The Consequences of Mexico's Mixed-Member Electoral System, 1988–1997." In *Mixed-Member Electoral Systems: The Best of Both Worlds?*, ed. Matthew S. Shugart and Martin P. Wattenberg, 447–74. New York: Oxford University Press.

Weyland, Kurt. 1996. *Democracy without Equity: Failures of Reform in Brazil.* Pittsburgh: University of Pittsburgh Press.

White, Leonard D. 1951. *The Jeffersonians: A Study in Administrative History, 1801–1829.* New York: Macmillan.

Whiteley, Paul F., and Patrick Seyd. 1999. "Discipline in the British Conservative Party: The Attitudes of Party Activists toward the Role of Their Members of Parliament." In *Party Discipline and Parliamentary Government*, ed. Shaun Bowler, David M. Farrell, and Richard S. Katz, 53–71. Columbus: Ohio State University Press.

Index

accountability, 1–4, 7–9, 11, 16, 29–36, 43, 45, 46, 51–55, 63, 64, 65 68–70, 74, 80, 82, 85, 89–91 92, 93, 165–172, 175, 176
  collective, 1, 2, 9, 10, 12–14, 20–21, 24, 29, 92, 166, 168–176
  individual, 1–3, 9, 12, 13, 15–16, 20, 21, 32, 36, 41, 44, 166–168 170–172
  rendiciones de cuentas, 33
Afghanistan, 9–13, 172
agenda powers, 5, 17, 18, 25, 44, 48, 76, 77, 78, 81, 91, 125–128, 132 134–136, 166
American Legion, 54
American Medical Association, 54
American Political Science Association, 4, 23, 170
Ames, Barry, 47, 97, 125
Antigone. *See* Sophocles
Anti-Saloon League, 54
Argentina, 15, 45, 50, 58, 59, 60, 61, 64, 71, 75, 81, 90, 98, 99, 105, 107, 108, 140, 141, 142
Austen-Smith, David, 33
Australia, 103, 105, 107, 108, 109, 141

Bagehot, Walter, 23, 139, 141
Baltodano, Mónica, 28, 29, 80, 89, 136
Blanco Oropeza, Carlos, 84, 89, 91
Bolivia, 25, 26, 28, 31, 32, 41, 42, 45, 49, 56, 58, 67, 76, 78, 80

Brazil, 15, 18, 25, 45, 47, 58, 60, 61, 71, 75, 88, 105, 108, 110, 125, 141, 142, 144, 155, 156, 157, 163
Burke, Edmund, 69, 70, 91

Calvo, Ernesto, 47, 135
campaign contributions, 85
Canada, 103, 104, 105, 107, 108, 141, 142, 154, 155
Carazo Odio, Rodrigo, 79
Cardoso, Fernando Henrique, 110, 155, 156
Chavez, Hugo, 27, 32, 33, 34, 90, 137
Chile, 37, 45, 58, 60, 61, 71, 88, 104, 105, 107, 108, 140, 141, 173 174, 175
CLOSE score, 104, 116
coalitions, 6, 15, 16, 21, 22, 29, 47, 48, 53, 64, 65, 75–77, 78, 80, 88, 90, 92, 93, 99, 109, 110, 113, 126–127, 135, 155–163, 166–169, 173 174–176
  governing, 159
  opposition, 159, 161
cohesiveness, 7, 27, 123, 126–129 132, 162
Coleman, William, 52
Colombia, 25, 26, 27, 38–41, 45, 49, 57, 58, 60, 61, 64, 66, 71, 78, 79 80–84, 90
Combellas, Ricardo, 27, 32, 33, 34, 90, 137

Compensation Act of 1816, 52
competing principals, 3, 15, 17, 18, 126, 127, 132–134, 143, 156, 158, 162, 164, 169
Confederate Congress, 6
confidence vote, 134, 139–146, 147, 150, 153, 154, 159, 163, 169
Costa Rica, 25, 26, 28, 32, 41, 45, 49, 56, 57, 59, 60, 61, 64, 71, 78, 79, 136, 137
Cox, Gary, 5, 6, 7, 9, 12, 29, 45, 71 113, 126, 127, 128, 139, 141 172, 175
cross-voting. *See* discipline
cycling problem, 5
Czech Republic, 99, 102, 103, 104, 105, 108, 140, 141

de la Rua, Fernando, 50
deadlock, 1
decisiveness, 1, 4–8, 14
Desposato, Scott, 25, 59, 72, 123, 142, 163, 172
direct democracy, 30
discipline, 1, 7, 8, 24–31, 36, 38, 41, 44, 51, 54, 61, 75, 76, 80, 88, 89, 97, 126–136, 137, 155, 163, 171
disproportionality, 10
district magnitude, 10, 12, 71, 72, 98, 123, 133, 168, 173, 175

Ecuador, 25, 26, 27, 31, 45, 49, 56, 57, 58, 67, 71, 78, 105, 107, 108, 141
El Salvador, 25, 28, 45, 49, 59, 67, 71, 75, 77, 78
electronic voting, 46, 49, 51, 54–67 73, 76–80, 82, 83, 86, 89, 90 120, 167
European Union, 18

Farm Bureau, 54
federalism, 4, 15, 125, 127, 134, 148, 154
Federalist Party, 52
floor votes. *See* legislative votes
France, 103, 105, 107, 108, 139, 141, 142

Frente Sandinista (FSLN), 28, 136
Fujimori, Alberto, 38, 63, 82, 86

gender quotas, 10, 12
Germany, 32, 33, 89
Gioja, José Luis, 50
governors, 4, 15, 18, 74, 142
gridlock. *See* deadlock
Guatemala, 31, 45, 56, 57, 58, 105, 107, 108, 141

hand raising. *See* signal voting
Hix, Simon, 18, 125, 133
Hurtado, Carlos, 27, 86, 136, 149
hybrid regimes, 45, 134, 135, 139, 143, 146, 158

indiscipline. *See* discipline
individualism, 2, 12, 14–22, 27, 29, 36, 40, 41, 42, 61, 62, 71, 133, 143, 157, 166–173, 175
instability problem. *See* cycling problem
interest groups, 4, 15, 39, 54, 73, 74, 80, 167
intraparty competition. *See* individualism
Iraq, 9, 10, 11, 12, 13, 14
Israel, 103, 104, 106, 107, 108, 109, 110, 111, 140, 141, 142
Italy, 32, 171

Japan, 32
Jefferson, Thomas, 52, 53
Jenkins, Jeffrey, 6, 53, 54, 75
Jordan, 11

Kwasniewski, Alexander (President of Poland), 143

Latin America, 7, 20, 21, 24, 25, 29 30, 31, 32, 33, 36, 40, 41, 44, 46 49, 50, 51, 55, 56, 61, 64, 65, 66 71, 74, 75, 87, 88, 90, 98, 166 167
Latinobarómetro, 30, 187
legislative votes, 3, 33, 42, 48, 49, 66, 68, 69, 70, 73, 74, 76, 87, 87, 92, 103, 122, 127, 128, 137, 167, 176

manipulation of, 76, 77
thresholds, 56, 57, 64, 97, 100, 101, 106, 113, 115, 120, 122, 143
Linz, Juan, 31, 134
Lula (Luiz Ignacio da Silva, president of Brazil), 155

Mainwaring, Scott, 24, 113, 125, 139, 142, 162, 163
Mayhew, David, 52, 54
Mexico, 25, 28, 31, 41, 45, 56, 58, 59, 60, 61, 64, 65, 75, 81, 106, 108, 137, 141
mixed member electoral systems, 13, 33, 41
Monroe, Burt, 9
Morgenstern, Scott, 59, 126
multimember district (MMD) elections, 44, 71

National Rifle Association, 54
New Zealand, 32, 98, 100, 103, 106, 107, 108, 141
NGOs, 72, 81, 90
Nicaragua, 25, 28, 45, 49, 57, 58, 60, 61, 64, 71, 78, 80, 86, 87, 89, 97, 106, 107, 108, 120, 121, 122, 136, 137, 141, 143
nonvotes, 94–100, 107–122, 146, 154, 165, 173
nonvoting equilibria, 99

Odegard, Peter, 54
Orduz, Rafael, 79, 83

Panama, 31, 45, 49, 57, 58, 59, 60, 61, 63, 64, 76, 78, 81, 90
Paniagua, Valentín, 86
parliamentarism, 21, 22, 29, 30, 31, 125, 135, 138, 139, 142, 149, 153–158, 161, 162, 169, 171, 174
party labels, 8, 17, 30, 32, 169
party leaders, 4, 7, 8, 15, 18, 20–22, 25, 27, 29, 31, 32, 36–41, 46, 49, 53–56, 58, 61, 62, 65, 74, 72–76, 79–83, 88, 89, 97, 101, 126–135, 137, 149, 157, 162–164, 167 169, 170

party unity, 2, 3, 7, 16–22, 23, 24, 42, 47, 59, 80, 89, 107, 92–116, 120, 122, 123, 125–135, 137–147, 151, 158–163, 165, 166, 168, 169, 170, 175, 176
measurement, 92, 113, 115, 116, 117, 126, 128–131, 132
mobilization, 85, 98, 100, 110–116, 146, 155, 169, 173
partyarchy, 33, 90, 176
Pease, Henry, 85
Peronist Party (Argentina), 50, 98
personal preference votes, 171, 173
Peru, 25, 37, 38, 45, 49, 51, 56, 58 60, 61, 63, 64, 71, 82, 85, 86, 88 89, 90, 91, 98, 101, 104, 106 107, 108, 141, 143, 144
Philippines, 32, 106, 107, 108, 131, 141
Poland, 103, 106, 107, 108, 141, 142, 143, 144, 146
political parties, 1, 3, 4–7, 13, 20, 24 30, 32, 44, 92, 169
age of, 140
dissident legislators, 76
dissident members, 21, 53, 73, 74, 75, 80, 90
governing parties, 21, 30, 76, 90, 98, 110, 135, 138, 147–158, 161, 169, 174, 175
leaders, 7, 8, 14–20, 31, 36, 39, 41, 47, 80, 133, 135, 137, 138, 168
measuring unity in small parties, 85, 101, 102, 122, 154
party groups, 25, 26, 75, 104, 124, 134, 136
party labels, 1, 7, 33, 93, 140, 170
partyarchy, 34
rank-and-file legislators, 46, 53, 54, 61, 73, 74, 75, 97, 100, 101, 132, 137
preference votes, 10, 17, 22, 41, 71, 148, 162, 173, 175, see individualism
presidentialism, 11, 18, 21, 29, 30 45, 46, 56, 59, 81, 104, 125 126, 127, 134–139, 143, 146, 147, 152–159, 161–164, 167, 169, 171, 173, 174

presidents, 4, 15–18, 24, 39, 40, 74, 82, 125, 134, 135, 137, 139, 149, 154, 157, 158, 163, 164, 169, 170, 171, 175
principals, 3, 4, 14–22, 23, 36, 37, 38, 39, 69, 70, 72, 74, 90, 127, 133, 134, 135, 137, 138, 139, 162 166–170
proportional representation, 8, 9, 31, 143, 168, 172
   closed lists, 8, 10, 41, 125, 133
Proyecto de Elites Latinoamericanas, 36
public votes, 44, 45, 46, 49, 50, 51 53, 54, 58, 66, 68, 69, 75, 79, 81 82, 91

Quinn, Kevin, 46, 47

recall elections, 33, 34
recorded votes, 21, 22, 36, 46, 47, 51, 55, 57, 59, 60, 62, 65, 76, 78, 79 80, 81–90, 94, 102, 103, 104 143, 167
reform, 8, 31
regimes, age of, 141, 148
Republican Party (United States), 24, 52
responsible party government, 23, 24, 91
responsiveness, 1, 3, 8, 29–33, 41, 52, 69, 74, 89, 127, 133, 134, 162, 169, 170, 171
rhetorical ideal point estimation, 46, 47
RICE index, 94, 95, 96, 102, 112, 115, 116, 117, 122, 123, 124, 129, 130
Rice, Stuart, 94
RLOSER index, 96, 99, 100, 101, 101, 102, 108, 109, 110, 111, 112, 118, 119, 120, 154
roll call voting. See recorded votes
Rose-Ackerman, Susan, 43, 171
Rousseau, Jean Jacques, 68, 69, 91
Russia, 32, 97, 103, 104, 106, 107, 108, 120, 141, 143

Samper, Jorge, 28, 86, 87, 136, 137
Sanchez de Lozada, Gonzalo, 28, 76, 81
secret ballot, 53, 68
secret voting, 50, 55
separation of powers. See presidentialism
signal voting, 50, 70, 72, 74, 77
single non-transferable vote (SNTV) elections, 11, 12, 172
single-member district (SMD) elections, 9, 13, 44, 71
Sophocles, 20
Stokes, Susan, 43, 125, 140, 170

Taiwan, 11
Tarek Saab, William, 32, 34, 90
Texas, state legislature, 76, 85, 90
Toledo, Alejandro (president of Peru), 86, 98
transparency, 2, 21, 44, 45, 46, 63, 68, 69, 74, 78, 80–84, 87, 90, 102, 165, 166, 167, 176
   monitoring, 2, 21, 48, 49, 50, 52, 53, 54, 59, 70–75, 81, 88, 165, 167
   monitoring votes, 21, 50, 54, 55, 56, 68, 69, 72–75, 83, 167
   Web sites, 50, 59, 63, 64, 65, 76, 81
Transparency International, 81, 87, 88
U.S. Congress, 6, 7, 47, 49, 51, 52, 53, 55, 57, 60, 64, 103, 111, 113, 127, 176
   Legislative Reorganization Act of 1970, 55
   Speaker of the House, 54

Ukraine, 32
ULOSER index, 96, 99, 100, 101, 102, 108, 109, 110, 111, 112, 118, 119, 173
United States, 21, 24, 43, 44, 45, 49 51, 52, 54, 55, 57, 58, 65, 68, 74 76, 85, 86, 87, 91, 103, 104, 106, 107, 108, 110, 112, 116, 141 144, 167, 176
UNITY index, 95, 96, 102, 112, 115, 116, 117, 123

Index

Uribe, Alvaro (presidnt of Colombia), 82

Uruguay, 45, 56, 57, 58, 59, 104, 106, 107, 108, 141, 144

Vanuatu, 11

Venezuela, 25, 27, 31, 32, 33, 34, 37, 38, 41, 42, 45, 49, 56, 58, 60, 61, 64, 78, 90, 137

1999 Constitution, 27, 33

visible votes, 21, 45, 51, 55, 61, 62, 72, 73, 74, 79, 84, 87

vote records, 2, 44, 56, 59, 60, 61, 104

VoteWorld, 103

Weldon, Jeffrey, 31, 41, 127, 137

WRICE index, 99, 100, 101, 102, 108, 109, 110, 111, 112, 121, 130, 160

Other Books in the Series *(continued from page iii)*

Catherine Boone, *Political Topographies of the African State: Territorial Authority and Institutional Change*

Michael Bratton and Nicolas van de Walle, *Democratic Experiments in Africa: Regime Transitions in Comparative Perspective*

Michael Bratton, Robert Mattes, and E. Gyimah-Boadi, *Public Opinion, Democracy, and Market Reform in Africa*

Valerie Bunce, *Leaving Socialism and Leaving the State: The End of Yugoslavia, the Soviet Union, and Czechoslovakia*

Daniela Caramani, *The Nationalization of Politics: The Formation of National Electorates and Party Systems in Europe*

Kanchan Chandra, *Why Ethnic Parties Succeed: Patronage and Ethnic Headcounts in India*

José Antonio Cheibub, *Presidentialism, Parliamentarism, and Democracy*

Ruth Berins Collier, *Paths toward Democracy: The Working Class and Elites in Western Europe and South America*

Christian Davenport, *State Repression and the Domestic Democratic Peace*

Donatella della Porta, *Social Movements, Political Violence, and the State*

Alberto Diaz-Cayeros, *Federalism, Fiscal Authority, and Centralization in Latin America*

Gerald Easter, *Reconstructing the State: Personal Networks and Elite Identity*

M. Steven Fish, *Democracy Derailed in Russia: The Failure of Open Politics*

Robert F. Franzese, *Macroeconomic Policies of Developed Democracies*

Roberto Franzosi, *The Puzzle of Strikes: Class and State Strategies in Postwar Italy*

Geoffrey Garrett, *Partisan Politics in the Global Economy*

Miriam Golden, *Heroic Defeats: The Politics of Job Loss*

Jeff Goodwin, *No Other Way Out: States and Revolutionary Movements*

Merilee Serrill Grindle, *Changing the State*

Anna Grzymala-Busse, *Rebuilding Leviathan: Party Competition and State Exploitation in Post-Communist Democracies*

Anna Grzymala-Busse, *Redeeming the Communist Past: The Regeneration of Communist Parties in East Central Europe*

Frances Hagopian, *Traditional Politics and Regime Change in Brazil*

Gretchen Helmke, *Courts under Constraints: Judges, Generals, and Presidents in Argentina*

Yoshiko Herrera, *Imagined Economies: The Sources of Russian Regionalism*

J. Rogers Hollingsworth and Robert Boyer, eds., *Contemporary Capitalism: The Embeddedness of Institutions*

John D. Huber and Charles R. Shipan, *Deliberate Discretion? The Institutional Foundations of Bureaucratic Autonomy*

Ellen Immergut, *Health Politics: Interests and Institutions in Western Europe*

Torben Iversen, *Capitalism, Democracy, and Welfare*

Torben Iversen, *Contested Economic Institutions*

Torben Iversen, Jonas Pontussen, and David Soskice, eds., *Unions, Employers, and Central Banks: Macroeconomic Coordination and Institutional Change in Social Market Economies*

Thomas Janoski and Alexander M. Hicks, eds., *The Comparative Political Economy of the Welfare State*

Joseph Jupille, *Procedural Politics: Issues, Influence, and Institutional Choice in the European Union*

Stathis Kalyvas, *The Logic of Violence in Civil War*

David C. Kang, *Crony Capitalism: Corruption and Capitalism in South Korea and Philippines*

Junko Kato, *Regressive Taxation and the Welfare State*

Robert O. Keohane and Helen B. Milner, eds., *Internationalization and Domestic Politics*

Herbert Kitschelt, *The Transformation of European Social Democracy*

Herbert Kitschelt, Peter Lange, Gary Marks, and John D. Stephens, eds., *Continuity and Change in Contemporary Capitalism*

Herbert Kitschelt, Zdenka Mansfeldova, Radek Markowski, and Gabor Toka, *Post-Communist Party Systems*

David Knoke, Franz Urban Pappi, Jeffrey Broadbent, and Yutaka Tsujinaka, eds., *Comparing Policy Networks*

Allan Kornberg and Harold D. Clarke, *Citizens and Community: Political Support in a Representative Democracy*

Amie Kreppel, *The European Parliament and the Supranational Party System*

David D. Laitin, *Language Repertories and State Construction in Africa*

Fabrice E. Lehoucq and Ivan Molina, *Stuffing the Ballot Box: Fraud, Electoral Reform, and Democratization in Costa Rica*

Mark Irving Lichbach and Alan S. Zuckerman, eds., *Comparative Politics: Rationality, Culture, and Structure, Second Edition*

Evan Lieberman, *Race and Regionalism in the Politics of Taxation in Brazil and South Africa*

Julia Lynch, *Age in the Welfare State: The Origins of Social Spending on Pensioners, Workers, and Children*

Pauline Jones Luong, *Institutional Change and Political Continuity in Post-Soviet Central Asia*

Doug McAdam, John McCarthy, and Mayer Zald, eds., *Comparative Perspectives on Social Movements*

Beatriz Magaloni, *Voting for Autocracy: Hegemonic Party Survival and Its Demise in Mexico*

James Mahoney and Dietrich Rueschemeyer, eds., *Historical Analysis and the Social Sciences*

Scott Mainwaring and Matthew Soberg Shugart, eds., *Presidentialism and Democracy in Latin America*

Isabela Mares, *The Politics of Social Risk: Business and Welfare State Development*

Isabela Mares, *Taxation, Wage Bargaining, and Unemployment*

Anthony W. Marx, *Making Race, Making Nations: A Comparison of South Africa, the United States, and Brazil*

Bonnie Meguid, *Competition between Unequals: The Role of Mainstream Parties in Late-Century Africa*

Joel S. Migdal, *State in Society: Studying How States and Societies Constitute One Another*

Joel S. Migdal, Atul Kohli, and Vivienne Shue, eds., *State Power and Social Forces: Domination and Transformation in the Third World*

Scott Morgenstern and Benito Nacif, eds., *Legislative Politics in Latin America*

Layna Mosley, *Global Capital and National Governments*

Wolfgang C. Muller and Kaare Strøm, *Policy, Office, or Votes*

Maria Victoria Murillo, *Labor Unions, Partisan Coalitions, and Market Reforms in Latin America*

Ton Notermans, *Money, Markets, and the State: Social Democratic Economic Policies since 1918*

Aníbal Pérez-Liñán, *Presidential Impeachment and New Political Instability in Latin America*

Roger Petersen, *Understanding Ethnic Violence: Fear, Hatred, and Resentment in Twentieth-Century Eastern Europe*

Simona Piattoni, ed., *Clientelism, Interests, and Democratic Representation*

Paul Pierson, *Dismantling the Welfare State? Reagan, Thatcher, and the Politics of Retrenchment*

Marino Regini, *Uncertain Boundaries: The Social and Political Construction of European Economies*

Marc Howard Ross, *Cultural Contestation in Ethnic Conflict*

Lyle Scruggs, *Sustaining Abundance: Environmental Performance in Industrial Democracies*

Jefferey M. Sellers, *Governing from Below: Urban Regions and the Global Economy*

Yossi Shain and Juan Linz, eds., *Interim Governments and Democratic Transitions*

Beverly Silver, *Forces of Labor: Workers' Movements and Globalization since 1870*

Theda Skocpol, *Social Revolutions in the Modern World*

Regina Smyth, *Candidate Strategies and Electoral Competition in the Russian Federation: Democracy without Foundation*

Richard Snyder, *Politics after Neoliberalism: Reregulation in Mexico*

David Stark and László Bruszt, *Postsocialist Pathways: Transforming Politics and Property in East Central Europe*

Sven Steinmo, Kathleen Thelen, and Frank Longstreth, eds., *Structuring Politics: Historical Institutionalism in Comparative Analysis*

Susan C. Stokes, ed., *Public Support for Market Reforms in New Democracies*

Duane Swank, *Global Capital, Political Institutions, and Policy Change in Developed Welfare States*

Sidney Tarrow, *Power in Movement: Social Movements and Contentious Politics*

Kathleen Thelen, *How Institutions Evolve: The Political Economy of Skills in Germany, Britain, the United States, and Japan*

Charles Tilly, *Trust and Rule*

Daniel Treisman, *The Architecture of Government: Rethinking Political Decentralization*

Lily Lee Tsai, *Accountability without Democracy: How Solidary Groups Provide Public Goods in Rural China*

Joshua Tucker, *Regional Economic Voting: Russia, Poland, Hungary, Slovakia, and the Czech Republic, 1990–1999*

Ashutosh Varshney, *Democracy, Development, and the Countryside*

Jeremy M. Weinstein, *Inside Rebellion: The Politics of Insurgent Violence*

Stephen I. Wilkinson, *Votes and Violence: Electoral Competition and Ethnic Riots in India*

Jason Wittenberg, *Crucibles of Political Loyalty: Church Institutions and Electoral Continuity in Hungary*

Elisabeth J. Wood, *Forging Democracy from Below: Insurgent Transitions in South Africa and El Salvador*

Elisabeth J. Wood, *Insurgent Collective Action and Civil War in El Salvador*